First World War
and Army of Occupation
War Diary
France, Belgium and Germany

15 DIVISION
46 Infantry Brigade
Highland Light Infantry
12th (Service) Battn
4 July 1915 - 31 January 1918

WO95/1952/2

The Naval & Military Press Ltd
www.nmarchive.com
Published in association with The National Archives

Published by

The Naval & Military Press Ltd

Unit 10 Ridgewood Industrial Park,

Uckfield, East Sussex,

TN22 5QE England

Tel: +44 (0) 1825 749494

www.naval-military-press.com

www.nmarchive.com

This diary has been reprinted in facsimile from the original. Any imperfections are inevitably reproduced and the quality may fall short of modern type and cartographic standards.

© **Crown Copyright**
Images reproduced by permission of The National Archives, London, England, 2015.

Contents

Document type	Place/Title	Date From	Date To
Heading	1952/2 12 Battalion Highland Light Infantry		
Heading	15th Division 46th Infy Bde 12th Bn High'd Lt Infy Jly 1915-Jan 1918 To 35 Div 106 Bde		
Heading	15th Division 12th H.L.I. Vol. I July To 30 August 15		
War Diary	Chiseldon	04/07/1915	10/07/1915
War Diary	Boulogne	11/07/1915	12/07/1915
War Diary	Louches	13/07/1915	14/07/1915
War Diary	Arques	15/07/1915	15/07/1915
War Diary	Norrent-Fontes.	16/07/1915	16/07/1915
War Diary	Allouagne	17/07/1915	04/08/1915
War Diary	Noeux Les Mines	04/08/1915	11/08/1915
War Diary	Les Brebis	11/08/1915	11/08/1915
War Diary	Maroc	12/08/1915	18/08/1915
War Diary	Les Brebis	19/08/1915	20/08/1915
War Diary	Maroc	21/08/1915	26/08/1915
War Diary	Les Brebis Houchin Labeuvriere	27/08/1915	31/08/1915
War Diary	Labeuvriere	31/08/1915	31/08/1915
Heading	46th Inf. Bde. 15th Div. War Diary 12th Battn. The Highland Light Infantry. September 1915		
War Diary	Labeuvriere	01/09/1915	07/09/1915
War Diary	Mazincarbe	08/09/1915	08/09/1915
War Diary	Noeux	09/09/1915	20/09/1915
War Diary	Quality St.	21/09/1915	26/09/1915
War Diary	Mazingarbe	27/09/1915	27/09/1915
War Diary	Haillicourt	28/09/1915	30/09/1915
Heading	Appendices 1, 2 & 3		
Miscellaneous	No 5 Column 12th Bn High. L.I.	01/10/1915	01/10/1915
Miscellaneous	12th Bn High. L.I. Short Narrative Of Events 25th/26th Sept. 1915	25/09/1915	25/09/1915
Miscellaneous	Headquarters, 46th Infy. Bde	13/10/1915	13/10/1915
Miscellaneous	12th Bn High. L.I. Report of the O.C. No. 5 Column 25th and 26th September 1915	25/09/1915	25/09/1915
Heading	15th Div. 12th H.L.I. Vol. 2 Oct-Dec		
War Diary	Haillicourt	01/10/1915	03/10/1915
War Diary	Lillers	04/10/1915	12/10/1915
War Diary	Noeux Les Mines	13/10/1915	20/10/1915
War Diary	Quarries Sector D2	21/10/1915	25/10/1915
War Diary	Old British Front Line	26/10/1915	28/10/1915
War Diary	Old Germany Front Line Sector D1	29/10/1915	30/10/1915
War Diary	Sector D2	31/10/1915	31/10/1915
War Diary	Noeux Les Mines	01/11/1915	06/11/1915
War Diary	Old Germany Front Line C 2	07/11/1915	09/11/1915
War Diary	Philosophe	10/11/1915	12/11/1915
War Diary	Old Germany Front Line Sector C 2	13/11/1915	15/11/1915
War Diary	Old British Line	16/11/1915	18/11/1915
War Diary	Verquin	19/11/1915	23/11/1915
War Diary	Vermelles	24/11/1915	25/11/1915
War Diary	Old British Front Line	26/11/1915	27/11/1915
War Diary	Vermelles	28/11/1915	30/11/1915
War Diary	Jermyn Street	01/12/1915	03/12/1915

War Diary	Vermelles	04/12/1915	05/12/1915
War Diary	K.2	06/12/1915	06/12/1915
War Diary	Verquin	07/12/1915	12/12/1915
War Diary	Raimbert	13/12/1915	31/12/1915
Heading	12 H.L.I. 15th Div. Vol 3		
War Diary	Raimbert	01/01/1916	04/01/1916
War Diary	Ernay St Julien	05/01/1916	06/01/1916
War Diary	Raimbert	07/01/1916	12/01/1916
War Diary	Ninth Av.	13/01/1916	14/01/1916
War Diary	Philosophe	15/01/1916	15/01/1916
War Diary	9th Av.	17/01/1916	19/01/1916
War Diary	Noeux	20/01/1916	25/01/1916
War Diary	Philosophe	26/01/1916	29/01/1916
War Diary	Loos.	30/01/1916	06/02/1916
War Diary	Noeux	07/02/1916	12/02/1916
War Diary	Philosophe	13/02/1916	16/02/1916
War Diary	9th Av.	17/02/1916	20/02/1916
War Diary	10th Av.	21/02/1916	24/02/1916
War Diary	Philosophe	25/02/1916	29/02/1916
Heading	12 H.L.I. Vol 4 15th		
War Diary	Philosphe	01/03/1916	01/03/1916
War Diary	Loos	02/03/1916	14/03/1916
War Diary	Noeux-Les Mines	15/03/1916	19/03/1916
War Diary	Hulluch	20/03/1916	25/03/1916
War Diary	Philosphe	26/03/1916	26/03/1916
War Diary	Raimbert	27/03/1916	31/03/1916
Miscellaneous	The Officer i/c Adjutant-General Office Base	03/06/1916	03/06/1916
War Diary	Raimbert	01/04/1916	07/04/1916
War Diary	Serny	08/04/1916	09/04/1916
War Diary	Floringhem	10/04/1916	23/04/1916
War Diary	Annequin	24/04/1916	24/04/1916
War Diary	Hohenzollern Sector	25/04/1916	27/04/1916
War Diary	Hohenzollern	28/04/1916	30/04/1916
Miscellaneous	To 46 I.B. Operations Night Of 26.4.16	26/04/1916	26/04/1916
War Diary	Hohenzollern	01/05/1916	02/05/1916
War Diary	Bethune	03/05/1916	10/05/1916
War Diary	Noyelles	11/05/1916	11/05/1916
War Diary	Vermelles	12/05/1916	15/05/1916
War Diary	Hulluch	16/05/1916	26/05/1916
War Diary	Labourse	27/05/1916	03/06/1916
War Diary	Hohenzollern	04/06/1916	19/06/1916
War Diary	Verquineul	20/06/1916	23/06/1916
War Diary	Sailly Labourse	24/06/1916	27/06/1916
War Diary	Hulluch	28/06/1916	30/06/1916
Heading	Confidential War Diary 12 Highland L.I. From 1st July 1916 To 31st July 1916 Volume 13 12 H.L.I. Vol 8		
Miscellaneous	46th I.B. Volume 13	01/08/1916	01/08/1916
War Diary	Hulluch	01/07/1916	13/07/1916
War Diary	Bethune	14/07/1916	20/07/1916
War Diary	Maries Les Misses.	21/07/1916	21/07/1916
War Diary	Heuchin	22/07/1916	25/07/1916
War Diary	Hericourt	26/07/1916	26/07/1916
War Diary	Villers L'Hopital	27/07/1916	27/07/1916
War Diary	Berneuil	28/07/1916	30/07/1916
War Diary	Flesselles	31/07/1916	31/07/1916
Miscellaneous	A Form. Messages And Signals.		

Operation(al) Order(s)	Operation Order No. 1 by Lt. Col. Heyman Comdg 12th Bn. High L.I.	30/06/1916	30/06/1916
Map	Sketch Of Operations.		
Miscellaneous	46th I.B.	17/07/1916	17/07/1916
Miscellaneous	Scheme for Raid on Enemy's Front Line Trenches.		
Heading	46th Brigade. 15th Division. 1/12th Battalion Highland Light Infantry August 1916		
Miscellaneous	46 I.B	08/09/1916	08/09/1916
Miscellaneous	D.A.G. 3rd Echelon	09/09/1916	09/09/1916
War Diary	Flesselles	01/08/1916	03/08/1916
War Diary	Molliens-au-Bois	04/08/1916	04/08/1916
War Diary	Faranvillers	05/08/1916	06/08/1916
War Diary	Albert	07/08/1916	07/08/1916
War Diary	Trenches	08/08/1916	08/08/1916
War Diary	S of Martinpuich	09/08/1916	12/08/1916
War Diary	Dingle Near Fricourt	13/08/1916	17/08/1916
War Diary	Trenches S of Martin Puich	18/08/1916	18/08/1916
War Diary	Albert in Bivouac	19/08/1916	27/08/1916
War Diary	Trenches between Highwood and Bazentin Le Petit	28/08/1916	31/08/1916
Heading	War Diary of 12th. H.L.I. From 1st.9.16 To 30.9.16 Vol 10		
War Diary	Bazentin Le Petit	01/09/1916	04/09/1916
War Diary	Fricourt	05/09/1916	12/09/1916
War Diary	Martin Puich	13/09/1916	16/09/1916
War Diary	Contalmaison	17/09/1916	17/09/1916
War Diary	Lavieville	18/09/1916	18/09/1916
War Diary	Lahoussoye	19/09/1916	30/09/1916
Map	15th Div. Map No. 6		
Map	15th Div Map No. 8A		
Miscellaneous	46 I.B.	12/09/1916	12/09/1916
Miscellaneous	To G.O.C. 46th Inf. Bde.	19/09/1916	19/09/1916
Heading	War Diary 12th H.L.I. 1/10/16 31/10/16 Vol 11		
War Diary	Albert	01/10/1916	09/10/1916
War Diary	Lozenge Wood	10/10/1916	20/10/1916
War Diary	Cutting Contalmaison	21/10/1916	25/10/1916
War Diary	Le Sars	26/10/1916	31/10/1916
War Diary	Somme Front		
Heading	War Diary 12th. H.L.I. From 1/11/16 to 30/11/16		
War Diary	Lozenge Wood	01/11/1916	01/11/1916
War Diary	Millen Court	02/11/1916	05/11/1916
War Diary	Henen Court	06/11/1916	06/11/1916
War Diary	Millen Court	07/11/1916	12/11/1916
War Diary	Baizieux	13/11/1916	15/11/1916
War Diary	Naours	16/11/1916	30/11/1916
Heading	War Diary of 12th. (S) Bn. Highland Light Infantry. From 1.12.16 To 31.12.16. Vol 13		
War Diary	Warloy	01/12/1916	01/12/1916
War Diary	Becourt Camp	02/12/1916	21/12/1916
War Diary	Pioneer Camp	22/12/1916	23/12/1916
War Diary	Shelter Wood, North	24/12/1916	24/12/1916
War Diary	Shelter Wood (North) Camp.	24/12/1916	29/12/1916
War Diary	Villa Camp	30/12/1916	31/12/1916
Heading	12th Battn. Th Highland Light Infy January 1917		
War Diary		01/01/1917	04/01/1917
War Diary	Shelter Wood Camp (South)	05/01/1917	14/01/1917
War Diary	Pioneer Camp	15/01/1917	15/01/1917

War Diary	Shelter Wood (South)	16/01/1917	24/01/1917
War Diary	Villa Camp	25/01/1917	25/01/1917
War Diary	Acid Drop (South)	26/01/1917	27/01/1917
War Diary	Shelter Wood (South) Camp	28/01/1917	31/01/1917
Miscellaneous	Casualties during the month Officers-Nil		
War Diary	Shelter Wood (South)	19/01/1917	19/01/1917
Heading	12th Battn. The Highland Light Infy February, 1917		
War Diary	Albert	01/02/1917	03/02/1917
War Diary	Warloy	04/02/1917	12/02/1917
War Diary	Beauval	13/02/1917	13/02/1917
War Diary	Gezaincourt	14/02/1917	14/02/1917
War Diary	Bouret	15/02/1917	15/02/1917
War Diary	Izel-Lez-Hameau	16/02/1917	20/02/1917
War Diary	Arras	22/02/1917	28/02/1917
War Diary		20/02/1917	20/02/1917
Heading	War Diary of 12th High. L.I. for March 1917. Vol 16		
War Diary	Arras	01/04/1917	02/04/1917
War Diary	Noyelette	03/04/1917	04/04/1917
War Diary	Noyelette	05/03/1917	11/03/1917
War Diary	Mazieres	12/03/1917	18/03/1917
War Diary	Arras	19/03/1917	29/03/1917
War Diary	Trenches Arras I.E. Sector	30/03/1917	31/03/1917
War Diary	Habarcq	01/04/1917	04/04/1917
War Diary	Arras	04/04/1917	09/04/1917
War Diary	Battery Valley	09/04/1917	09/04/1917
War Diary	Orange Hill	09/04/1917	11/04/1917
War Diary	Monchy	11/04/1917	12/04/1917
War Diary	Arras	12/04/1917	14/04/1917
War Diary	Duisans	15/04/1917	20/04/1917
War Diary	Arras	22/04/1917	23/04/1917
War Diary	Shovel TV	23/04/1917	24/04/1917
War Diary	Blueline	24/04/1917	30/04/1917
War Diary	Duisans	30/04/1917	30/04/1917
Operation(al) Order(s)	12th Battalion Highland Light Infantry. Operation Orders No. 1 by Lieut. Col. W.E. St. John, Commanding 12th Battalion H.L.I.	06/04/1917	06/04/1917
Operation(al) Order(s)	12th Battalion Highland Light Infantry. Operation Orders No. 2	06/04/1917	06/04/1917
Miscellaneous	12th Battalion Highland Light Infantry. Intelligence Arrangements. Instruction No. 1	07/04/1917	07/04/1917
Miscellaneous	12th Battalion Highland Light Infantry. Synchronization Of Watches. Instruction No. 2	07/04/1917	07/04/1917
Miscellaneous	12th Battalion Highland Light Infantry. Signals. Instruction No. 6		
Operation(al) Order(s)	46th Infantry Brigade Order No. 180	22/04/1917	22/04/1917
Operation(al) Order(s)	March Table. Issued with 46th Infantry Brigade Order No. 180 dated 22-4-1917	22/04/1917	22/04/1917
Operation(al) Order(s)	46th Infantry Brigade Order No. 181	24/04/1917	24/04/1917
Miscellaneous			
Miscellaneous	Personnel WHO. Went Forward With Unit On "Z" Day.		
Miscellaneous	Lieut 12 H.L.I.	08/04/1917	08/04/1917
Miscellaneous	46 I.B.	08/04/1917	08/04/1917
Miscellaneous	List of Officers Wounded.		
Miscellaneous			
Miscellaneous	O.R's Casualties 22/27/4/17		

Miscellaneous	Officer Casualties 22/27/4/17		
Miscellaneous	Casualties Other Ranks 9/11 4.17	09/04/1917	09/04/1917
Miscellaneous	Messages And Signals.		
Miscellaneous	A Form. Messages And Signals.		
Map			
Map	Secret Map A		
Map			
Miscellaneous	Report No.		
Map			
Heading	War Diary of 12th High. L.I. from 1st May to 31st May 1917 Vol 18		
War Diary	Duisans	01/05/1917	07/05/1917
War Diary	Fosseux	08/05/1917	21/05/1917
War Diary	Gd. Roullecourt	22/05/1917	22/05/1917
War Diary	Bouquemaison	23/05/1917	23/05/1917
War Diary	Buire au Bois	24/05/1917	31/05/1917
Heading	War Diary of 12th Highland Light Infantry. From 1st June 1917 To 30th June 1917 Vol 19		
War Diary	Buire Au Bois	01/06/1917	17/06/1917
War Diary	Erie Camp	18/06/1917	19/06/1917
War Diary	Toronto Camp	20/06/1917	24/06/1917
War Diary	In the Line	25/06/1917	30/06/1917
Heading	War Diary 12th (S) Bn. Highland Lt. Infantry for the month July 1917 Vol 20		
War Diary	In the Line	01/07/1917	01/07/1917
War Diary	Erie Camp	02/07/1917	03/07/1917
War Diary	Watou	04/07/1917	05/07/1917
War Diary	Watou Area	05/07/1917	07/07/1917
War Diary	Broxelle Area	08/07/1917	17/07/1917
War Diary	Erie Camp	18/07/1917	19/07/1917
War Diary	H.16. &. 17	20/07/1917	20/07/1917
War Diary	Reserve Camp. H. 16	21/07/1917	24/07/1917
War Diary	In the Line	24/07/1917	28/07/1917
War Diary	Erie Camp	29/07/1917	29/07/1917
War Diary	Reserve Camp H.16.17	30/07/1917	30/07/1917
War Diary	In the Line	31/07/1917	31/07/1917
Map	B.3		
Miscellaneous	Message Form.		
Heading	War Diary Of 12th (S). Bn. Highland Lt. Infantry. for month of August. 1917 Vol 21		
War Diary	Ecole Ypres	02/08/1917	02/08/1917
War Diary	Winnizeele Area	03/08/1917	19/08/1917
War Diary	In the Line	20/08/1917	31/08/1917
War Diary	Thistle Camp	26/08/1917	31/08/1917
War Diary	Thistle Camp	23/08/1917	23/08/1917
Heading	12 (Service) Bn. Highland. Lt. Infantry. War Diary for September 1917 Vol 22		
War Diary	Field	01/09/1917	30/09/1917
Heading	War Diary Of 12th (Service) Batt. Highland Light Infantry. For Month Of October 1917 Vol 23		
Miscellaneous	To. 46. I.B.	31/10/1917	31/10/1917
War Diary	In the Field	01/10/1917	26/10/1917
War Diary	Field	27/10/1917	31/10/1917
Miscellaneous	To 46. Inf. Bde.	04/12/1917	04/12/1917
Heading	War Diary of 12th Bn. Highland Lt. Infantry for month of November. 1917 Vol 24		

War Diary	Arras	01/11/1917	02/11/1917
War Diary	In the Line	03/11/1917	11/11/1917
War Diary	Arras	11/11/1917	17/11/1917
War Diary	Fampoux	18/11/1917	25/11/1917
War Diary	In the Line	26/11/1917	30/11/1917
War Diary	Line	30/11/1917	30/11/1917
Heading	War Diary of 12th High L.I from 1st Dec. to 31st Dec 1917 Volume XXX 12 H.L.I. Vol 25		
War Diary	In The Line	01/12/1917	09/12/1917
War Diary	Arras	10/12/1917	28/12/1917
War Diary	In the Line	29/12/1917	31/12/1917
Heading	Confidential War Diary Of 12th Bn High. L.I. For January 1918 Vol 26		
War Diary	In the Line	01/01/1918	01/01/1918
War Diary	Arras	02/01/1918	02/01/1918
War Diary	Berneville	03/01/1918	31/01/1918

1052/2

12 Battalion Highland Light Infantry

15TH DIVISION
46TH INFY BDE

12TH BN HIGH'D LT INFY
JLY 1915 - JAN 1918

To 35 DIV
106 Bde

I.M.
18 sheets

121/7592

12th H.L.I.
Vol: I

30 August
July to Sept 15

July 15
Jan 18

Army Form C. 2118.

Sheet 1

WAR DIARY
or
INTELLIGENCE SUMMARY.
(Erase heading not required.)

Instructions regarding War Diaries and Intelligence Summaries are contained in F.S. Regs., Part II. and the Staff Manual respectively. Title pages will be prepared in manuscript.

Place	Date	Hour	Summary of Events and Information	Remarks and references to Appendices
	1915			I
Chiseldon	July 4th		On this date, mobilisation was ordered. This proceeded until on 2nd July 7th instructions were received that the Advance Party would embark for France on Friday, and the Remainder on Saturday. 3 officers and 111 men left on	
"	July 9th		Friday and Eantled to Southampton and HAVRE. The remainder 28 officers (one	
	July 10th		attached) under Major T.H. Purvis with 814 men went via FOLKESTONE and BOULOGNE.	
BOULOGNE	July 11th-12th		Spent the day in rest. camp (OSTROHOVE) nr BOULOGNE	
LOUCHES	July 13th	12.10 PM	Marched out from the camp to PONT-DE-BRIQUES Station. Were met by the advance party in train. Proceeded via CALAIS to AUDRUICQ. arrived in LOUCHES about 8 PM, when we went into billets, very scattered, mostly in barns or farms. Under instructions received outposts not put out.	
LOUCHES	July 14th		The Bn remained in billets all day. Orders received at 10.0 PM to move on 15th	
ARQUES	July 15th	5.20 AM	Left Billets at 5.20 AM. Marched via LOCTRAT - NORDAUSQUES - TILQUE - ST OMER to ARQUES. Trying march. Went into billets in ARQUES.	
MORBECQUE - FONTES.	July 16th	8.0 AM	Continued march. Behind to proceed further to join 4th Corps. Route. CAMPAGNE - RACQUINGHEM - WITTES - AIRE - LAMBRES. Went into billets at FONTES.	

1577 Wt.W10791/1773 500,000 1/15 D.D.&L. A.D.S.S./Forms/C. 2118.

Army Form C. 2118.

Sheet 2

WAR DIARY
or
INTELLIGENCE SUMMARY.
(Erase heading not required.)

Instructions regarding War Diaries and Intelligence Summaries are contained in F.S. Regs., Part II. and the Staff Manual respectively. Title pages will be prepared in manuscript.

Place	Date	Hour	Summary of Events and Information	Remarks and references to Appendices
ALLOUAGNE.	July 17th		Left NORRENT-FONTES at 10.15 am and marched in ST HILAIRE - LILLERS - to ALLOUAGNE. Went into billets, mostly half ruined barns and farm-houses. The place was in an extremely dirty condition.	
	July 18th – 20		Remained in billets. Route marching and visits to Baths at AUCHEL on alternate days. The Bn has now taken its place in IV Corps area.	
	20.	6pm	Capt Dixon (acting 2nd in command): M.G. officer and S.W.O. went for four day instruction to trenches, returning on Saturday 24th. Attached 1st Division 2 days, XLVII Div. 2 days. Routine for remainder of Bn as on three previous days. C.O. (Attd 2. H. Purvis) Adj. & 5 W.O.s attended similar instructional tour in trenches, attached 2 days 1st Div. & 2 days XLVII Div.	
	24.		2 Companies marched to MAZINGARBE and attached in W Section of Trenches to units of XLVII. Division. (London Regt.) Attachment for 48 hours. Appointment of Major Purvis to command to be Lt. Col. (London Gazette)	

Army Form C. 2118.

Sheet 3

WAR DIARY
or
INTELLIGENCE SUMMARY.
(Erase heading not required.)

Instructions regarding War Diaries and Intelligence Summaries are contained in F.S. Regs., Part II. and the Staff Manual respectively. Title pages will be prepared in manuscript.

Place	Date	Hour	Summary of Events and Information	Remarks and references to Appendices
ALLOUAGNE	July 26th		A & B Coys returned to ALLOUAGNE. Enemy aeroplane. No casualties had occurred. A.A. had been quiet on the front except intermittent shelling.	
	July 28th		C of Pauns, Adjt & Orderlies. 5 W.Os with 2 companies (C & D) returned to billets in ALLOUAGNE. No casualties.	
	July 29th 30th 31st		Routine work carried on as usual. Brig Gen T.G. Matteson arrived 29th to command 46th Brigade.	
	August 1st 2nd 3rd Aug 4th		Routine work carried on as usual. The XV Divn proceeded to relieve the XLVII Divn in sections W & X of the trenches. The 46th Inf Bde in reserve (Divi) to section W relief by 44th Inf Bde and section X held by 45th Inf Bde. Head Quarters of 44th Bde LSS BREBIS, 7th & 8th K.O.S.B. billeted, 45th MAZINGARBE 46th NOEUX LES MINES.	
NOEUX-LES- MINES			12th High.L.D. & 10th Sea Rgt at NOEUX-LES-MINES. The M.G. Section taken to the trenches to be relieved by Reserve M.G. Section. Orders received to have formed 4 M.G. off.	
	Aug 5th			

Army Form C. 2118.

Sheet 4

WAR DIARY
or
INTELLIGENCE SUMMARY.
(Erase heading not required.)

Place	Date	Hour	Summary of Events and Information	Remarks and references to Appendices
	Aug. 6th Aug. 7th		2.28 bedilluted men. Totalling 6 off. and 90 men after Draft of 79 men received. Casualties to date wounded 1 sent to Hospital sick 33. D. Great efforts made to clean the village by dropping of refuse. Prevalence of Diarrhoea etc owing to flies and insanitary conditions.	
	Aug. 8th		Continued in billets. Working party of 300 men sent out in the evening to dig along the GRENAY MAROC LINE. (2nd Line of Defence).	
	Aug. 9th Aug. 10th -11th		In billets. During the day in NOEUX-LES-MINES. No shelling was experienced. Left NOEUX-LES-MINES & proceeded by platoons to LES BREBIS as the Brigade (46) was taking over the line from 14th Bde. We were in Brigade Reserve at LES BREBIS in billets. No shelling during 9th & 10th.	
LES BREBIS Aug. 12 MAROC			Proceeded to relieve 7.K.O.S.B in section W.1. The relief was carried out entirely by daylight. The batt's moved by half platoons at 3 & 5 min interval. Relief begun at 3pm completed about	Ⓐ

1577 Wt. W10791/1773 500,000 1/15 D. D. & L. A.D.S.S./Forms/C. 2118.

WAR DIARY
or
INTELLIGENCE SUMMARY

Army Form C. 2118.

Sheet 5

Place	Date	Hour	Summary of Events and Information	Remarks and references to Appendices
Aug. 12th LES BREBIS @ 12th		7.30 p.m.	The trenches were in need of repair; and a great deal of work necessary. The notes on W.1. section are appended.	A.1.
MAROC Aug. 13th			The situation was quiet. Distribution of Companies were as follows:- In firing line A and B Coys. A on the right, B on the left. C Coy holding out post line; D Coy in Reserve. The Machine Gun sections were supplied and relief were arranged for the day under Different arrangements. The greatest part of the day was devoted to cleaning up & repair of trenches.	
MAROC	Aug 14th		Work continued in the trenches. The Head Quarters were in cellars about 1 mile behind the firing line hidden chiefly from observation except from aircraft. Great difficulty was experienced in hunting carrier-pigeons on the roofs of the men. All coding was done in a Railway cutting by daylight traces of these being obtained. No looking being permitted in the trenches. The French were on our

WAR DIARY
INTELLIGENCE SUMMARY
Army Form C. 2118.
Sheet 6

Place	Date	Hour	Summary of Events and Information	Remarks and references to Appendices
MAROC	14th		night and the remainder of the Bn on our left the system of reliefs was as follows 2 days in rear at LES BREBIS and 6 days in the trenches.	
	15th		All continued fairly quiet during the morning. During the furious night work had been carried on without any casualty.	
		5:30 pm	About 5:30 shells were dropped round Head quarters (5 in number) evidently searching for the Railway Cutting. Shelling was probably the result of a German aeroplane observation which had been made earlier in the day. During the afternoon	
		7:30 pm	the first casualties occurred 1 man being slightly wounded & returned to duty. Brother slightly wounded and sent to Hospital. During the evening the snipers were	
		9:0 pm	active, and a party of them about in the Gordons (9th) Working Party which was working in front. About 11:30pm a German aeroplane was caught up in the wire and though covered by our rifles, Lieut Alexander stopped firing	

WAR DIARY
or
INTELLIGENCE SUMMARY.

Army Form C. 2118.

Sheet 7

Place	Date	Hour	Summary of Events and Information	Remarks and references to Appendices
MAROC	15		with an escort to rejoin the men, who were calling "Camarade". As soon as Lt Alexander was near he shot him with his revolver. Having previously left his rifle leaning against the barbed wire. Lt Alexander died almost immediately. Situation was quiet on the front.	
	16		Occasional shelling of Battalion Head Quarters, and we of Trench Mortar Bombs on the Trenches. The weather was thundery with heavy showers so that the trenches became very muddy with water in places. Weather still wet and the condition of the trenches was bad as the water was knee deep in parts of the Comm. Trench. Work could not be carried on to any great extent.	
	17		During the previous night a party sent out to catch snipers happened to get lost and turned round and charged one of the party. It wounded a man in the side with a bayonet and himself received a bullet in the knee. Situation still normal and quiet.	

Army Form C. 2118.

Sheet 8

WAR DIARY
or
INTELLIGENCE SUMMARY.
(Erase heading not required.)

Place	Date	Hour	Summary of Events and Information	Remarks and references to Appendices
MARSC	18th		Relieved by 10th Sea. Rgt. Marching was of the Railway cutting. The relief was carried out in daylight, starting at 2.30 pm, finishing at 8 pm without event. Heavy bombardments by French guns at this time, stopped by 2 German aeroplanes which flew over. The war company Rd. runs is eaten going down the road, as the enemy were shelling French Battalion. Before leaving W.1 Battalion Headquarters were changed to a point nearer (C.T.) The chief Communication Trench. Rest in LES BREBIS.	
LES BREBIS	19. 20		Relief of 7 K.O.S.B. in W.2. in daylight starting at 2.30pm During the afternoon enemy shelled main road and one shell pitching in the centre of the road about 200 yards west of GRENAY CHURCH killed 2nd Lt J.D. Linville, a Lance Corporal and a Sapper and wounded one more major, several other Platoon Red' names scatter. The Battalion men in half Platoons from the level crossing to W.2. via the main road	

WAR DIARY
INTELLIGENCE SUMMARY

Army Form C. 2118.

Sheet 9

Place	Date	Hour	Summary of Events and Information	Remarks and references to Appendices
MAROC	August		After the casualties however any further casualties from one Company to work on a line of new trench, & form up the left and right of the Battalion. 8 Companies were in the firing line and one in billets in reserve; The working parties were covered by a covering party and were not shelled that night. Situation quiet. The Trenches required a considerable amount of work to be done on them.	
	21		The enemy's light field guns shelled the left of the line and billets & killed occasionally without casualties. Working party at night was fired on and the party driven in. On the left owing to some confusion the 2 men on the left retired with one man killed, and another wounded. But it appears from evidence that there were very few Germans near, and that the wounds were probably inflicted by our own men in mistake.	

1577 Wt. W10791/1773 500,000 1/15 D.D.&L. A.D.S.S./Forms/C. 2118.

WAR DIARY
or
INTELLIGENCE SUMMARY.

Army Form C. 2118.

Sheet 10.

Place	Date	Hour	Summary of Events and Information	Remarks and references to Appendices
MAROC	August 22		Very Quiet until about 5 p.m. when the Germans shelled SNIPERS HOUSE and set it on fire and then proceeded to shell our front trenches on the left which had been newly dug but were not occupied. Our artillery retaliated and the duel continued until about 8.30 p.m. The enemy firing light high velocity H.E. & Shrapnel. About 11.30 PM they again opened on the working parties and evening fatigues. Our artillery retaliating.	
	23		Quiet on the whole while intermittent shelling at intervals of our trenches and billets. in rear of Head Quarters. Quiet. Large trench mortar bombs which at the time were offered to the heavy stalls, were dropped at foot of crassier in which was the Battalion H.Q., were there bombs which were from a 9" Trench mortar found on great uneven by the bearers of the explosion, though they appeared to do comparatively little damage. Six of these bombs were found during the day.	
	24			

WAR DIARY
or
INTELLIGENCE SUMMARY

Army Form C. 2118.

Sheet 11

Place	Date	Hour	Summary of Events and Information	Remarks and references to Appendices
MAROC	August 24		No casualties resulted from Shere & hits. During the day, the enemy shelled the road in rear to LES BREBIS immediately. Night was quiet. Heavy shelling of our front line trenches, & killed & the road 2 or 24 O.pm artillery in rear and on the road. One man was shot by a sniper and another related.	
	25.		wounded by shrapnel.	
		12 mn.	At night our much lyn opened fire on German working parties. This being in cooperation with the artillery. The result could not be observed.	
	26.	2/pm	Trench mortar bomb dropped R.I. Coy. Dug out about 50 yds from H.Q. There R.I. but dug out could not withstand the explosion and caved in. A thing which caused more injury than the fragments of the shell. Casualties were one officer wounded, 1 man killed and 1 other died of wounds and another wounded.	

WAR DIARY
or
INTELLIGENCE SUMMARY.
(Erase heading not required.)

Army Form C. 2118.

Sheet 12

Place	Date	Hour	Summary of Events and Information	Remarks and references to Appendices
MAROC	August 26	8pm 11pm	Were relieved by the 1st LONDON Regt. Relief completed about 11.0 pm without casualties	
LES BREBIS HOUCHIN	27	10AM	at LES BREBIS and marched back to HOUCHIN where they bivouacked. Had breakfast and marched to LABEUVRIERE where the Bn. went into billets.	
LABEUVRIERE			1st time B. Coy which had been left at HOUCHIN while the Batt. was in the trenches joined at HOUCHIN and proceeded to LABEUVRIERE with them.	
	27		Billets were on the whole dirty with one or two exceptions. A great deal of fatigue work had to be done immediately the Batt. leaving the rest of the men who had been in the trenches.	
	28 29 30		Resting in billets. Resting in billets. Routine work.	
	31st		Routine work. Route marching by companies. Batt. went at TAUCHEL.	

12/H.L.I.
Sheet 13

WAR DIARY
or
INTELLIGENCE SUMMARY.

Army Form C. 2118.

Place	Date	Hour	Summary of Events and Information	Remarks and references to Appendices
LABEUVRIÈRE	August 31st		At this time the following changes in the Staff were made. Lieut E. A. McLellan took over the duties of Adjutant vice Lieut K.G. Campbell who proceeded to join B Company.	6

46th Inf.Bde.
15th Div.

WAR DIARY

12th BATTN. THE HIGHLAND LIGHT INFANTRY.

S E P T E M B E R

1 9 1 5

Attached:

Appendices 1, 2 & 3.

Instructions regarding War Diaries and Intelligence Summaries are contained in F.S. Regs., Part II. and the Staff Manual respectively. Title pages will be prepared in manuscript.

INTELLIGENCE SUMMARY.

September 1915

(Erase heading not required.)

12/H.L.I.

Place	Date	Hour	Summary of Events and Information	Remarks and references to Appendices
LABEUVRIÈRE	September 1st		Routine work. 1 coy on musketry and remainder of Batt. on fatigue. Capt. R. P.W. TORRANCE took over duties of 2nd in Command.	eamh
	2nd		Routine work. Route marching by companies. Working parties at night.	eamh
	3rd		Parades were under Coy. arrangements. 1 coy was on musketry. Watering.	eamh
	4th		The Batt. was on fatigue.	eamh
	5th		Divine Services. Working parties at night.	eamh
	6th		Parades under Company arrangements.	eamh
	7th		The Battalion moved at 9.0 am to VERQUIN where it halted for dinners. Leaving VERQUIN at 1.0 p.m. it marched via Noeux to its billets. B & C companies in dug-outs to the right of the SAILLY line, and A & D in billets in MAZINGARBE. LOOS ROAD KEEP & QUALITY KEEP NORTH were each occupied by 2 Platoons of A. company.	eamh
MAZINGARBE	8.		The Batt. moved at 2.0 p.m. to NOEUX and both over billets from the 1st Camerons.	eamh

Army Form C. 2118.

Sht 14

WAR DIARY
or
INTELLIGENCE SUMMARY.
(Erase heading not required.)

Place	Date	Hour	Summary of Events and Information	Remarks and references to Appendices
	1915			
NOEUX	Sep 9		The Battn was occupied in bathing, cleaning billets, & parades under company arrangements.	camp
	10		Fatigue duties, & parades under Coy. arrangements	camp
	11		Do Do	camp
	12		Do Do	camp
	13		Do Do	camp
	14		Do Do	camp
	15		Do Do	camp
	16		Capt H. STEVENSON joined as 2nd in Command.	camp
	17		Draft of 20 men joined	camp
	18		Do Do	camp
	19		Do	camp
	20		The Battn relieved the 11th A&SH in a portion of X2. The relief commenced at 2.0 pm & was concluded at 7.30 pm	camp
QUALITY ST.	21	7.0am	The bombardment of the enemy's lines commenced. A patrol under Capt Young went out at	camp

Instructions regarding War Diaries and Intelligence Summaries are contained in F. S. Regs., Part II. and the Staff Manual respectively. Title pages will be prepared in manuscript.

INTELLIGENCE SUMMARY

(Erase heading not required.)

Place	Date	Hour	Summary of Events and Information	Remarks and references to Appendices
QUALITY ST.	Sept. 22		The bombardment was continued all day	
	23		Do	
	24		Billets in MAZINGARBE & PHILOSOPHE. The bombardment was continued. Head quarters moved to into Battle Hq about 5.0 P.M.	
	25		The battalion was in position in the early hrs of the morning A & B Coys in front line system forming the 5th attacking Column & C & D Coys in C.T. 16 in support to the 10 Scottish Rifles, 3rd Columns, and 7th K.O.S.Bs, 4th Columns respectively. The Gas attack commenced at 5.50 am. The assaulting parties of A & B Coys went over the parapet at 6.30 am. At the same time C & D Coys moved up to the front line system and as soon as the S.R. & K.O.S.Bs were clear of it to the trenches they went over the parapet in support. Details of the action are given in the Attached. After the action the remains of the battalion were relieved withdrawn to our old front line system, where it was relieved at 10 p.m. front into billets at QUALITY ST. Capt. TORRANCE was Hospitaled (gassed concussion).	Attached Nos 1, 2 & 3
	26			

INTELLIGENCE SUMMARY

Place	Date	Hour	Summary of Events and Information	Remarks and references to Appendices
MAZINGARBE	Sep 27		The battalion moved from QUALITY ST and went into hutts at MAZINGARBE. It was 9 Officers and at 1400 O.R. strong. Its casualties were — Officers 7 killed and 11 wounded, O.R. 63 killed, 228 wounded, and 214 missing. The following officers were killed:— "A" Coy Capt Hartley, "B" Coy Capt Gemmell, Lt K.G. Campbell, Lt Pentone + 2Lt G. Adamson, "C" Lt B. Brown, D Coy Lt Nicoll. The following officers were wounded. Adjutant Lt McKellar, Transport Officer Lt Shaw, Quartermaster Lt Reuter, "A" Cy Capt Young, Lt Jones + 2Lt Lucas, "B" Lt/, "C" Coy Capt Brown 2Lt McNeil, "D" Coy Capt Shaw, Lt Hinton + 2Lt D.G. Campbell.	Aps
HAILLICOURT	28		The battalion moved from MAZINGARBE and went into hutts at HAILLICOURT. Lt Stevens was appointed acting Adjutant. The following officers took over temporary command Hay of Companies. Lt Hawley A Coy, Capt Stevenson B Cy, Capt. Wilson "C" Coy and 2Lt Murdoch D Coy. on turn it 26lt. 2Lt Sim joined.	Aps
"	29		Battalion refitting. Draft of 74 NCOs & men received.	Aps
"	30		Battalion refitting. Routine work. 2Lt McHardie joined posted to D Coy.	Aps

A P P E N D I C E S

1, 2 & 3 .

NO 5 COLUMN

12th Bn High. L.I.

Report on Operations of A. and B. Companies and
M.G. Section 12th Bn High. L.I. during attack
25th and 26th September.

  At the commencement of operations on 25th Sept.
A. and B. Companies 12th Bn High. L.I. forming the 5th
Column and commanded by Captain P.W. Torrance were in
position in our front line trench, A. Coy. on the
right B. Coy. on the left, the frontage covered
extending from the VERMELLES-LOOS ROAD on the right
to the LE RUTOIRE LOOS ROAD on the left.
They were supported by four Machine Guns, two of which
were kept under cover until such time as they should
advance.
  The objective of No 5 Column was the German front
line, communication and support trenches from LOOS ROAD
REDOUBT to SOUTHERN SAP, which when taken by the
Infantry were to be consolidated and held, the Machine
Guns being brought up for this purpose. At 6.30 a.m. on
the morning of the 25th September immediately on
cessation of the Gas A. and B. companies sent sections
of Infantry forward supported by Machine Gun fire, to
make way for the bombers who were to clear the German
trenches in LOOS ROAD REDOUBT and the SOUTHERN SAP
respectively. Owing to the condition of the wind
and the contour of our line on the right, many of
A. company's men suffered from the effects of our own
gas before leaving the trenches.

2.

B. Company were also apparently affected by it, but not to the same extent. Southern Sap on investigation proved to be only a track some inches deep and was responsible for many of the losses sustained by B. Company, who had looked for shelter in it. It was raked by Machine Gun fire constantly. All the company's Officers were killed, and all its sergeants either killed or wounded before reaching the German wire, but the Bombers got through and proceeded with their work of clearing the trenches and eventually met in with those of A. Company. On account of the losses sustained and a shortage of bombs, it was impossible to carry out the original idea of bombing along the trenches to the left to get into touch with the Bombers of the 1st Division who failed to put in an appearance.

Acting on orders from O.C. Column the Machine Guns were brought forward at 7.15 a.m. but owing to the German front line trenches being still held in places by the enemy, they met with considerable opposition both from Machine Gun and rifle fire. Three of our guns gained the trenches with about 50% of casualties but the fourth on the right and in charge of the M.G.O Sergeant was put out of action, being struck by a bullet, and the section at this point reduced to two men. Pte A.Ramage (17641) Acting No 1 on No 4 Gun is deserving of special mention for the cool and able manner he displayed in handling the gun under fire. At about 11.30 a.m. M.G.O. and SIGS entered the German front line trench at a point just N. of Southern Sap and found O.C. Column and some 80 men of A. and B. Companies barricading the fire trench, as a party of the enemy were still holding about 50 yds of their trench to our N.

Two machine guns of ours were covering operations at the time. About noon a bombing party of 6th Camerons arrived and endeavoured to clear the trench, with partial success. During this period the support line was put in a state of defence and emplacements and fire steps made and Machine Guns mounted.

About 3.30 p.m. some of the 1st Division arrived and completed the clearing of this trench. At 5 p.m. the 1st Division Bombers passed through. Owing to the 1st Division bombers not appearing the 5th Column found its position too much to the left and proceeded to occupy the frontage allotted in Brigade orders, which was put in a state of defence and held during the night 25/26th Sept. About 9.30 a.m. on the 26th September O.C. Column received orders to change his position and eventually took up a line in an enemy trench 36.B.G.29.c.39 to G. 29.B.03. This position was held until the evening of 26th September when orders were received for the troops to be withdrawn.

         (Sgd) J.H. Purvis, Lt·Col.

1.10.15.   Commanding 12th Bn High' L.I.

12th Bn High. L.I.

Short Narrative of events 25th/26th Sept. 1915.

On the morning of the 25th the 12th Bn High. L.I. was in position in the trenches as ordered, A. and B companies occupying a position in front line system forming the 5th attacking column, C. and D. Coys being in support to 10th Bn Sco. Rifles (3rd Column) and 7th Bn K.O.Sco. Bord. (4th Col) respectively. C. and D. Coys occupied C.T. 16.

I have no personal knowledge of the actions of the 5th attacking column and propose to deal only with the situation as I found it in my immediate vicinity.

C. Coy. moved up to the front system followed by D., and reached the front line parapet with a hitch.

The last of the leading Battalion had just left.

I then ordered my two Coys to advance in support and they crossed over to the German trenches.

From this point we advanced towards our objective without a pause until we reinforced the firing line in the neighbourhood of Puit 14 (Bis) This was taken by our left flank without opposition.

At this time I was on the extreme left and realised our line was gradually changing to a more Southerly direction and advancing on LENS instead of CITE ST AUGUSTE. Our left advancing along the LE BASSE-LENS ROAD in place of the road running East, marked "Metalled, but poor".

Further we were not in touch with the first Division which should have been on our immediate left at

2.

Puits 14 (bis) and our left flank was dangerously exposed.

These facts were reported by me to the Brigade at the time.

At this moment I saw Major Glenny of the 7th Bn K.O.Sco. Bord. and told him that we must endeavour to bring the attack back to the right direction and delay advancing until this was accomplished. He agreed with me and said he would get this carried out. The line was now continuing direct on Hill 70. Just before reaching the road junction at 31.B.3.5., I saw my orders were not being carried out and that the line had advanced too near the crest of the Hill. I then sent Captain Stevenson to Major Glenny to tell him I did not consider he should advance further, but should halt and get the line consolidated, Major Glenny told Captain Stevenson that he had no intention of going further.

I then sat down at the road junction (31.B.3.5.) and wrote a lengthy report of the situation. On getting up from this I found the whole of the firing line had passed over the crest of Hill 70. I immediately proceeded over the crest of the hill and found that they were hotly engaged with the enemy holding the line in front of the CITE ST LAURENT and were driven back by Machine Gun fire . I sat down to write a report to the Brigade and before I had finished it most of the line had retired. They were then rallied behind a small embankment running East and West just below the crest of the hill, where they dug themselves in . At this period realising the weakness of our exposed left flank I took steps to protect this by placing troops in the wood South

of BOIS HUGO and PUIT 14.(Bis), and also occupied
BOIS HUGO itself.

This was the state of affairs at nightfall on
the 25th.

That night about 9 p.m. I proceeded to Brigade
Headquarters to report situation. I then learned
the 62nd Brigade was to co-operate with us in the
defence of Hill 70 but that touch could not be obtained
with this Brigade

On my way back from Headquarters I met some of the
62nd Brigade and eventually fell in with the 13th
Northumberland Fusiliers whose Adjutant said they were
looking for the Brigadier, and that they were to come
under his orders.

I then guided them to a point on the road
50.N.2.1. and explained the whole situation to their C.O.

With the exception of one Company they remained
here for the night. The Company was sent up to
strengthen our left front-. They dug themselves in on
the North side of the wood at (B.31.5.9.)

At this stage I sent a message to Brigade
Headquarters, reporting situation but received no
acknowledgement.

At 2 a.m. I went myself to report to the Brigadier.

The situation, therefore of all troops at Hill 70
on the morning of the 26th was precisely the same as
at nightfall on the 25th excepting that we had been
reinforced by one Battalion (13th Northumberland
Fusiliers).

When the Hill was shelled by our guns on the
morning of 26th the troops holding the trench just
under the crest were badly shelled by our own guns
and in some places shelled out of it, and were also
fired on by some of the relieving troops.

From this time onwards I can make no statement

as to any definite movement being carried out.

The proceedings resolved themselves into stray bodies of men being rallied and collected by any Officer in their vicinity.

Eventually we were driven back to the South side of the LOOS-HULLUCH road.

I then wnet in search of my No 5 Column which had been left in the German Trenches. Not finding it I went on to Quality Street where I collected 120 men, these I took up to our front line trenches where we remained until relieved at 10 p.m. the same evening.

29.9.15. (Sgd) J.H. Purvis, Lt. Col.
Commanding, 12th Bn High. L.I.

Headquarters,
       46th Infy. Bde

   I submit a report received from
Captain Torrance, who commanded No 5
Column on 25th September . The previous
report rendered was drawn upm by Lt.
Laird in Captain Torrance's absence.

                    (Sgd) J.H. Purvis, Lt. Col.
   13.10.15   Commanding 12th Bn High L.I.

12th Bn High. L.I.

Report of the O.C. No 5 Column
25th and 26th September 1915.

The gas attack commenced at 5.5 a.m. on the 25th.

Unfortunately two (or three) of the gas cylinders burst and several more were leaky and we had several casualties through men being "gassed."

This I can only attribute to carelessness as the helmets were most efficient.

At 6.30 a.m. prompt the assault began. I could see the left, or "B" assaulting party deploying but owing to the thickness of the smoke I was unable to see the right, or "A" party, going out. Owing to the smoke, visual signalling was impossible, and as I had no word from either "A" or "B" party, at about 6.50 a.m. I sent across a runner to each party for information. Neither of these runners returned. At about 7.10 a.m., after speaking to the Brigade Major on the telephone, I was about to take my reserve over to the German trenches when I received word from both ="A" and "B" Company Commanders. From "A" Company that the German front line and support trenches were taken, and from "B" Coy that Southern Sap was taken. I immediately sent on these messages to the Brigade and at once proceeded across with the Reserve, half of which I sent by Southern Sap, and the other half I took myself by LOOS ROAD REDOUBT

On arriving in the German trenches I found they were indeed taken, but the casualties were very heavy" I found myself the only unwounded officer there. I set the men with me at work fire stepping and reversing the parapet in the German support trench and made my way to the north of Southern Sap, where our men under the direction of C.S.M. Bruce "A" Coy. were bombing up the German front line and support trenches. We had cleared about 100 yds of these trenches to the North of SOUTHERN SAP when we ran out of bombs, so many of the bomb carriers having become casualties on the way across to the German trenches. We were able to secure a quantity of German bombs, but as the quantity of these was limited, and the force at my disposal had suffered so severely and was inadequate to hold the section of trenches allotted to us I decided to stop the offensive till I got mre bombs and bombers. I sent messages to the Brigade asking for these to be sent. The position at this time was rather critical. The Germans counter attacked strongly down their front line trench, but we had blocked this trench, and L/Cpl Anderson of "A" Coy made some excellent practice with the German bombs. The enemy made an attempt to come at us across the open between the front line and support trenches, but we had got our Machine Guns mounted in a communication trench, and we had no difficulty in keeping the Germans from coming out.

Shortly after this the M.G.O. Lt Laird and the Signal Officer Lt Hawley got across to the trenches we were occupying and they were both of great assistance to me. Bombs were now coming across

to us, brought by a party under Sgt McGarry
and we were able to resume the offensive.
About 11 o'clock, a bombing party of the
6th Camerons under 2nd Watson came to our
assistance and this Officer led the bomb attack
up the German front line, and C.S.M. Bruce of
"A" Coy. led the bomb attack up the German support
line. In this way we cleared another 300 yds
of the German trenches in the 1st Divisional area,
but as there was still no sign of the 1st Divisional
Bombers meeting us, I ordered the trenches to be
blocked again, as I considered that in the event
of a heavy counter attack across the open, we
would be holding too wide a front for the number
of men we had. About three o'clock in the afternoon
the 1st Divisional troops came across, and I
withdrew my command and occupied the trenches allotted
to No 5 Column in 46th Brigade operation order No 11.
My dispositions were ;- H.L.I. in the front line
or original German Support trench, Camerons in the
original German firing line trench. The usual
night sentries were posted, and most of the night
was spent in making fire steps.
On the morning of the 26th, on the authority of the
Brigade Major, I sent back parties to LENS ROAD KEEP
to get water. Dixies came up from QUALITY STREET
with tea and provisions which the men shared with
the Camerons. After breakfast, in accordance
with orders received from the Brigade, I was
proceeding with my command to the place allotted to
us when I saw a retiral over on the right near the
LENS ROAD. and, knowing that there were some of
our own troops in front of us, I moved up to the

German second line trench in front of LOOS, and reported to the Brigadier in this trench about 200 yds north of the VERMELLES-LOOS ROAD. There I received orders from the Brigadier to take up a defensive position across the VERMELLES-LOOS ROAD, and to report to him when this was done. This would be about 10 a.m. I was on my way back to report to the Brigadier that this had been done when I was knocked down by the explosion of an H.E. shell close to me.

When I got to my senses and reached the place where I had left the Brigadier he was gone, but I reported to the Brigade M.G.O.

7.10.15.   (Sgd. P.W. TORRANCE"

Oct - Dec

12th Wkly.
vol: 2

7958/31

15th/5/51

L.M.
11 sheets

WAR DIARY
or
INTELLIGENCE SUMMARY.
(Erase heading not required.)

Army Form C. 2118.

Sheet 1.

Place	Date	Hour	Summary of Events and Information	Remarks and references to Appendices
HAILLICOURT	Oct. 1		Battalion inspected by G.O.C. IV. Corps, who expressed his admiration of the work done by the Brigade on the 25/26 Sep.	
HAILLICOURT	2		Routine work. Company parades. Inspected by G.O.C. XI. Division at 10.45 a.m.	
	3		Divine Services not held. Battalion moved to LILLERS. Billeted.	
	4		Routine work. Company parades. Following changes made. Capt. STEVENSON resumed his duties as 2nd in Command & 2nd Lieut. LAIRD takes over temp. Coy command of "B" Coy. Capt. WILSON appointed Quartermaster & 2nd Lieut. SIM takes over temporary command of "C" Coy. Draft of 46 N.C.O.s & men arrived.	
LILLERS	5		Routine work. Company parades.	
	6		Routine work. Route march. Capt. STEVENSON appointed 2nd in Command & granted temporary rank of Major from 16-9-15. 2nd Lts. MILLIGAN, DRURY-LOWE, LEITCH, CRAIK and GORDON arrived.	
	7		Routine work. Company parades. 2nd Lts. ROBERTSON, SLOAN, ADAMSON and STEWART arrived.	
	8		do. 2nd Lt. AITCHISON takes over Machine Guns, 2nd Lt. STEWART 2 Lt.	
	9		Reserve M.G. Officer and 2nd Lt. ROBERTSON R.E. Transport Officer. Routine work. Company parades.	
	10		Divine Services. 2nd Lts. SMITH and TOD joined.	

Army Form C. 2118.

WAR DIARY
or
INTELLIGENCE SUMMARY
(Erase heading not required.)

Sheet 17

Place	Date	Hour	Summary of Events and Information	Remarks and references to Appendices
LILLERS	Oct 11		Routine work. Company parades.	[initials]
	12		The battalion left LILLERS by train at 7.31 a.m. for NOEUX LES MINES. Transport proceeded by Road at 6 p.m. via ALLOUAGNE, LOZINGHEM, MARLES LES MINES and moved into South of HOUCHIN. 2nd Lt ADIE joined.	[initials]
NOEUX LES MINES	13.		Battalion billeted. Resting until put on half-an-hour notice to move from noon. Notice to move cancelled at night. 2nd Lt MILLIGAN the signal officer.	[initials]
	14		Routine work. Company parades. Lt. Col. PURVIS proceeded to England on sick leave. Major STEVENSON took charge of the battalion.	[initials]
	15		Routine work. Company parades.	[initials]
	16		do	[initials]
	17		do	[initials]
	18		Divine Service. Fatigue parties.	[initials]
	19		Routine work. Company parades. Fatigue parties.	[initials]
	20		— do —	[initials]
QUARRIES Section D2	21		The battalion paraded at 12.30 p.m. marched to HERMELLES and relieved the Essex Regt & Royal Fusiliers in Section D2 near the QUARRIES. Relief completed by 5.30 p.m. H.Q. BETHUNE joined proceeded to 'B' Coy at BETHUNE. The 2nd K.O.S.B. were	[initials]

Army Form C. 2118.

WAR DIARY
or
INTELLIGENCE SUMMARY.
(Erase heading not required.)

Sheet 18

Place	Date	Hour	Summary of Events and Information	Remarks and references to Appendices
QUARRIES Sec^n D2	Oct 22		On the night and 7th K.O.S.B. on the left.	
	23		Fairly heavy shelling and continuous sniping on part of the enemy. Companies changed men in afternoon during relief. Enemy bombed ESSEX TRENCH, killing and wounding several men. 2/Lt AITCHISON, M.G.O. went out to rally the men in the trench and was killed by a bomb. Enemy's bombing was silenced by our bombers. Rest of day/night was quiet.	
	24		Quiet day. A little shelling, but not at night.	
	25		do.	
Old British front line	26		Battalion relieved in afternoon by 10 Scottish Rifles – went back to support trenches in Old British System. One Company went out to VERMELLES for the night.	
	27		D Company relieved from VERMELLES. C & B Coys went out to VERMELLES for the night.	
	28		C & B Companies relieved. A Coy went out to VERMELLES for the night.	
Old German front line Sec^n D1.	29		Battalion relieved 8th K.O.S.B. in Sec^n D1 in the morning. A Coy coming straight in from VERMELLES at 1 hour. Night quiet.	
	30		Heavy shelling about 1 hour. Shell struck dug out in which were a number of men, killing eight wounding four. Rest of day quiet.	

Army Form C. 2118.

WAR DIARY
or
INTELLIGENCE SUMMARY.
(Erase heading not required.)

Sheet 19

Place	Date	Hour	Summary of Events and Information	Remarks and references to Appendices
Sectⁿ D2	Oct 31.		Quiet day. Heavy shelling at night in reply to our bombardment.	
NOEUX LES MINES	Nov. 1		Relieved by 11th A. & S. H. Relief completed by 4 p.m. Companies marched independently to NOEUX LES MINES where the battalion went into billets	
	2		Routine work. Company parades. Very wet weather. Fatigue parties sent to trenches	do.
	3			do.
	4			do.
	5			do.
	6		Fine day.	
	7		Brigadier General Pelham lectured all Officers at 3.30pm. Battalion paraded at noon marched to VERMELLES where they relieved the 8th Seaforths in	
Old German front line C.2			C.2 (just north of HULLUCH RD in front of ST ELIE). 7th K.O.S.B. on right, 4th St L.B. on left.	
	8		Heavy shelling all day on front line. Trenches badly knocked about - 8 men killed 7 wounded — working parties all night repairing damage. 2/Lt DRURY-LOWE went to HOSPITAL.	
	9		Quiet day. Our heavy guns shelled German front line trenches	
PHILOSOPHE	10.		Relieved by 10th Scottish Rifles. Relief completed by 9 p.m. Scottish Rifles having moved their way up. Companies marched independently to PHILOSOPHE where they billeted.	

WAR DIARY
or
INTELLIGENCE SUMMARY.
(Erase heading not required.)

Army Form C. 2118.

Sheet 20

Place	Date	Hour	Summary of Events and Information	Remarks and references to Appendices
	Nov.			
PHILOSOPHE	11		Resting in huts. Fatigue parties	
	12		do.	
Old German Front Line Section C.2	13		Paraded at 11am moved up to trenches when the battalion took over Section C.2 relieving 10th Scottish Rifles. Relief completed by 1.30pm.	
	14		Quiet day. Some shelling but no damage.	
	15		Heavy shelling morning & afternoon. Two men killed & trench knocked about badly. Fatigue parties at night repairing damage.	
Old British 2nd Line	16		Battalion relieved by 10th Scottish Rifles moved back into support trenches in Old British System. Working parties in afternoon.	
	17		Working parties all day. Very quiet. 2nd Lt MYLES joined, posted to "D" Coy	
	18		do.	
VERQUIN	19		Battalion moved out of trenches at 9.30am & Companies marched independently to VERQUIN when the battalion went into billets	
	20		Resting in billets. Cleaning up	
	21		Robes Hats & Equipment examined. C/S Divine Service held.	
	22		Routine Work. Company Parades. Bathing Parade. 2/Lt HUMPHRIES joined, posted "A" Coy	

Army Form C. 2118.

WAR DIARY
or
INTELLIGENCE SUMMARY.
(Erase heading not required.)

Sheet 22

Place	Date	Hour	Summary of Events and Information	Remarks and references to Appendices
	Nov.			
YERQUIN	23		Routine Work, Company parade. Baths	
VERMELLES	24		Battalion moved to VERMELLES, two Companies marching there Companies by buss. Took over billets from 9th Essex Regt. Battalion in support under ½ hour notice to move. 2nd Lt ADAMSON went to hospital.	
	25		Fatigue parties in trenches. 2nd Lt GORDON went to hospital.	
Old British front line	26		Paraded at 8 am. relieved 6 Yth K.O.S.B in D1 (S.E Julian of HOHENZOLLERN REDOUBT) On left 10th Scottish Rifles on right 4th L.I.B.	
	27		Quiet day. Cold frosty weather	
VERMELLES	28		Relieved by 7th K.O.S.B went back to old billets in VERMELLES. Relief completed before 10 p.m.	
	29		Fatigue parties in trenches	
JERMYN STREET	30		Battalion paraded at 6.30 am relieved 1/4th Seaforths (T.F.) in D.2. by noon.	
	Dec. 1		Quiet day. Some shelling	
	2		Quiet day. A little shelling trench mortars	
	3		do	
VERMELLES	4		Very wet night. trenches in bad state falling in. About 9.30 am seven or eight Germans	

WAR DIARY or INTELLIGENCE SUMMARY.

Army Form C. 2118.

Sheet 23.

Place	Date	Hour	Summary of Events and Information	Remarks and references to Appendices
	4		Showed himself at not less than 1 this sap's one night 9 of our line opposite Sap 4. One of them advanced with his hands up & handed a note from 9 of our men who went to meet him. The note was written on a German field postcard read "We are here – How are well off – and welcome – not cheot." The enemy threatened almost immediately. The rest of day was quiet. At 11 a.m. the battalion was relieved by 10th Scottish Rifles & got back to its old Billets in VERMELLES at 3.30 p.m.	
VERMELLES	5		Fatigue parties. Some shelling in morning. Rest of day quiet.	
K2	6		Battalion started at 8.30 a.m. relieved 4th Seaforths (T.F.) in D3. Quiet day.	
VERQUIN	7		Battalion relieved by 1st CAMERONS 45' I.B. by 11 a.m. Four Companies marched thro'	
	8		Companies by bus. Battalion billeted at VERQUIN – Same billets as before	
	9		Resting in billets, cleaning up	
	10		Erskine WNR, Company parades & baths	
	11		do Company parades & baths, working party to trenches. 2nd Lt ADAMSON returned from hospital.	
	12		do Company parades & baths	
	13		Divine Service	
RAIMBERT			Battalion handed moved off at 8.15 a.m. marched to RAIMBERT, via VAUDRICOURT, HESDIGNEUL	

WAR DIARY
or
INTELLIGENCE SUMMARY.

Army Form C. 2118.

Sheet No.

Place	Date	Hour	Summary of Events and Information	Remarks and references to Appendices
RAIMBERT	Dec. 14		GOSNAY - LES CHARTREUSES - MARLES AND AUCHEL. Battalion billeted at RAIMBERT by 1 p.m. Routine work - Company paraded. Platoon drill etc. starts.	
	15		" Working party to R.F.C. Ground Hesdigneul.	
	16.		" "A" Coy on range from 9 two n.	
	17		"	
	18		" "B" Coy on range from 1-4 p.m.	
	19		Divine Services. lined streets at 11.15 a.m. Sir John French motored through about noon.	
	20		Routine work - Company parades. Company drill etc. starts. "C" Coy on range from 9 two n.	
	21.		"	
	22		" Baths.	
	23		" Lecture on R.E. work by R.E. officer	
	24		" Officers & duty depts attended practical work by R.E.	
	25.		" "D" Coy on range from 9 to noon. 2/Lieuts ? Curtis & Harris	
	26.		Divine Services. Holiday.	
	27		Routine work. Company parades. " " "A" Coy on range from 1 to 4 p.m.	
	28		" "	

Army Form C. 2118.

WAR DIARY
or
INTELLIGENCE SUMMARY.
(Erase heading not required.)

Sheet 25.

Place	Date	Hour	Summary of Events and Information	Remarks and references to Appendices
RAIMBERT	29		Routine work. Company parade. M.G. Section Range from 1pm to 4pm	Ref Des Flt
	30		" " Draft of 34 men arrived from Base. Both	
	31		Brigade Route March. Arrived back hr at 1.35 p.m.	

/2 H.L.I.

15th Div

Vol 3

46.

B.M.

Army Form C. 2118.

WAR DIARY
or
INTELLIGENCE SUMMARY.
(Erase heading not required.)

Sheet 26

Instructions regarding War Diaries and Intelligence Summaries are contained in F.S. Regs, Part II. and the Staff Manual respectively. Title pages will be prepared in manuscript.

Place	Date	Hour	Summary of Events and Information	Remarks and references to Appendices
	1916 Jan 1		Routine Work. B Sqn M.G. Section on range. Divine Service	
RAIMBERT	2		Divine Services, C Sqn on range. Draft of 20 men arrived from Base	
	3		Brigade Route March - Route BURBURE, ECQUEDECQUES, LIÈRES, AUCHY-AU-BOIS and FERFAY.	
	4		Routine - Battalion drill - D Sqn on range	
	5		Brigade Exercise commenced. Marched at 8.45 a.m. via AUCHY-AU-BOIS to ERNIAST JULIEN about 12 mls. Arrived at about 11 p.m. and went into billets. C sqn by bit outpost The Bn formed part of adv guard to the division marching in a N.W. direction through DELETTE	
ERNIAST ST JULIEN	6		marching the place the adv halted and troops billeted. The Bn bivouacing Bivouaced. On returning the Bn was taken up a line of outpost with Gen PELIENT - relieving them returning to billets a 3 p.m. The Bde marched back to former billets arriving a.m. RAIMBERT at -	
RAIMBERT	7		2 p.m.	
	8		Routine work - B Sqn on range	
	9		Divine Services - Baths	
	10		Routine work. M.G. section on range	
	11		Routine work.	
	12		Routine work. Preparing trench work trenches	

Army Form C. 2118.

WAR DIARY
or
INTELLIGENCE SUMMARY.
(Erase heading not required.)

Sheet 27.

Place	Date	Hour	Summary of Events and Information	Remarks and references to Appendices
	1916			
NINTH AV.	Jan 13		Entrained at Lillers and detrained at Noeux - marched straight into kitchens (HULLUCH Secli) and took over from 1st Cameron Hqrs. Rations were taken at NOEUX.	
	14		Quiet day. Some shelling which mattered. Capt HANLEY accidentally injured.	
PHILOSOPHE	15		Relieved by 10. S. R. moved back to PHILOSOPHE (West). Under 1/2 hours notice to move in Brigade Reserve. 2Lt SMITH killed by Artillery fire. Right	
9t AV.	17th/6?		Moved into trenches at 11.30pm relieved 10.S.R. in Right Sub Section HULLUCH Sechn	
	17		Quiet day. Some shelling, killed mortars rifle grenades	
	18		do	
	19		do	
NOEUX	20		Relieved by 4 & 5 I.B. moved back to NOEUX	
	21		Routine work. Cleaning up	
	22		Baths. Routine work	
	23		Divine Service. Working parties. Received draft 18 men.	
	24		Routine work Company parades.	
	25		Working parties	
PHILOSOPHE	26		Battalion moved to PHILOSOPE (East) in Brigade Reserve with "C" Cy Connaught Rangers attached	

1577 Wt. W10791/1773 500,000 1/15 D. D. & L. A.D.S.S./Forms/C. 2118.

Army Form C. 2118.

WAR DIARY
or
INTELLIGENCE SUMMARY. Sheet 58.
(Erase heading not required.)

Instructions regarding War Diaries and Intelligence Summaries are contained in F. S. Regs., Part II. and the Staff Manual respectively. Title pages will be prepared in manuscript.

Place	Date	Hour	Summary of Events and Information	Remarks and references to Appendices
	1916			
PHILOSOPHE	Jan 27		for instruction. Battalion under 4 hours notice to move.	
			10 S.R. in left Sub. Section 14 Bde Sectn attacked battalion moved up relieved with 10th AVENUE	
	28		returned billets on situation becoming normal.	
	29		Routine Work	
	30		Routine Work	
			Battalion paraded & went into trenches at 6.15 pm relieving 7 & K.O.S.B. in the Centre Sub. Section	
LOOS.	31		14 Bde Sectn	
	Feb 1		Quiet day in the whole. 2Lt SANDERS & 2Lt NUENSCH arrived for duty	
	2		do	
	3		do	
	4		do	
	5		do	
	6		2Lt TOOVEY arrived for duty	
			Heavy bombardment about 200 yds either side of HAY ALLEY for 2 hours in afternoon	
	7		Relieved returned to billets in NOEUX — killed at 3am. 2Lt JEFF arrived for duty.	
NOEUX	8		Baths. Routine Work & Cleaning up	

Army Form C. 2118.

WAR DIARY
or
INTELLIGENCE SUMMARY.
(Erase heading not required.)

Sheet 29.

Place	Date	Hour	Summary of Events and Information	Remarks and references to Appendices
	1916			
NOEUX	Feb. 9		Under orders to move at 2 hrs notice. Routine work	
	10		Working parties	
	11		Routine work	
	12		Routine work	
	13		Battalion moved at 9.15am to PHILOSOPHE (West). In Brigade Reserve under orders to move at ½ hours notice.	
PHILOSOPHE	14		Routine work. Capt Dixon arrived for duty.	
	15		Routine work. Working parties. 2/Lt LUCAS arrived for duty.	
	16		Routine work	
	17		Relieved the 10th S.R. in Curly Sub Section HULLUCH Section	
9th AV.	18		Quiet day on the whole 2/Lt MACKAY arrived for duty.	
	19		do	
	20		do	
10th AV.	21		Relieved 10th S.R. in Brigade Support in 10th AVENUE	
	22		Working parties in trenches	

Army Form C. 2118.

WAR DIARY
or
INTELLIGENCE SUMMARY.
(Erase heading not required.)

Sheet No 30.

Instructions regarding War Diaries and Intelligence Summaries are contained in F. S. Regs., Part II. and the Staff Manual respectively. Title pages will be prepared in manuscript.

Place	Date	Hour	Summary of Events and Information	Remarks and references to Appendices
	1916			
10th A.V.	Feb 25		Working parties in trenches	
	26		do.	
			Draft 35 O.R. received.	
PHILOSOPHE	27		Relieved & marched to PHILOSOPHE (East) but to 44th I.B. acting as Brigade Reserve. Under orders to move at ½ hour notice. (Relieved by 45th I.B. — 13.R.S.)	
			Routine work. Cleaning up	
	26		Working parties day & night.	Routine work
	27		do.	Routine work
	28		do.	Baths at MAZINGARBE
	29		do.	Routine work
	Mar 1			

1577 Wt. W10791/1773 500,000 1/15 D. D. & L.   A.D.S.S./Forms/C. 2118.

46

12 H L 1

Vol 4
15-cv

H. M.

Army Form C. 2118.

WAR DIARY
or
INTELLIGENCE SUMMARY.
(Erase heading not required.)

Sheet No. 31.

Instructions regarding War Diaries and Intelligence Summaries are contained in F. S. Regs., Part II. and the Staff Manual respectively. Title pages will be prepared in manuscript.

Place	Date	Hour	Summary of Events and Information	Remarks and references to Appendices
PHILOSPHE	March 1st		In Brigade reserve to 44th I.B.	ASD
	March 2nd		Relieved 7th Camerons in right sub-section 14 Bis sector.	ASD
	3rd		Quiet day. 1 Coy of the 7th Royal Inniskillen Fusiliers attached for instruction	ASD
	4th		do.	ASD
	5th		Major H.H. McD Stevenson rejoined 2nd H.L.I. Capt. A.A.S. Heyman joined and took over Command of the Bat".	ASD
	6th		Quiet day.	ASD
	7th		" " Relieved by 10th S.R. 1 Coy & Coy 7th R.S.F. went into Brigade Reserve in PHILOSPHE	ASD
	8th		" " Relieved by 10th S.R. ASD 3 Coys in Brigade Support in 10th Avenue	ASD
	9th		7th K.O.S.B's relieved Coys. in Brigade Support. They joined the 2 Coys in Brigade Reserve in PHILOSPHE.	ASD
LOOS.	10th		Fatigues in LOOS. Draft of 37 N.C.O.'s & Men arrived for duty.	ASD
	11th		Relieved 8th K.O.S.B's in Left sub-section 14 Bis sector.	ASD
	12th		Quiet day. Slight shelling. 2nd Lt. F.R. Sim wounded.	ASD
	13th		" "	ASD
	14th		Relieved by 6th Camerons & 2 Coys A & S. Highrs. went into Divisional Reserve at Noeux-les-Mines. 2nd Lt W. McHardie & 2nd Lt T.D. Adie wounded.	ASD

Army Form C. 2118.

WAR DIARY
or
INTELLIGENCE SUMMARY.
(Erase heading not required.)

Sheet N° 32.

Place	Date	Hour	Summary of Events and Information	Remarks and references to Appendices
	March			
Noeux-les-Mines	15th		General Routine. Cleaning up.	RSD
	16th	"	Route March in the morning.	RSD
	17th	"	Capt H.G.S. Mackay, 2nd Lt A. Kincaid-Smith & 24 O.R. joined for duty.	RSD
	18th		Work party of 200 men under R.E. in reserve trenches.	RSD
	19th		General Routine. Church Parades. Gen Gough. G.O.C. 1st Corps inspected Church parade. Working of 200 men at Night.	RSD
Hulluch	20th		Relieved 7th Camerons in Brigade Support in 10th Avenue Hulluch sector. Found working parties.	RSD
	21st		Found working parties.	RSD
	22nd		Relieved 7th K.O.S.B's in Left Sub sector. Quiet day.	RSD
	23rd		Quiet day.	RSD
	24th		" "	RSD
	25th		" "	RSD
	26th		" " Relieved by 9th Royal Munster Fusiliers. Went into Brigade reserve in Philosphe to 48th S.B.	RSD
Philosphe				RSD
Raimbert	27th		Marched to Noeux-les-Mines and trained to Lillers. Then marched to billets at Raimbert, where we were in corps reserve.	RSD

Army Form C. 2118.

WAR DIARY
INTELLIGENCE SUMMARY.
(Erase heading not required.)

Sheet No 33.

Place	Date	Hour	Summary of Events and Information	Remarks and references to Appendices
RAIMBERT	28th		General routine. Cleaning up.	RDD
	29th		" " " Musketry etc. Draft 66 O.R. joined for duty.	RDD
	30th		" " " Inspected by Gen Matheson G.O.C. 4th G.B. 2nd Lt R. M°P. Cowper joined for duty	RDD
	31st		" " " " Range practice.	RDD

The Officer
i/c Adjutant-General's Office,
BASE.

Herewith please find
Army Form C. 2118 (War Diary)
for month of April, 1916

J.C. Sloan.
Captain & A/Adjt
for O.C. 13th High. L.I.

3. 6. 16.

WAR DIARY or INTELLIGENCE SUMMARY.

Army Form C. 2118.
Sheet No 34.

12. HLI Vol 3

Place	Date	Hour	Summary of Events and Information	Remarks and references to Appendices
RAIMBERT	April 1st		General Routine. Baths.	ASD
	2nd		Church Parades.	ASD
	3rd		General Routine. Range practice. 2nd Lt S.S. Murdoch transferred to 1st Br Royal Highlanders.	ASD
	4th		General Routine. C.O. inspected a Company. Draft of 69 O.R. reported.	ASD
	5th		General Routine	ASD
	6th		"	ASD
	7th		Divisional Training marched to SERNY.	ASD
SERNY	8th		Divisional Training. Brigade practised the attack. Returned to billets at SERNY.	ASD
	9th		End of Divisional Training. Marched back to FLORINGHEM	ASD
FLORINGHEM	10th		General Routine. 2nd Lt T.A.G. Aitchison reported for duty. Draft of 140 O.R. reported: lecture by the G.O.C. 4th I.B. Capt J. Stratton. C.F. reported for duty.	ASD
	11th		"	ASD
	12th		"	ASD
	13th		" Capt E.J. Qullan. C.F. transferred to 3rd Casualty clearing Station.	ASD
	14th		" Capt V.T. Shaw returned for duty. S.O.C. 46 S.B. inspected wiring squads.	ASD
	15th		"	ASD
	16th		Church Parades. A/t & Q.M. J. Carpenter returned for duty.	ASD

Army Form C. 2118.

WAR DIARY
or
INTELLIGENCE SUMMARY.
(Erase heading not required.)

Sheet 35

Instructions regarding War Diaries and Intelligence Summaries are contained in F.S. Regs., Part II. and the Staff Manual respectively. Title pages will be prepared in manuscript.

Place	Date	Hour	Summary of Events and Information	Remarks and references to Appendices
FLORINGHEM	April 17th		General Routine. ~~Gas~~ Smoke demonstration.	RSD
	18th		" " Baths. C.O. inspected Coys. 2nd Lt D.G. Campbell returned for duty.	RSD
	19th		" "	RSD
	20th		" "	RSD
	21st		" "	RSD
	22nd		" " Church parades.	RSD
	23rd		" " C.O. Coy commanders etc. visited the trenches.	RSD
			Church Parades.	
ANNEQUIN	24th		Marched to LILLERS. Trained to NOEUX. Marched to ANNEQUIN to billets. 2nd Lt H.M. Austin joined.	RSD
HOHENZOLLERN Sector	25th		Relieved 7th East Surrey Regt 12th Div. in left sub-section HOHENZOLLERN Sector. Dr Blew mine at 7.30pm. Under enemy crater. Slight Shelling during afternoon.	RSD
	26th		Quiet Morning. Slight Shelling in Afternoon increasing at Dusk. At 7.30pm. enemy attacked Craters 3 & 4. They were driven back. Heavy Bombardment with rifle grenades. Minenwerfer and artillery. Situation normal at 10.30pm.	RSD
	27th		5.30 A.M. GAS attacked on our right. Wind S.E. Enclosed passed over trenches. East of Hill 645. Enemy then again attacked Craters 3 & 4 But was driven back. Situation normal by 9 A.M. Relieved by 10th Sco Rifs. went into Rest trenches. Casualties 10ff killed 5 O.R. 1 off wounded 70 O.R. 2nd Lt Gunfrey killed. 2nd Lt Bethune wounded.	RSD

1577 Wt.W10791/1773 500,000 1/15 D.D.&L. A.D.S.S./Forms/C. 2118.

Army Form C. 2118.

WAR DIARY
or
INTELLIGENCE SUMMARY.
(Erase heading not required.)

Sheet 36.

Place	Date April	Hour	Summary of Events and Information	Remarks and references to Appendices
Hohenzollern	28th		Quiet day, slight shelling of reserve line. Supplied fatigue parties	RSD
	29th		Quiet day. Slight shelling of reserve line supplied fatigue parties	RSD
	30th		Quiet day slight shelling of reserve line. Supplied fatigue parties	RSD

To 46 I.B.

Operations Night of 26.4.16.

6.30 pm   Enemy bombarded our right & centre support reserve trenches with every description of shell. They also bombarded our front line with shrapnel, T.M. and rifle Grenade. We retaliated at once.

7 pm   The enemy attacked craters 3 and 4 simultaneously from direction of A and C craters. Our bombers kept them off & a continuous chain was at once put in motion carrying bombs up from CLARKS KEEP to the front line. Major Dixon was sent to the QUARRY to superintend the forwarding of the bombs & advise on the situation. Apparently the object of the enemy was to cut off Crater 4, make the garrison prisoners & destroy our mine galleries which, I understand, are centered here. Captain MACKAY immediately took charge of the fighting in Nº 4 Crater & reports to me that 2 Lt LUCAS and Pte HALL R.E. did splendid work in bombing the enemy. Two attempts were made on this Crater & repulsed.   At Nº 3 Crater Captain HUMPHRIES took charge & very good work was also done there in beating off the enemy.

The reserve Company at this time had only one platoon left in Reserve & in reply to the request from Capt. MACKAY for reinforcements, was sent to his assistance.

A working party of the 10 S.R and the personnel of the Tunnelling Cos rendered great assistance in pushing up adequate supplies of bombs.

10 pm   The attacks died away & gradually the situation reverted to normal.

At no time was any part of our line occupied by the enemy, nor were any of our men taken prisoners. Considerable damage was done to RUSSIAN SAP, Nº 12 SAP and portions of CRATER LOOP. These were repaired during the night.

AASteyman
       Lt G
27.4.16.   Eng 10th L.I.

WAR DIARY or INTELLIGENCE SUMMARY

Army Form C. 2118.

Sheet 37.

Place	Date	Hour	Summary of Events and Information	Remarks and references to Appendices
Hohenzollern	May 1st		Relieved 10th Scot Rifs. Quiet day on the whole. Enemy snipers very active. Slight shelling	RSD
	2nd		Quiet morning. ab 2 p.m. enemy shelled support trench & Quarry Alley with 5.9". Very quiet night	RSD
Bethune	3rd		The 11th A & S. Highlanders & 5th L.B. relieved us. Marched to billets in BETHUNE.	RSD
	4th		General routine. Inspection of Bn. by The Lord Provosts of Edinburgh and Glasgow and G.O.C. 15th Div.	RSD
	5th		Supplied working party.	RSD
	6th		General Routine. Brigade exercise. Baths.	RSD
	7th		General Routine. Brigade exercise.	RSD
	8th		Church Parade.	RSD
	9th		General Routine. Supplied working parties. 2nd Lt. R.L. Hannah reported for duty.	RSD
	10th		General Routine. Supplied working parties with H.C. Black rep.	RSD
Noyelles	11th		Relieved 9th Black Watch. H.H.M.G.B. in Brigade Reserve. HQ and 2 Coys Noyelles, 2 Coys Vermelles. 4 p.m. intense enemy bombardment of trenches near the KINK and VERMELLES. Batt.n Stood to. "A" Coy occupied Keeps. D Coy moved to VERMELLES. 7 p.m. "C" Coy occupied Village Line. HQ and "B" Coy moved to VERMELLES. "D" Coy reinforced K.O.S.B.s in Village LINERS O.B.1. Enemy took the Kink about 7 p.m. The Batt.n had few casualties.	RSD
Vermelles	12th		Situation normal by 2 A.M. A-D Coys returned to VERMELLES. Supplied working & carrying parties.	RSD

WAR DIARY
or
INTELLIGENCE SUMMARY

Army Form C. 2118.

Sheet 38.

Place	Date	Hour	Summary of Events and Information	Remarks and references to Appendices
VERMELLES	MAY 13th		Quiet day. Supplied Working and Carrying parties.	RSD
	14th		At 7 p.m. after a bombardment 5th K.O.S.B.s delivered a counter attack at the KINK without much success. "A" & "B" Coys were employed carrying bombs. "C" & "D" Coys reinforced and went to O.B.1 > O.B.5 respectively. Moving later to HULLUCH ALLEY.	RSD
	15th		Quiet day. Supplied working parties. Draft of 100 O.R. reported from 10/11 High L.I. 2nd Lt. H.A. Marten reported for duty.	RSD
Hulluch.	16th		Relieved the 9th R.Munster Fusiliers and 1 Coy R.Dublin Fus. in the HULLUCH sector Quiet day Draft of 101 O.R. reported.	RSD
	17		Quiet day except for rifle grenade activity. Enemy blew small Camouflet without effect.	RSD
	18th		Quiet day. We blew small mine and occupied near lip of the Crater. Considerable rifle grenade activity.	RSD
	19th		Quiet day usual rifle grenade activity. Patrol of 8 O.R. under Lt Todd went behind the Craters. They were seen and fired on by a M.G. and with bombs. Lt Todd was wounded but brought in good information. Four men were missing 1 killed & 3 wounded. Two men returned up on the morning of the 21st with good information.	RSD
	20th		Quiet day except for rifle grenade activity. Capt N.Leitch killed by a rifle grenade.	RSD
	21st		7/8 K.R.S.Bs still relieved the Batth. which went into Brigade Reserve. Supplied working parties.	RSD
	22nd		Quiet day. Supplied Working parties.	RSD
	23rd		Relieved the 10th S.R. in the centre Sub-section. Quiet day.	RSD
	24th		Quiet day. 2nd Lt. H.C. Black reported for duty.	RSD
	25th		Quiet day. Draft of 28 O.R. reported.	RSD

WAR DIARY
or
INTELLIGENCE SUMMARY.

Army Form C. 2118.

Sheet 39.

Place	Date	Hour	Summary of Events and Information	Remarks and references to Appendices
Hulluch	May 26th		Quiet day.	RSD
	27th		Were relieved by 13th Royal Scots 45th I.B. and moved into billets at LABOURSE. were put on ½ hour notice	RSD
	28th		Were ordered to "Stand to" at 10:30 p.m.	RSD
LABOURSE	29th	12:30 A.M.	"C" & "D" Coys were ordered to move to NOYELLES. "A" & "B" Coys relieved them at 8 A.M. Quiet day. Supplied working parties. Draft of 40 O.R. reported. Capt. A. Mather, 2nd Lt. Christie, A. Stewart, J.S. Hamilton, J. McLellan, R.F. Sheil, W.W. Crawford, A.S. Mackenzie, R.R. Marshall, S.W. Hutchin, Lt. J. Duncan reported for duty	RSD RSD RSD
	30th		"A" & "B" Coys returned to LABOURSE. General Routine. Baths for C. Coy.	RSD
	31st		General Routine D Coy abled Baths.	RSD

12 H.L.I. June

Army Form C. 2118.

WAR DIARY
or
INTELLIGENCE SUMMARY.
(Erase heading not required.)

Sheet 40.

Instructions regarding War Diaries and Intelligence Summaries are contained in F.S. Regs., Part II. and the Staff Manual respectively. Title pages will be prepared in manuscript.

Vol 7

7.M
3 whubs

Place	Date	Hour	Summary of Events and Information	Remarks and references to Appendices
LA BOURSE	June 1st		General routine.	RSD
	2nd		General routine. Draft of 38 O.R. reported.	RSD
	3rd		General routine. Baths for A & B Coys.	RSD
HOHENZOLLERN	4th		Relieved 9th Black Watch in centre subsection Hohenzollern Sector. Quiet day.	RSD
	5th		Quiet day except for rifle grenade & Trench Mortar activity	RSD
	6th		Relieved by 10th S.R. went into reserve in Lancashire Trench supplied working parties.	RSD
	7th		Quiet day. Supplied working party.	RSD
	8th		Relieved the 7th 1/15th K.O.S.B's in the Right Subsector. We blew two mines in the HAIRPIN Group one on each flank. 8 2nd Lt We occupied the northly of the craters losing 2nd Lt Aitcheson killed and 2nd Lt R.F.O'D Shiell & 2 O.R. killed & 6 wounded.	RSD
	9th		Quiet day except for rifle grenade & trench mortar activity. Draft of 13 O.R. reported.	RSD
	10th		We bombarded trenches in rear of the HAIRPIN with howies. Fairly quiet day	RSD
	11th		Quiet day except for rifle grenade & trench mortar activity	RSD
	12th		Quiet day except for rifle grenade & trench mortar activity	RSD
	13th		Quiet day.	RSD
	14th		Relieved by 10th S.R. went into reserve in Lancashire trench. Supplied working parties. Quiet day.	RSD

Army Form C. 2118.

WAR DIARY
or
INTELLIGENCE SUMMARY. A.D.

Sheet 41.

(Erase heading not required.)

Instructions regarding War Diaries and Intelligence Summaries are contained in F. S. Regs., Part II. and the Staff Manual respectively. Title pages will be prepared in manuscript.

Place	Date	Hour	Summary of Events and Information	Remarks and references to Appendices
HOHENZOLLERN	Jan 15th		Quiet day. Supplied working parties.	RSD
	16th		Relieved by the 7th/8th K.O.S.Bs. in the Left subsector. Quiet day.	RSD
	17th		Quiet day. Strong patrol went out to try and get prisoner without success.	RSD
	18th		Quiet day. Strong patrol went out again without success.	RSD
	19th		Quiet day	RSD
	20th		Relieved by the 11th A. & S. Highlanders, went into Divisional reserve. HQ and Left half Battn.	RSD
VERQUINEUIL			VERQUINEUIL. Right half Battn. BETHUNE.	RSD
	21st		Cleaning up and Mustered parade. Baths for C. Coy	RSD
	22nd		General routine. Baths for D Coy. Supplied working parties of 100 men. G.O.C. 46th I.B. inspected billets	RSD
	23rd		General routine. Baths for A & B Coys. Supplied working parties of 100 men. G.O.C. I Corps inspected billets.	RSD
Sailly LABOURSE	24th		Marched into billets in SAILLY LABOURSE. D Coy going to NOYELLES. Supplied working parties. Received Draft of 81 O.R. Lt. R.R. Brown & 2nd Lt. D. Drury-Lowe rejoined for duty.	RSD
	25th		Church Parades. 2nd Lts A Bryan, G Cross & W.G. Notman & R.B.O. Moir reported for duty.	RSD
	26th		General routine supplied working parties.	RSD
	27th		General routine.	RSD
Hulluch	28th		Relieved 8th/10th Gordons in the centre sub section Hulluch Sector. Quiet day	RSD

Army Form C. 2118.

WAR DIARY
or
INTELLIGENCE SUMMARY. R.E.
(Erase heading not required.)

Sheet 42.

Instructions regarding War Diaries and Intelligence Summaries are contained in F. S. Regs., Part II. and the Staff Manual respectively. Title pages will be prepared in manuscript.

Place	Date	Hour	Summary of Events and Information	Remarks and references to Appendices
Hulluch	June 29th		Quiet day. Blew small mine on left of St Elie Group and occupied the crater.	ASD
	30th		Quiet day. 2nd Lt Deenah wounded on patrol.	RSD

40/15
July

12.H.L.I.
vol 8

S.M.
6 sheets

CONFIDENTIAL

WAR DIARY

12- Highland L.I.

From
1st July 1916
to
31st July 1916

VOLUME 13

C/o
46th I.B.

Volume 13.

Herewith please find War Diary for month of July, 1916 for transmission to Division.

S. Watson Capt + Adj

JN Lt. Col
Commg. 17th Highland
Light Infantry

1-8-16.

WAR DIARY
or
INTELLIGENCE SUMMARY. RSD

Army Form C. 2118.

Sheet 43

Place	Date	Hour	Summary of Events and Information	Remarks and references to Appendices
Hulluch.	July 1st		Quiet day except for rifle grenade activity in the afternoon. Received draft of 6 O.R.	RSD
	2nd		Relieved by 10th K.S.R. Went into Brigade Reserve. Supplied working parties	RSD
	3rd		Supplied working parties	RSD
	4th		Relieved the 7/8th K.O.S.B's in left sub-section. Considerable trench mortar activity. Blew a mine on the left of the Lookout Group 2. Occupied the new left crater. Lt. McLellan wounded	RSD
	6th		Considerable Trench Mortar activity. Gas discharge on right and left.	RSD
	7th		Quiet day. Slight shelling. Received draft of 5 O.R.	RSD
	8th		Quiet day	RSD
			Quiet Morning. Shelled in afternoon. Heavily shelled on right Coy front from 8.30 to 10 p.m. enemy raided Batts on our right.	RSD
	9th		Quiet day. Blew mine in front of Look Out Sap	RSD
	10th		Relieved by the 10th S.R. Went into Brigade reserve. Supplied working parties	RSD 52
	11th		Supplied working parties.	RSD
	12th		Relieved 7th/8th K.O.S.B's in right sub-section. Quiet day.	RSD
	13th		Quiet day. Enemy blew mine on the right of the Hulluch Group doing no damage	RSD
Bethune	14th		Relieved by 13th Royal Scotts. Went into Divisional Reserve in Bethune	RSD

Army Form C. 2118.

WAR DIARY
~~INTELLIGENCE SUMMARY.~~ R.S.D.   Sheet 4

(Erase heading not required.)

Place	Date	Hour	Summary of Events and Information	Remarks and references to Appendices
Bethune	July 15th		General Routine. Cleaning up.	RSD
	16th		Church parade.	RSD
	17th		General routine. Bathing.	RSD
	18th		General routine. Bathing.	RSD
	19th		General routine. Supplied working parties.	RSD
	20th		General routine. Bathing. H.Q.s by Commanders visited trenches.	RSD
Marles les Mines	21st		Brigade Marched to billets in Marles Les Mines.	RSD
Heuchin	22nd		Marched as a Brigade and went into billets at Heuchin	RSD
	23rd		Church parade.	RSD
	24th		General trudne practised offensive out post attack	RSD
	25th		General routine	RSD
Hericourt	26th		Marched as Brigade and went into billets in Hericourt.	RSD
Villers l'Hôpital	27th		Continued march. H.Q. and 2 coys went into billets in Villers l'Hôpital and 2 coys billeted in	RSD
			Noeux	
Bernevil	28th		Continued march and went into billets in Bernevil	RSD
	29th		Rested. General routine.	RSD

Army Form C. 2118.

Sheet 45

WAR DIARY
or
INTELLIGENCE SUMMARY.

(Erase heading not required.)

Place	Date	Hour	Summary of Events and Information	Remarks and references to Appendices
Berneuil	July 30th		Church parade.	R.S.F.
Flesselles	31st		Continued march. Billeted at Flesselles.	R.S.F.

"A" Form. Army Form C. 2121.
MESSAGES AND SIGNALS.

SECRET

TO: O.C 12th H.L.I

Sender's Number: BM 986 Day of Month: 16th   AAA

1. The Brigadier directs that you carry on with making arrangements for a raid against enemy trenches.

2. Please submit scheme and proposals as to what is to be practised.

J Work Capt
Brigade Major
46th IB

Secret   Copy No 2

            Operation Order No 1.
            by Lt. Col. Heyman Comdg. 12th Bn. High L.I.

Map Ref. Brigade trench map and attached Sketch.
                General Idea

1. In accordance with orders received the battalion will, on the night of the 4th/5th July 1916, carry out the following operation.

2. The batt'n. will be holding the left sub-section of the HULLUCH Sector.

3. The batt'n operation will consist of two attacks on the enemy's trenches opposite.
   A. A bombing attack on the enemy's posts in the QUARRY Group of Craters.
   B. Simultaneously a raid on the enemy trenches between G 12 C 4½. 9½ and G 12 C 5, 8½.

4. The object of this raid is:—
   I. To destroy raid the enemy's trenches.
   II. To destroy their bombing posts
   III. To destroy all deep "Dug-Outs.

11

4. (continued)
 D To secure prisoners and all identification possible
 E To destroy any mine shafts in the area. (For this purpose a party of R.E from the 91st Field Coy will be attached & their services however will not be called upon until actually required.)

5. The ideal to be attained in carrying out this operation will be for the two attacks to meet at point "J" on the sketch

Special Idea.

4. The attacking columns will be composed as follows:-
A/ Bombing assault column under command of 2nd Lt Austin consisting of 2 off. 6 N.C.O's, and 22 men.
B/ Raiding party under 2nd Lt D.G. Campbell consisting of 2 off. 8 N.C.O's & 40 men. (R.E. detachment will be attached to this party)

IV

push on to 'g'.
No 3 party will meanwhile have split
into two parties and following parties 1 & 2
will occupy sapheads "A & B", which they
will destroy.
They will cover the retirement of parties
1 & 2
The bombing party at 'F' is not to
proceed further. Should the "raiding
party" not succeed in reaching this
point the senior present will withdraw
the whole party at his own discretion.
The party at 'C' will conform.

'B' The Raiding Column.
1. The raiding platoon under 2nd Lt D.G. Campbell
will be divided into two equal parties.
    They will leave our trenches at
Bayan 8 9 and will be conducted by
the scout officer and scout corpl. to
two openings in enemy wire marked
'g' & 'h' on sketch, where they will
effect an entrance into the enemy
trenches.
    The party entering at 'g' will detach
a party of 1 N.C.O and 5 men who will

III

"A". Bombing Assault Column.

I The bombing assault column will be divided into three parties;
1st party 1 off 2 N.C.O's & 8 men.
2nd party 1 off 2 N.C.O's & 8 men.
3rd party 1 off 2 N.C.O's & 6 men.
Each party is to be a complete bombing party carrying its own supply of bombs (60).
Composition of each party.
  3 bayonette men
  1 thrower
  1 carrier
  3 or 1 spare men.

II The objective of the attack will be Sap heads marked "A" & "B" on the attached sketch. The parties attacking over the ridge between SEAFORTH and LOOKOUT Craters.
No 1 party attacking Saphead "A"
No 2 party attacking Saphead "B"
and both bombing down respective saps.
At "C" No 1 party will leave 1 bayonet man and 1 bomber and proceed to "E"
At "d" No 2 party will leave 1 bayonet man and 1 bomber and with remainder will

V

remain and establish a post there.
The remainder will proceed south towards
the junction of the next communication
trench with the front line shown on
sketch immediately above 'F'. They will
also establish a post there and proceed
to bomb the Dug-outs between G and
this point

Meantime the party which entered at
"H" will bomb their way down to
point 'J', leaving a post of 1 NCO and 5
men at the junction of the Communication
trench just N. of point 'J'. (This post will
follow on & rejoin their party on arrival
of the party which entered at 'J')

Should the bombing assault column
not have arrived at that point, they
will bomb up towards 'd' & 'c'
endeavouring to take the enemy
posts in A & B in rear.

General Instructions

1. The paths to be followed by the raiding
column to 'g' & 'h' will be taped out
the previous night by the scout
officer, so that there will be

VI

no question of the guides not leading these parties correctly.

2. The detail and composition of the "raiding party" has been already communicated to the officer in charge.

3. The hour at which the action will begin will be notified later.

4. Arrangements will be made with the French mortars to concentrate on the M.G. emplacement N of 'g'

5. Two rifle grenade batteries of 4 rifles will be posted under command of 2nd Lt Goff so as to fire on enemy support trench in rear of the craters. He will register these batteries previously

6. The R.E. party will only be sent for, if on entering the enemy lines their services are found to be required for demolition.

VII

7. The watches of all officers in the Battn are to be synchronised at 4 p.m. on the afternoon of the 1st July and O.C. Coys will report at that hour accordingly.

8. The period allowed for the operation will be 30 mins. from the moment the attack begins.

30.6.16. R S Dixon Major
for O.C. 12th (S) B" High L.I.

Copy No 1 File
Copy No 2 46 I.B.
"   No 3 O.C. D Coy
"   No 4 2nd Lt Atkin
"   No 5 All Coys.

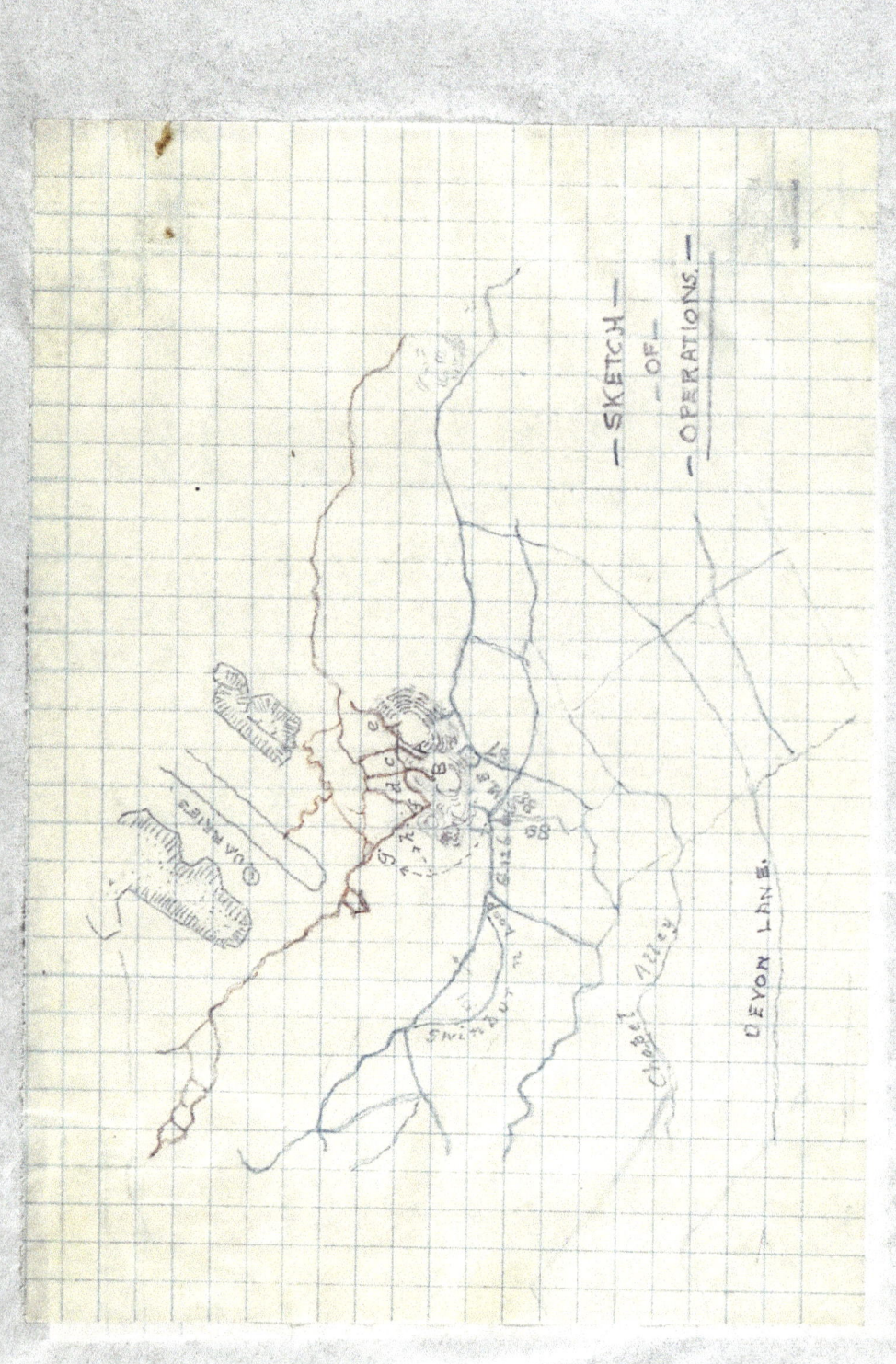

C.C.15.

SECRET.

　　To/

　　　　46th I. B.

　　Reference your B.M.986 of yesterday I submit herewith the general outline of the Scheme I wish to adopt.
　　If this scheme is approved of I would like to dig replica trenches and practice the raid for two or three days.
　　In addition I would also like to be able to give a demonstration to the men of the effect of, say, 2 Bangalore torpedoes on 40 feet of good wire

Aastupman
Lt.Col.
commg. 12th High. L. Infty.

17-7-16.

SECRET.

Scheme for Raid on Enemy's Front Line Trenches.

1. <u>General Idea.</u> The plan suggested is based with a view to retain the element of surprise in our raids. The main principle will be the employment of Bangalore torpedoes for the destruction of the enemy wire. No previous artillery bombardment- A short and rapid raid on explosion of the torpedoes by a party previously drawn up in front of enemy wire at point to be raided- The Artillery to cooperate by creating a box barrage round the selected spot immediately on the explosion of the torpedoes- The withdrawal to be covered by "P" bombs dropped in enemy trench and smoke barrage by T.Ms.

2. <u>Site of trenches to be raided.</u> The site proposed is the trench junction at G.5.c.5½.2¼. and frontage proposed is from suspected M.G. emplacement on left to suspected T.M. emplacement on right- about 100 yds. (Air photo 25 J.248 Square G.4.5.10.11. taken 8th July 1916. attached).

3. <u>Strength and Composition of Parties.</u> Raiding party to consist of 5 Officers and 100 O.R. divided up as follows:-
    (a.) <u>Torpedoe party</u> - One Officer 20 O.R.
    (b.) <u>Remainder</u> of party 4 Officers and 80 O.R. armed with knobkerries and bombs to be drawn up in extended order one pace interval opposite trench junction to be raided.

4. <u>Detail of Parties.</u>
    (a). Torpedoe party will place 6 Bangalore torpedoes in wire at trench junction at G.5.c.5½.2¼. and 3 torpedoes on either flank at places appointed for the exit of the raiders and withdraw to our trenches leaving 2 men to observe the wire until appointed time.
    (b) On explosion of the torpedoes the whole raiding party will immediately rush the enemy's trench and work outwards.
        i. One party will work to the suspected M.G. emplacement.
        ii. One party will work to the suspected T.M. emplacement.
        iii. Special parties to block the two converging Communication trenches will work up to a point 40 yds. from junction with front line trench.
    (c). Torpedoe party will form up in extended order in rear of the raiding party. On the raiding party going forward the torpedoe party will take up its position just short of the enemy parapet and be ready to cover the withdrawal of the raiders by throwing "P" bombs into the evacuated trenches on a given signal. When the raiding party has passed through the torpedoe party the latter will withdraw.

5. <u>Co-operation Required.</u>
    R.A. and Medium T.Ms. to form a box barrage on explosion of torpedoes.
    At the same time Light T.Ms. to bombard the front line trenches on either flank and engage known M.G. emplacements in the vicinity.

    R.E. party to be supplied for the purpose of correctly charging, connecting up and firing the Bangalore torpedoes under the orders of the Officer in charge of the operation.

46th Brigade.

15th Division.

1/12th BATTALION

HIGHLAND LIGHT INFANTRY

AUGUST 1 9 1 6

Confidential

To. 46.I.B.   C 149

Herewith War Diary for
August 1916

                    C.A.Strymann
                         Lt. Col.
7.9.16   C.O. 10 H.L.I.

              A.A. & Q.M.G.
                  15

        forwarded.

8.9.16.
                         M. Fox
                         Capt.
                         for Brigade Cmdr. 46 I.B.

D.A.G.
3: Echelon

Forwarded in continuation of my A/38/23 of 6: inst.

SECRET

[signature] Capt
for MAJOR GENERAL
COMMANDING 15th DIVISION.

HEADQUARTERS
15th DIVISION.
9 - SEP. 1916.
Reg. No. A/38/23.

WAR DIARY
INTELLIGENCE SUMMARY.
(Erase heading not required.)

Sheet 43

Instructions regarding War Diaries and Intelligence Summaries are contained in F.S. Regs., Part II. and the Staff Manual respectively. Title pages will be prepared in manuscript.

Place	Date	Hour	Summary of Events and Information	Remarks and references to Appendices
	Aug.			
Flixecourt	1/8/16		General Routine	
	2		General Routine. Received a draft of 13 O.R.	
	3		Brigade exercise. Practising new Attack formation. Received a draft of 31 O.R.	
MOLLIENS-AU-BOIS	4		Continued march and billeted at MOLLIENS-AU-BOIS	
FARANVILLERS	5		Continued march to FARANVILLERS and billeted there.	
	6		Church Parades	
ALBERT	7		Marched to trenches and relieved 30th DURHAM L.T. Infy. 23rd Division 3rd Corps ## South of MARTINPUICH	
TRENCHES	8		Trenches heavily shelled especially by night	
Sq MARTINPUICH	9		At 6 p.m. the Germans heavily barraged our Support line for an hour but no infantry action took place	
	10		Customary heavy shelling otherwise nothing of importance	
	11		Usual day and night barrages by enemy. Received a draft of 62 O.R.	
	12		At 10.30 p.m. after artillery preparation, the Battn. attacked part of GERMAN SWITCH LINE in conjunction with the 45th Brigade on our left. Order of Attack Regt. B Coy Centre C Coy Right A Coy Reserve D Coy Assaulting troops formed up in their positions 50 yds the parapet at 10 p.m. The assault was delivered on the barrage lifting at 10.32 p.m. but in spite of determined efforts the enemy M.G crews stopped the attack. Those who were left stayed in Shell holes near the German line until ordered to return to their	

INTELLIGENCE SUMMARY.

Sheet 44.

Place	Date	Hour	Summary of Events and Information	Remarks and references to Appendices
DINGLE near FRICOURT	13		Many original positions. The Casualties in this action amounted to 16 officers and 236 OR 1 Coy 10/11th HLI and 1 Coy 7/8 KOSB were sent up to assist hold the line.	
	14		Relieved by 10/11 H.L.I. The Battn went into Brigade Reserve near the DINGLE with a strength of roughly 140 per Coy.	
	15		Battalion reorganising and refitting. All officers left behind at Reinforcement Camp rejoined.	
	16		Usual working parties	
	17		As above	
Trenches S of MARTIN P.RICH	18		As above Relieved the 10/11th H.L.I. in the same Sub Section. By this time most of the GERMAN SWITCH LINE and 5 prisoners were captured. 1½ Coys 10 4/11th H.L.I. were attached to us in Support & Reserve the Battn only to be strong enough to hold the front line and immediate Support.	
ALBERT in BIVOUAC	19		Brigade relieved by 45th Brigade and went into Divisional Reserve. The Battn was relieved by the 13th Battn Royal Scots and moved into Bivouac immediately E of ALBERT	
	20		Refitting & Supplying Working Parties and usual Church Parades	
	21		Usual Combat and Working Parties	
	22		As above. Draft 7/17 OR Received	

INTELLIGENCE SUMMARY.

(Erase heading not required.)

Sheet 45.

Place	Date	Hour	Summary of Events and Information	Remarks and references to Appendices
ALBERT in Bivouac	Aug 23		Usual Pointing and Working parties	
	24		As above. 2/Lt W.M Crawford wounded when in charge of a working party. Draft 9 2 OR received	
	25		As above. Draft of 95 OR (Bantams) received	} M.
	26		As above. Draft of 60 SR chiefly Ayrshire Yeomanry received.	
	27		Draft 62 OR Bantam Draft returned as unsuitable to Reinforcement Camp. 29 OR Bantam Draft held at Transport lines pending medical board there being Physical unfit. 3 of the draft received on 25/8/16 were considered fit for duty with the Battⁿ. The Battalion Brigade relieved the 3rd Brigade, this Battalion relieving the 2nd Welch Regt in trenches between HIGH WOOD and C.T.S	
TRENCHES between HIGH WOOD and BAZENTIN LE PETIT	28		BAZENTIN LE PETIT. Very heavy shelling all night on C.T.S. Usual shelling. Much work was done by all ranks in the Battⁿ digging SWANSEA Trench, a new trench running parallel with ∧ INTERMEDIATE LINE and 200 yards in front of which was still in the hands of the enemy	} M.
BAZENTIN LE PETIT	29.		The Battⁿ was relieved by 10/11 High L.I. in the front line and moved back to Brigade Support in O.C.1.	
"	30.		Quiet day. A and B Coys proceeded to <s>th</s> SWANSEA TRENCH as a working party with orders to take over that line at 4 am on 31st from the 10/11th H.L.I. Principally as a result of work	

WAR DIARY
or
INTELLIGENCE SUMMARY. Sheet 46.
(Erase heading not required.)

Place	Date	Hour	Summary of Events and Information	Remarks and references to Appendices
Between HIGH WOOD & BAZENTIN LE PETIT	30		Work. Referred to on 28.8.16. 4 Officers and 130 O.R. were surrendered and surrendered to and the 45th Brigade.	10/11 HLI W.D.
	31		Relieved 10/11 HLI in the same line as 27.8.16. Shelling slightly less than usual.	

Vol 10

10. M.
8 sheets

Mean Dining
"
12" H. 6 9

from 18. 9. 16
To   30. 9. 16

WAR DIARY
or
INTELLIGENCE SUMMARY.
(Erase heading not required.)

Army Form C. 2118.

Sheet 47

Place	Date	Hour	Summary of Events and Information	Remarks and references to Appendices
BAZENTIN LE PETIT	Sept 1st		Normal shelling on all C.T.s & intermediate line. During the night Swansea Trench was deepened & joined with the 45th Brigade on our left.	RSD
	2nd		Relieved by 10/11 H.L.I. & went to O.G.1. Supplied a carrying party of 110 men.	
	3rd		Quiet day.	
	4th		Relieved 10/11 H.L.I. in the front line. Usual shelling which was especially heavy at night.	
	5th		Relieved by 7th Camerons. I went into Divisional reserve at the Dingle. 30 off. & 190 O.R. reported.	RSD
FRICOURT	6th		Cleaning up & refitting. Supplied working party of 100 men.	
	7th		Cleaning up & refitting. Supplied same working party.	
	8th		General Routine work. Supplied same working party.	
	9th		General Routine work. Supplied working party. 2 off. reported for duty.	
	10th		General Routine. Supplied working party. Received draft of 34 O.R.	
	11th		General Routine. Supplied working party.	
	12th		Relieved the Northumberland Fusiliers 103rd Brigade at 3 A.M. The relief was shelled with gas shells. Work was done joining up & deepening saps to make jumping of places for the attack. 2 off. & 193 O.R. joined.	RSD

WAR DIARY
or
INTELLIGENCE SUMMARY.
(Erase heading not required.)

Army Form C. 2118.

Sheet 48

Place	Date	Hour	Summary of Events and Information	Remarks and references to Appendices
	Sept		Cameron	
MARTIN Puich.	13th		Heavy Shelling all day. At night trench was joined and deepened.	RSD
	14th		Heavy Shelling all day. The Bn was relieved by the three assaulting Battns at 6 p.m. and into support.	RSD
	15th		At 6.20 the attack on MARTINPUICH commenced. At 6.30 A.M. BOTTOM TRENCH the 1st objective was captured and we immediately established bomb Stores. At 7.22 the final objective was taken and we established bomb stores in factory line and Martinpuich property A & B.D Coys occupied & consolidated the first objective. About 11 p.m. we took over the captured positions from the assaulting troops. Heavy shelling all night.	RSD attached
	16th		During the Day two strong points were commenced in front of Gun Pit Road. Relieved at 6.30 P.M. by 8/10 Gordons and moved back to GOURLAY TRENCH. Received draft of Sgt & 40 O.R.	RSD
CONTAIMAISON	17th		Moved back to trenches near CONTAIMAISON.	
LAVIEVILLE.	18th		Moved into Corps reserve & marched to LAVIEVILLE where we bivouaced	RSD
LAHOUSSOYE	19th		Marched to billets in LAHOUSSOYE	
	20th		Cleaning up & refitting	
	21st		General routine. Draft of 160 O.R reported.	

WAR DIARY
or
INTELLIGENCE SUMMARY.
(Erase heading not required.)

Army Form C. 2118.

Sheet No. ___

Place	Date	Hour	Summary of Events and Information	Remarks and references to Appendices
LA HOUSSOYE	Sept 22nd		Coy Parades. Supplied small working party for the R.E. Bombing ladder commenced.	Nil.
	23rd		Coy Parades. 1 OR reported for duty.	
	24th		Church Parades.	
	25th		Bombing ladder exercise commenced. Draft of 22 O.R. reported.	
	26th		Coy parades A & B Coys went to the range. Draft of 6 O.R. reported	
	27th		Coy parades practising the attack. Draft of 1 off & 70 O.R. reported	Nil.
	28th		Coy Parades. B & C Coys went to the range	
	29th		Coy Parades. Draft of 26 O.R. reported	ASD
	30th		Coy Parades practising the attack. A & B Coys went to the range. Draft of 50 arrived.	ASD
	21st		The Coys practised the attack. Marched into billets in ALBERT.	

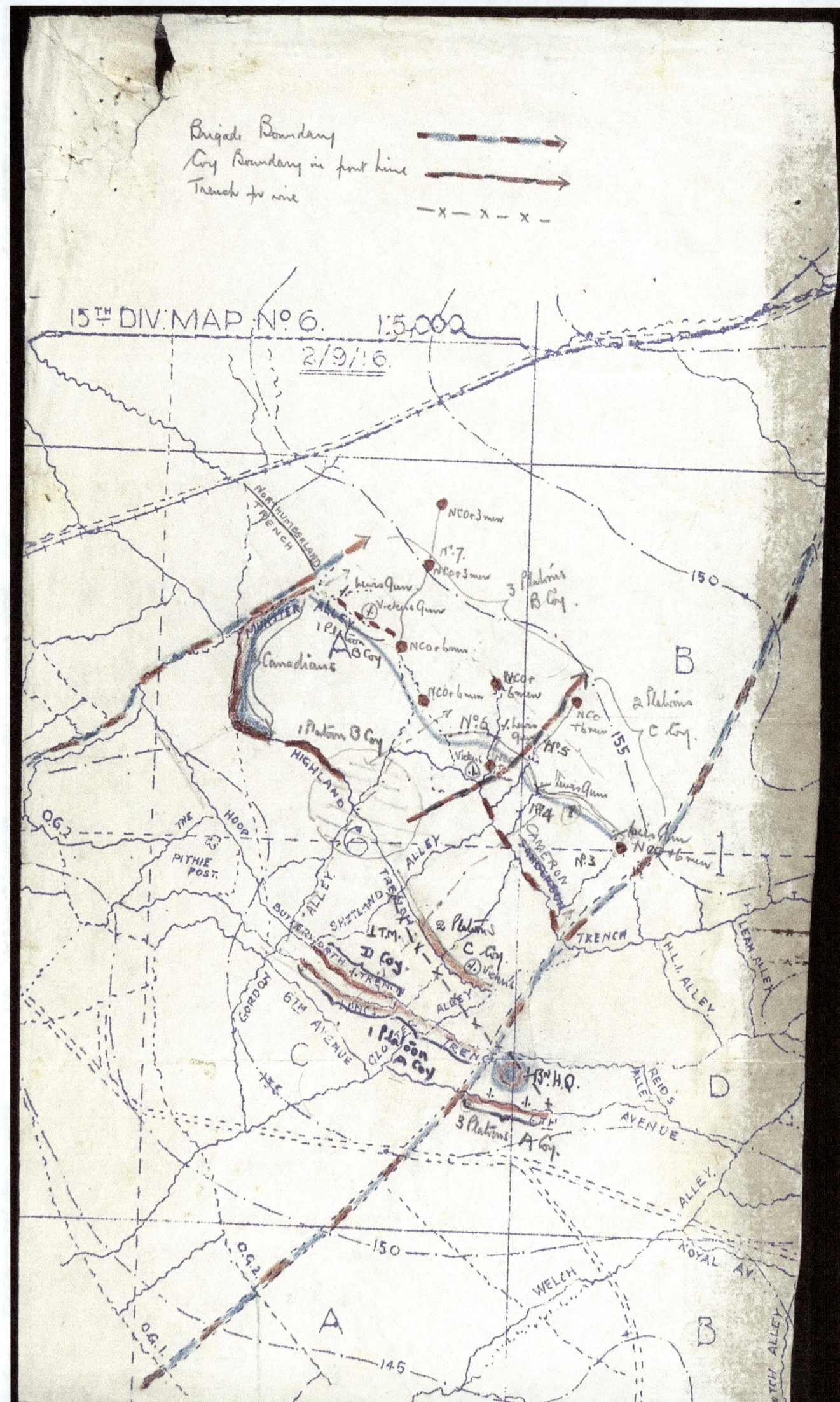

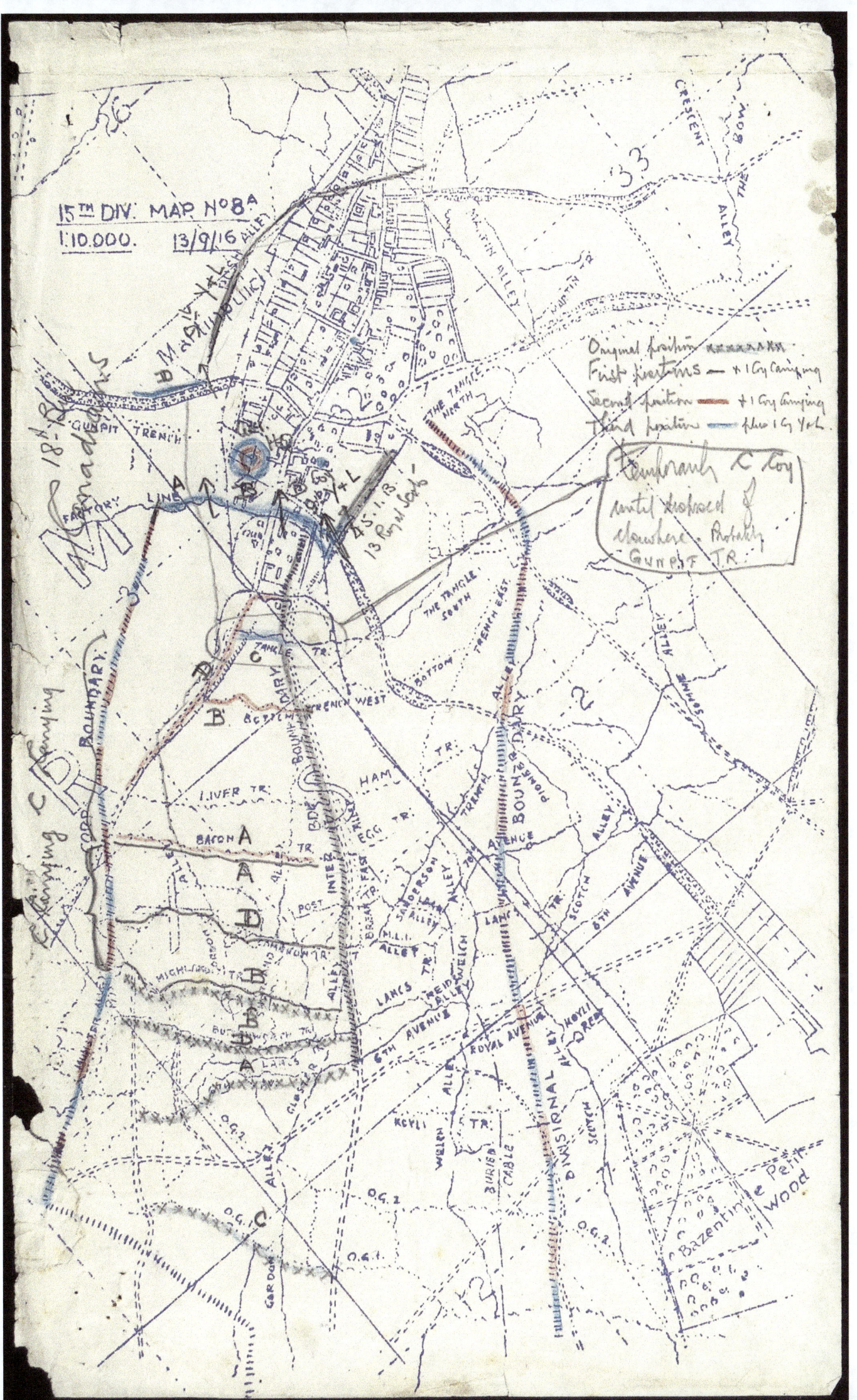

To
46 I.B.
C.159

I beg to report that my dispositions are as shown in attached sketch map —

1. FRONT LINE Right   2 Platoons C Coy to No 6 Sap (exclusive)
                Left   3 "   B . No 6 Sap to MUNSTER TR
   HIGHLAND TR Right 2 Platoons C Coy
              Left   1 Platoon B Coy
   BUTTERWORTH TR (Between SHETLAND + NEW GLOSTER)
              D Coy.
   LANCS TR   1 Platoon A Coy
   6th AV. (on right of road) 3 Platoons A Coy.

2. The CANADIANS occupy MUNSTER TR from its junction with NORTHUMBERLAND TR, then along HIGHLAND TR as shown on map.

3. LANCS TR is in very bad condition + offers little cover so I have occupied it with one platoon placing the rest of the Reserve Coy out of our area in 6th AV as shown on map. This area was unoccupied + is in fairly good condition. These three platoons will work on their own area + will move in as soon as this is habitable.

4. There is a trench mortar (2") in SHETLAND

2.

ALLEY South of HIGHLAND TR. This mortar cannot be fired as it is out of range & its crew occupies two good dug out which could be utilised as a battalion HQ. They are splinter proof only.

5. From the present Battn HQ there is a new trench cut for burying cable. If this could be left open it would make an excellent assembly trench and is a very quick way to the centre of my area. Trench marked —x—x— on map.

6. Tonight I propose to carry out the following work.
a/ Complete trench joining up Saps 3, 4, 5, 6 and CAMERON TRENCH and hence CAMERON TRENCH to NORTHUMBERLAND TRENCH (marked in blue on map. I hope to get this down to average depth of 6 ft.
b/ Dig out Sap 6 to average depth of 6 ft.

A.W. Heymans
N.G.
Cmg 10 HLI

12.9.16
7.16

To
G. O. C.
46th Inf. Bde.

Sir,

I have the honour to report on the operation of the 15th/16th September 1916.

At 6pm on the 14th the battalion moved out of the front line system after having been — A Company took up a position in front of LIVER TRENCH covering the Brigade front, the remaining Companies withdrawing C Coy to O.G.1, D Coy to BUTTERWORTH TRENCH and B Company to HIGHLAND TRENCH. After the assaulting battalions had taken up their positions in the front system A Company was withdrawn to 6TH AVENUE, the battalion then forming BRIgade Support.

At 6.20am the attacking troops went over and at the same time A and D Companies were moved up to BACON and CAMERON trenches respectively. At the same time C Coy went forward to to advanced bomb etc. stores having been organised as in carrying parties for the attacking battalions. Parties were also told off from this Company to deal with prisoners and they took up their position at the same time.

At 6.30 am it was reported that the first objective had been gained and advanced bomb etc. stores were immediately established in BOTTOM TRENCH.

At 6.58am our troops were reported advancing into MARTINPUICH and at 7.12am well into the village. At 7.22am the final objective was reported as gained and our troops consolidating.

At 9am D Company was sent up from CAMERON TRENCH to occupy the SUNKEN ROAD and B Coy from HIGHLAND TRENCH to occupy BOTTOM TRENCH and the Southern portion of the SUNKEN Road. These Companies relieved parties of the 10/11 H. L. I. on the left and 7/8 K.O.S.B. on the right who pushed on to support their battalion at the final objective.

B. and D. Companies both did excellent work in consolidating their positions and before they were ordered forward had dug themselves in with 5/6 ft of cover, and firestepped in places. C Company assisted by a platoon from A Company carried up stores from the advanced stores to the firing line, and as far as can be ascertained satisfied all requirements.

The battalion was ordered to relieve all portions of 10/11 H. L. I., 7/8 K.O.S.B and 10 Sco. Rif. in GUN PIT ROAD and FACTORY LINE between the Brigade boundaries. This movement commenced at 6.30pm. Advanced Headquarters were established at the S. W. side of MARTINPUICH between the FACTORY LINE and GUN PIT ROAD and the relief was completed about midnight. B Company of the 9th Yorks & Lancs were attached to this battalion for this relief.

The original dispositions ordered were.-

GUN PIT ROAD - D Coy and half of C Coy
FACTORY LINE -xRightx - A Coy, Centre B. Coy and half Right
      Left
     B Coy 9th Yorks & Lancs.
TANGLE TRENCH Half of C Coy to occupy this line temporarily
      until it was known whether the whole Company
      was required in GUN PIT ROAD.

Touch was established with the 18th Battn. CANADIANS andx on left and 15th Royal Scots on the right and it was found that GUN PIT ROAD would be strongly with one Company. Half of D Company therefore took up position along the Northern portion of the SUNKEN ROAD.

The battalion continued the work of consolidating throughout the day with little interference from the enemy.

FACTORY LINE, however, received a fair amount of attention from the enemy's artillery especially on the left.

In the afternoon two strong posts were commenced about 60 yards in front of GUN PIT ROAD.

At 6.30pm the 8/10th GORDONS arrived at FACTORY LINE to relieve this battalion.

On relief the battalion was withdrawn to GOURLAY TRENCH being relieved there by the 11th ARGYLL & SUTHERLAND HGRS the following day.

I have the honour to be, Sir,

Your obedient Servant

Lt. Col.
Commg. 12th High. L. I.

19.9.16.

Confidential

War Diary

12th H.L.I.

4/10/16
31/10/16

WAR DIARY
INTELLIGENCE SUMMARY

Army Form C. 2118.

Sheet 44. 50 7b.

Place	Date	Hour	Summary of Events and Information	Remarks and references to Appendices
ALBERT	October 1.		Usual Church parade & general routine	
	2.		Coy parades. "B" Coy gave a successful concert.	
	3.		Coy parades – musketry. ALBERT shelled	
	4.		Coy parades. B. & C. Coy gave combined concert	
	5.		Coy parades. ALBERT again shelled by H.V. probably from MIRAUMONT	
	6.		Coy parades & general routine	
	7.		Coy routine. ALBERT again shelled. Lt Col The Earl of Rothes MC, Major R.S. Dixon, Capt & Adjt D.F. Watson MC, Capt W.D. Blews, Capt the Rev D.F. Stretton MC, Lt G.J. McCarthy RAMC were all casualties. Shell striking the house where they were billeted. A few minutes later, Lt/P. McDougald was also struck whilst in the street by a small piece of shrapnel. Lt R Russell Byrn took command of the batt. until relieved by Major M.H.B. Dennis DSO of the 4/8 KOSB	
	8.			
	9.		Company Routine & Church parades	

WAR DIARY
or
INTELLIGENCE SUMMARY.
(Erase heading not required.)

Army Form C. 2118.

Vol 5 1/7 51 28

Place	Date	Hour	Summary of Events and Information	Remarks and references to Appendices
ALBERT.	9/8/16		Battn. left ALBERT & relieved the 10th Duke of Wellington's Regt. of the 69th Inf. Bde. in the Reserve Bde Area at LOZENGE WOOD. Battn. accommodated in tents & bivouacs. Transport lines at BECOURT WOOD.	
LOZENGE WOOD.	10/8/16		General routine. Coy. parades.	
	11/8/16		Do — including Bombing under Bde bombing officer.	
	12/8/16		General routine. Coys. practise attack. 2Lt A.S.M. McKenzie transferred to R.F.C.	
	13/8/16		General routine. Bombing under Bde B. officer. Coys. in attack.	
	14/8/16		Battn. relieved 4th CAMERONS. in 44th Inf. Bde. Relief complete by 10.0. p.m. Draft of 50 Bantams brought up from TRANSPORT LINES. Capt. R.M. JOHNSTONE took over command of "B" Company. Dispositions A Coy. O.G. FLERS LINE. B Coy. CRESCENT ALLEY; "C"&"D" Coy. PRUE TRENCH.	
	15/8/16		A fine sunny day. Enemy artillery active — own more active.	
	16/8/16		Heavy shelling of O.G.I. Casualties few. Our artillery very active.	

WAR DIARY
or
INTELLIGENCE SUMMARY
(Erase heading not required.)

Army Form C. 2118.

Sheet 46. 57. 2.6

Date	Hour	Summary of Events and Information	Remarks and references to Appendices
17/8/16		Artillery activity on our part all day. Battn relieved 10th S.R. in front line in front of LE SARS. 'A' Coy in O.G. FLERS LINE. 'B' Coy CHALK PIT TRENCH. 'D' Coy. BUTTE TRENCH. 'C' Coy in LE SARS SUNKEN Rd. & Stg post on right. Battn warned that Div. on right (9th) was to attack at 3.40 a.m. of the 18th & all arrangements were made for supporting fire etc.	
18/8/16		Relief was completed by 10.30 p.m. Steady rain began to fall. O.P. established on right of LE SARS on Sunken road. Communication established by runner with LEFT BATTn of 9th Div. & arrangements made for 12+LT Battn of Battn of 9th Div. & our own were advanced to p. of Lupe. Battn of 9th Div. & link up with BUTTE TRENCH GAP. on our right, with a view to locating position for strong posts to link up information was obtained by Intelligence Officer 2nd Lt F.T. GARDINER commanding left the PIMPLE Scout Sgt SMITH Sgt TAYLOR & Pte WILDING. A. Dr posts struck BUTTE Tr. OP during day.	479
19/8/16	2.50 AM	Patrol under 2nd Lt	

WAR DIARY
or
INTELLIGENCE SUMMARY.

Army Form C. 2118.

Sheet No. 7. Sheet 57 7B

Place	Date	Hour	Summary of Events and Information	Remarks and references to Appendices

19/8/16.

A.M. 3.10.
Having investigated an old line of Hun dugouts, I obtained the necessary information re enemy posts.

3.20.
Party dug out in open & directed direction of a wiring party which was repairing enemy wire in front of Beaumont Hamel on this sector.

A.M. 6.20.
Spent twenty three hours of daylight day at O.P. in Sunken road, & O.P. in BUTTE SAP watched progress of fight between bombing parties of 9th Div. & Huns the South of BUTTE DE WALLENCOURT. Runs & Lewis Guns of D'Coy & Snipers actively were fired on by Lewis Guns of D'Coy & Snipers from BUTTE SAP.

The wire was laid from our Butt. Hd Qrs to Batt. H.Q. Hrs of South Africans on our left, & reels of our observations given.

Rain fell heavily throughout the day. Visibility was low & observation difficult. There were two attempts on division.

770.

Army Form C. 2118.

WAR DIARY
or
INTELLIGENCE SUMMARY.
(Erase heading not required.)

Sheet N° 8 of 76

Place	Date	Hour	Summary of Events and Information	Remarks and references to Appendices
			& fell in among them. Enemy steadily humbered LE SARS & casualties were high. A congratulatory message was received during the day from the Brigadier.	4/9
		6.0 pm	Relief by 8/10th Gordons began. 12 H.L.I. to go into Div. Reserve at the CUTTING. CONTALMAISON. Rain continued.	
	20/9/16	a.m 4:30	Relief completed. Total nil of casualties from 14th/15th — morning of 20th = 49. N.C.O.s & men.	
CUTTING CONTALMAISON	21/9/16		During the day Major. W.E. D^{st} JOHN YEOMANRY & Capt. the Rev. Steuart joined the Batt^n.	
	22/9/16		Evening up & working parties on roads.	
	23/9/16		Usual Church Parades. Working parties & Burning parties. Rations party. Following officers reported. MAJOR R. CHALMERS. 2 L^{ts} M. GUILLE, R.T. HALL, T.A.R. DALGLISH, L.D. HAMMOND, Neil McLean, G.S. Gordon, & M. Wallace.	

Army Form C. 2118.

WAR DIARY
or
INTELLIGENCE SUMMARY.
(Erase heading not required.)

Instructions regarding War Diaries and Intelligence Summaries are contained in F. S. Regs., Part II. and the Staff Manual respectively. Title pages will be prepared in manuscript.

Sheet # 9. 55 B

Place	Date	Hour	Summary of Events and Information	Remarks and references to Appendices
CONTALMAISON	24	2.0 pm	Ordered to be ready to move at 4.30 p.m. Moved at 4.45pm. Relieved 4th CAMERONS in CRESCENT ALLEY & RUE TRENCH. Heavy rain. Slight shelling of CRESCENT ALLEY by enemy. — no casualties.	
	25.		Trenches very wet & falling in. Weather improved. Stale shelling of dump at HIGH WOOD & the Valley.	
LE SARS	26.		Relieved 8th SEAFORTHS in front of LE SARS. A.R.E. in time in Pulka Road Attack by the 15th Div. on the LITTLE WOOD trenches in front of OG.1 LE SARS had been planned for the 26th but this had to be postponed on account of the heavy rains.	12-21HT
	27.		Steady rain. Our artillery very active. Enemy very quiet.	
	28.		At 9.30 pm when he artillery active. Trenches in very bad condition. Work almost impossible in consequence. Relieved by 10th S.R. Moved back to CRESCENT ALLEY & RUE TRENCH.— Support line.	
	29.		Rain, rain, rain. LE SARS shelled by enemy in morning.	

1577 Wt. W10791/1773 500,000 1/15 D. D. & L. A.D.S.S./Forms/C. 2118.

WAR DIARY or INTELLIGENCE SUMMARY

Army Form C. 2118.

Place	Date	Hour	Summary of Events and Information	Remarks and references to Appendices
	30/9/16		Five officers rejoined by five others from the Reinforcement Camp at ALBERT. BUTTE de WARLENCOURT heavily shelled by our artillery. A very wet day. Trenches very uncomfortable, many dugouts fell in & several men buried, but no deaths resulted. LE SARS was again heavily shelled. Batt. expected to be relieved during the night but order was cancelled & Batt. stood fast.	Sheet 57.S.E. 57.9.
	1/10/16		Relieved by 9th BLACK WATCH. Marched to LOZENGE WOOD & bivouaced. Hun aeroplane came over during the evening but no damage was done although 2 several bombs were dropped in the vicinity. Total No: of Casualties NCO's & men 36 officers NIL.	

Army Form C. 2118.

WAR DIARY
or
INTELLIGENCE SUMMARY.
(Erase heading not required.)

Instructions regarding War Diaries and Intelligence Summaries are contained in F. S. Regs., Part II. and the Staff Manual respectively. Title pages will be prepared in manuscript.

Place	Date	Hour	Summary of Events and Information	Remarks and references to Appendices
SOMME FRONT.	Mart 5th 26		The following honours have been granted to the Battn since coming to the SOMME FRONT. Military Cross :- Capt J. Stratton. (R.C. padre); 2/Lt A. Bryan; Military Medal :- 17441 Sgt A Ramage; 17569 Sgt A Mc Alpine 19164 Sgt Wm The Lab; 19946 Sgt E. Heatley 23156. S/Sgt E Brearley; 17544 Pte Young W; 19541 Pte Mc Henry G; 18645 Pte John Mc Lean	

Confidential

War Diary

12r. H.L.I.

From 1/11/16 to 30/11/16

Army Form C. 2118.

No. Vol #51r

WAR DIARY
or
INTELLIGENCE SUMMARY.
(Erase heading not required.)

12.M
5 sheets

99G

Hour, Date, Place	Summary of Events and Information	Remarks and references to Appendices
LOZENGE WOOD. 1/11/16. 1.0 p.m.	Left for MILLENCOURT. Billets good.	
MILLENCOURT. 2/11/16.	Cleaning up & refitting	
3/11/16.	Co. Working parties for the town ameis.	
2.0 p.m.	General Coy. routine.	
4/11/16.	General routine. Half holiday in the afternoon.	
5/11/16.	Usual Church parades. Circled the major Dennis, DSO. HENENCOURT. Units very busy. Major St John took	
	returned to 7/8. K.O.S.B. and the command of the battn.	
HENENCOURT. 6/11/16.	Returned to MILLENCOURT.	
MILLENCOURT. 7/11/16.	Heavy rain. Kit inspections.	
8/11/16.	General Coy routine & training. Lecture by C.O. to all officers on observation.	
9/11/16.	Bombing & Musketry.	
2.0 p.m.	Battn inspected by C.J. Douglas Haig.	
10/11/16.	Battn route march. LAVIEVILLE - TRESLÉ - HENENCOURT. Battery practice artillery formation in march.	

WAR DIARY
or
INTELLIGENCE SUMMARY.
(Erase heading not required.)

Army Form C. 2118.

Place	Hour, Date	Summary of Events and Information	Remarks and references to Appendices
MILLENCOURT.	11/XI/16.	Coy. routine.	
	12/XI/16.	Usual church parades.	
BAIZIEUX.	13/XI/16.	Battn. marched to BAIZIEUX. accommodated in tents.	
	14/XI/16.	Coy. routine.	229.
	15/XI/16.	Left for NAOURS. via BEAUCOURT. & TALMAS. whole Battn. billeted.	
NAOURS.	16/XI/16.	Very good, Shire & billets inspection of billets	
	17/XI/16.	Coy. in the attack. Inspection of billets by Brigadier General Watching	
	18/XI/16.	Inspection of Battn. by Brig. & Div. Lieut.	
	19/XI/16.	Usual church parades, & billets inspection by C.O.	
	20/XI/16.	Working parties & Coy. routine.	
	21/XI/16.	Practice of Battn. in the attack.	
	22/XI/16.	Battn. attack inspected by the Brigadier	

Army Form C. 2118.

WAR DIARY
or
INTELLIGENCE SUMMARY.
(Erase heading not required.)

Instructions regarding War Diaries and Intelligence Summaries are contained in F. S. Regs., Part II., and the Staff Manual respectively. Title pages will be prepared in manuscript.

Hour, Date, Place	Summary of Events and Information	Remarks and references to Appendices
NOOURS. 23/XI/16. 9.0 – 11.0. 2.30 – 5.30	Batta drill under the C.O. Inspection of 46th Inf. Bde by General Sir W. Pulteney.	779
24/XI/16. pm 5.0 – 7.0	Coy routine. Night operations.	
25/XI/16.	Coy routine & hutting. Cinema performance in the afternoon.	
26/XI/16.	Grand church parade.	
27/XI/16.	Batta moved to WARLOY via TALMAS.	
28/XI/16.	Practice in marching out. Strong posts. Coy routine.	
29/XI/16.	Inspection of batta in training by G.O.C. 15th Division.	
30/XI/16.	Coy routine.	

Confidential.   Vol /3

War Diary,
of
1st. (S) Bn. Highland Light Infantry.

From :-   1 . 12 . 16
To :-   31 . 12 . 16 .

Army Form C. 2118.

WAR DIARY
or
INTELLIGENCE SUMMARY.
(Erase heading not required.)

73.

13.M.
9 sheets

Hour, Date, Place		Summary of Events and Information	Remarks and references to Appendices
WARLOY	1/12/16	Marches via Albert to Becourt Camp. Weather cold wet frosty. Roads fairly good. Officers and men billeted in Huts, some of which not quite complete &c.	
BECOURT CAMP	2/12/16	Company Routine, and work carried out in General improvement of Camp. Camp Inspection by Commanding Officer.	
	3/12/16	Large Working Parties in repairing Roads and completing Construction of Brigade Camp Lines. Usual Church Parade.	
	4/12/16	Parades: Physical Training: Musketry: Bayonet fighting: Company in Attack, and Bombing. Inspection of Camp by Brigadier General.	
	5/12/16	Large Working Parties on Road Repair and Camp construction. Inspection of Great Defences by all available subaltern Officers, and Lecture	

Army Form C. 2118.

WAR DIARY
or
INTELLIGENCE SUMMARY.
(Erase heading not required.)

Instructions regarding War Diaries and Intelligence Summaries are contained in F. S. Regs., Part II., and the Staff Manual respectively. Title pages will be prepared in manuscript.

Hour, Date, Place	Summary of Events and Information	Remarks and references to Appendices
BECOURT CAMP (contd) 5/12/16	to Subaltern Officers. 2nd Lieut. E.H. Wrench rejoined the Battalion	
6/12/16	Parades: Bombing; Physical Training; Bayonet fighting; Musketry.	
7/12/16	Large working parties in Road repair and Camp Construction.	
8/12/16	Very wet. Kit Inspection, and Lectures to N.C.Os & men. Baths for men in afternoon.	
9/12/16	Large Working Parties in Road repair & Camp Construction	
10/12/16	Usual Church Parade. Major A.H.O. Devenish (2nd Black Watch) took over Command; vice Lt.Col. H.E. St Lott C.C. to Hospital	
11/12/16	Large working parties in Road repair & Camp Construction	
12/12/16	Parades: Physical Training; Musketry; Bayonet fighting; Digging Strong Point & Fitting Sheet Iron. Major H. Larkin took over Command.	
13/12/16	Large Working Parties in Road repair, Camp Construction. Draft of 106 N.C.Os and men joined Battn. All fairly trained men of average Physique	

:**WAR DIARY**
or
INTELLIGENCE SUMMARY.
(Erase heading not required.)

Army Form C. 2118.

Hour, Date, Place	Summary of Events and Information	Remarks and references to Appendices
BECOURT CAMP 14/10/16	Relief of 48th Division by 15th Division commences. Battalion left Becourt Camp and moved into left Support area in MARTINPUICH, relieving 4th Glosters. Having Runners on tour at SCOTS REDOUBT SOUTH CAMP. Relief complete by 7.30 p.m.	1/5
15/10/16	Moved into Centre Battalion area, front line relieving 9th Worcesters. 'B' 'D' Coys, Front Line. 'A' Coy Support. 'C' Coy Reserve. Relief complete 8.30 p.m.	} S
16/10/16	Commenced Digging new Strong Point. Moving out & consolidating position generally. Situation on the whole, Normal. Weather Conditions very trying.	
17/10/16	Relieved by 16th Scottish Rifles. Moved back into Centre Support area Headquarters SEVEN ELMS. Relief complete 10.30 p.m.	

Army Form C. 2118.

WAR DIARY
or
INTELLIGENCE SUMMARY.
(Erase heading not required.)

76

Hour, Date, Place	Summary of Events and Information	Remarks and references to Appendices
18/1/16.	In Support area. Supplying Working parties for Brigade fatigues.	
19/1/16.	Relieved 10th Scottish Rifles in Front Line. Relief complete 8.30 p.m. Slight fall of snow, and conditions frosty. A+C Coys Front Line, D Coy Support, "B" Coy Reserve.	
20/1/16.	Good nights work done moving right Company's front and part of left Company front. Auck Boards carried up and placed in position in Strong points.	
21/1/16.	Congratulatory note received from Brigadier General re last nights good work. In Brigade instructions relieving Battalion to carry up material for the nights work and Battalion being relieved to leave parties to work until midnight. 10th S.R. on Relieving carried up morning material.	

Army Form C. 2118.

WAR DIARY
or
INTELLIGENCE SUMMARY.
(Erase heading not required.)

77.

Hour, Date, Place	Summary of Events and Information	Remarks and references to Appendices
21/1/16 (contd.)	Front Line Companies left behind for work until midnight. Owing to the late arrival of a carrying party of the S.R., "A" Coy. kept for duty until 6 A.M. Relief reported complete 10.30 pm. Battalion went back to Reserve again during the night was shelled but without any casualties to this Battalion.	PIONEER CAMP
PIONEER CAMP 22/1/16	Cleaning up and drying Camp. In spite of all cautions and very attention being paid to feet, about 30 cases of trench feet had to be evacuated during the spell of 7 days in the trenches.	
23/1/16	Brigade relieved. Move to SHELTER WOOD CAMP, NORTH. "D" Coy on Hutts. Other 3 Companies in tents. Very stormy and wet.	
SHELTER WOOD, NORTH 24/1/16	80% of Battalion employed on working parties. R.E.	

WAR DIARY
or
INTELLIGENCE SUMMARY.
(Erase heading not required.)

78.

Army Form C. 2118.

Hour, Date, Place	Summary of Events and Information	Remarks and references to Appendices
SHELTER WOOD (NORTH) CAMP. 24/12/16 (cont.)	R.C. midnight service in Divisional Recreation Tent.	}
25/12/16	Christmas Day. Weather: very wet. No working parties. Christmas Dinner Battalion of in tents. Beer lales to arrive until 5 p.m. Every officer, N.C.O., man in Battalion received from Officers, "Socks, bun, Tobacco, & Cigarettes" from institutions at home. Officers Christmas Dinner held at night.	
26/12/16	Brigade Tactical Scheme (without troops). Taking up positions of assembly to support own Division, whose front lines are presumed to be broken. Officers Commanding Companies proceeded up line to inspect new area to be taken over in Left Sector. Very wet and stormy. Col. Thomson, 8th Gordons took over temporary Command of Brigade vice Brigadier General Matheson on leave.	

WAR DIARY
or
INTELLIGENCE SUMMARY.
(Erase heading not required.)

Army Form C. 2118.

79

Hour, Date, Place	Summary of Events and Information	Remarks and references to Appendices
27/12/16	Moves up to Right Battalion Front Line of Left Sector, relieving 8th Seaforths. Dispositions:- Front Line "D" Coy. 2nd Support "B" Coy. Secret Support "A" - Reserve "C". Relief complete 10-30 p.m. Work carried out in strong points	
28/12/16	Scheme submitted for advancing positions of Battalion and approved of by Actg. Brigadier General. "C" Coy. vacated Reserve area, and took over right end of frontage of "D" Coy. New Dispositions of Front Line Company:- C & D Coys had each 2 platoons in Front Line and 2 platoons in Check Support. 3 new strong points dug. So far as possible Duckboard carried up and placed in position	VR
29/12/16	Relieved	

Army Form C. 2118.

WAR DIARY
or
INTELLIGENCE SUMMARY.
(Erase heading not required.)

80.

Hour, Date, Place	Summary of Events and Information	Remarks and references to Appendices
VILLA CAMP. 29/12/16	Relieved by 10th Scottish Rifles. Owing to misunderstanding on their part relief delayed and not completed till 3 a.m. Battalion went back into support area at Villa Camp, "C" Coy being stationed in MARTINPUICH. Very stormy and wet. VILLA CAMP shelled. No Casualties.	} R
29/12/16	Working Parties supplied to Brigade	
30/12/16	Relieves 10th S.R. Dispositions A. & B. Coys. Front Line. "C" Coy. First Support. D. Coy. Second Support. Relief complete by 10.30 p.m.	
	Casualties during the Month 2nd Lieut. Heller, M.A. slightly wounded Killed 5 O.R. Wounded 2 O.R.	

WAR DIARY
or
INTELLIGENCE SUMMARY.
(Erase heading not required.)

Place	Date	Hour	Summary of Events and Information
	31/12/16		**Casualties during Month.** (Cont²)
			In addition, several O.R. were evacuated owing to Trench feet and other sickness.
			2nd Lieut Cuddeford, AWJ evacuated to Hospital on 14th Dec, returned to duty 30th Dec.
			Capt Chalmers R evacuated to England on 14th Dec.
			Promotions in Battalion during past Month.
			Temporary Capt. M.D. Shaw to be temporary Major 7/3/16
			Temporary Lieut. R.R. Brown " " Capt. 7/3/16
			Temporary Lieut. W. McHardie " " Capt. 2/9/16
			Temporary 2nd Lt. (actg Capt.) T.B. Myles to be temporary Lieut. 7.3.16
			Temporary 2nd Lt. (actg Capt.) R.L. Hannas " Lieut. 2.9.16
			Capt and Adjt. D.J. Trotman granted permanent Commission with Seniority from 2/12/16

Graham Major
O/C 12. 17/2.

12th Battn.
The Highland Light Infy.
January, 1917

14. M.
18 sheets

Army Form C. 2118.

WAR DIARY
or
INTELLIGENCE SUMMARY.
(Erase heading not required.)

91.

Place	Date	Hour	Summary of Events and Information	Remarks and references to Appendices
	1/1/17		Support coys engaged in carrying up wiring materials duckboards etc to front line coys. "A" and "B" Coys employed in wiring in front of the posts: also deepening the strong points, laying duckboards, + improving them generally	M.
	2/1/17		Relieved by 10th Scottish Rifles. Relief complete by 11 p.m. and battalion went back to Acid Drop Camp (South). During the afternoon the enemy very heavily shelled Chalk Walk, /e Avro cutting, O.G. 1, 26th Avenue	3/2

Army Form C. 2118.

WAR DIARY
or
INTELLIGENCE SUMMARY.
(Erase heading not required.)

Instructions regarding War Diaries and Intelligence Summaries are contained in F. S. Regs., Part II. and the Staff Manual respectively. Title pages will be prepared in manuscript.

Place	Date	Hour	Summary of Events and Information	Remarks and references to Appendices
	2/1/17		26th Avenue, and MARTINPUICH.	M.
	3/1/17		Inspection of rifles & equipment under Coy. arrangements.	
	4/1/17		Battalion moved to Shelter Wood Camp (South) and relieved 13th Bn. The Royal Scots	
SHELTER WOOD CAMP (SOUTH)	5/1/17		Working parties supplied by battalion to work on the roads under 5th Sussex (Pioneer) Bn.	317

WAR DIARY
or
INTELLIGENCE SUMMARY.

Army Form C. 2118.

83

314

Place	Date	Hour	Summary of Events and Information	Remarks and references to Appendices
SHELTER WOOD CAMP (SOUTH)	6/1/17		Working parties supplied to R.E.'s for digging cable trench and also repairing railway	M.L.
			Parades for remainder of battalion under Coy arrangements inspection of arms, equipment etc	
	7/1/17		Usual Church Parades. There were also two or three small working parties.	
	8/1/17		Before moving up the line special precautions were taken to avoid trench feet by each	

Place	Date	Hour	Summary of Events and Information	Remarks and references to Appendices
	8/1/17		each man dipping two pairs of socks in hot whale oil and wringing them dry. One pair of socks were then put on while the reserve pair was carried in the haversack. Bathing parade for the battalion from 9.30 am - 11 am. The Battalion relieved the 8th Seaforths in the left subsector of the Right Sector. Relief complete by 8.30 pm.	

WAR DIARY
or
INTELLIGENCE SUMMARY.

Army Form C. 2118.

85

Place	Date	Hour	Summary of Events and Information	Remarks and references to Appendices
	8/1/17		Dispositions Front line. Right "C" Coy. Left "D" Coy. Support Right "B" Coy. Left "A" Coy. Battalion Headquarters M.22.b.22.3. Rations, water and material carried up to front line coys. Work carried out in front line: - wiring & laying boards. Major J. C. Grahame D.S.O. took over temporary Col: W.E. tt John to hospital.	M.3

316

Army Form C. 2118.

WAR DIARY
or
INTELLIGENCE SUMMARY.
(Erase heading not required.)

96

317

Place	Date	Hour	Summary of Events and Information	Remarks and references to Appendices
	9/1/17		General improvement of posts carried on.	
	10/1/17		Support coys relieved front line coys	17th
			"A" & "B" Coys in front line	
			"C" & "D" Coys in support.	
			Good work was done by front line coys in strengthening the existing wire.	
	11/1/17		The left front company sent out a patrol which was, however, greatly handicapped by the ground being covered with a thin layer of snow.	

Army Form C. 2118.

WAR DIARY
or
INTELLIGENCE SUMMARY.

(Erase heading not required.)

Place	Date	Hour	Summary of Events and Information	Remarks and references to Appendices
	11/1/17		Usual carrying parties by supports coys while front companies continued the wiring.	
	12/1/17		The Battalion relieved the 10th Scottish Rifles in the centre support area. Relief completed by 9 p.m.	
			Dispositions "A" Coy - Rutherford Alley (Seven Elms)	
			"B" Coy - Starfish Lane	
			"C" Coy - Prue trench (left of Crescent)	
			"D" Coy - Prue trench (right) Alley)	
			H.Q. - Seven Elms.	

318

WAR DIARY
or
INTELLIGENCE SUMMARY.

(Erase heading not required.)

Army Form C. 2118.

88

Place	Date	Hour	Summary of Events and Information	Remarks and references to Appendices
	13/1/17		Large carrying parties supplied by battalion carrying material under the R.E.'s from MARTINPUICH to MAXWELL SUPPORT.	M.3
			Although every precaution had been taken to ensure against trench feet a large number of men had to be evacuated to hospital on this account.	
			Whilst the battalion occupied the front line support areas, however, the ground was particularly muddy and wet and in many cases even the trench [wards]	

319

Army Form C. 2118.

WAR DIARY
or
INTELLIGENCE SUMMARY.
(Erase heading not required.)

320

Place	Date	Hour	Summary of Events and Information	Remarks and references to Appendices
	13/1/17		Iards did not protect the feet from mud in the first.	
	14/1/17		Battalion relieved in Support Area by 7/8 K.O.S.B. Relief complete by 8.30 pm. The Battalion went back to the Reserve Area PIONEER CAMP	
PIONEER CAMP	15/1/17		Cleaning up & inspections under Coy. arrangements.	
SHELTER WOOD (SOUTH)	16/1/17		Battalion moved to Shelter Wood Camp (South) where it relieved 6th Camerons.	

WAR DIARY
or
INTELLIGENCE SUMMARY.

Army Form C. 2118.

Place	Date	Hour	Summary of Events and Information	Remarks and references to Appendices.
SHELTER WOOD (SOUTH)	17/1/17		Working parties under the R.E.s clearing roads. During the early morning the camp was shelled for about half an hour, the shed near the Orderly Room being destroyed.	90
	19/1/17		Working parties as usual. Remainder of Battalion employed cleaning rifles, kit etc. The ground was covered with snow but not very cold.	721

WAR DIARY
or
INTELLIGENCE SUMMARY.

Army Form C. 2118.

722

Place	Date	Hour	Summary of Events and Information	Remarks and references to Appendices
SHELTER WOOD (SOUTH)	19/1/17		Inspection of rifles, gasmasks, equipment, iron rations, field dressings, gum boots etc previous to moving up the line.	See appendix I Sheet 96
	20/1/17	9.30 p.m.	The Battalion relieved the 7th Camerons in the right sub-sector of the left sector. Relief complete by ≡ 9.30 p.m. On this occasion packs were taken into the trenches instead of haversacks. Dispositions Front Line Right "C" Coy. Left "D" Coy: Support "B" Coy in OG.1 (1 Platoon in Lestrement Farm) Reserve "A" Coy in 26th Avenue. HQ 26th Avenue.	M.L.

Place	Date	Hour	Summary of Events and Information	Remarks and references to Appendices
	20/1/17		The weather was clear but exceedingly cold. The hard frost had rendered the duck-board tracks and other paths very slippy & dangerous.	
	21/1/17		Reserve support coys engaged in carrying up ammunition, duck-boards, sandbags, picks, shovels, rations, water etc to front line coys who carried on good work improving the posts and laying extra boards in them.	
	22/1/17		"A" Coy 26th Avenue relieved "D" Coy front (left) "B" Coy O.G.1 " "C" Coy front (right) Usual carrying parties by reserve support coys. Front coys employed in improving existing cover	

Army Form C. 2118.

WAR DIARY
or
INTELLIGENCE SUMMARY.
(Erase heading not required.)

93

324

Place	Date	Hour	Summary of Events and Information	Remarks and references to Appendices
	23/1/17		Hard frost continued and not much digging could be done.	
	24/1/17		Work:- Making the wire continuous between posts. Battalion relieved in right sub-sector of left sector by 10th Scottish Rifles. Relief complete by 11 p.m.	
VILLA CAMP			Headquarters and "D" Coy moved down to support area VILLA CAMP: "A" "B" + "C" Coys accomodated in MARTINPUICH.	
	25/1/17		Working parties supplied to Brigade.	
HCID DROP (SOUTH)	26/1/17		Battalion relieved in SUPPORT AREA, VILLA CAMP by 7/8th KOSB and moved to RESERVE AREA ACID DROP CAMP (SOUTH)	

Army Form C. 2118.

WAR DIARY
or
INTELLIGENCE SUMMARY.

(Erase heading not required.)

325

Place	Date	Hour	Summary of Events and Information	Remarks and references to Appendices
ACID DROP SOUTH	27/1/17	10.30 am - 12.30 pm	Inspection of arms, ammunition, ankle boots, clothing and equipment. Examination of feet carried out under coy arrangements.	94
SHELTER WOOD (SOUTH) CAMP	28/1/17		Battalion moved to Shelter Wood Camp (South) and relieved the 6th Camerons.	M.G.
"	29/1/17		Whole battalion employed in working parties. One large party under 9th Gordons (Pioneer Bn.) working on the Bazentin - Martinpuich Road.	
"	30/1/17		Working parties for employment on road	
"	31/1/17	10 am - 3 pm	The battalion moved to billets in ALBERT. Physical drill parade Lt. Col. W.E. Johns returned to the battalion.	

1577 Wt. W10791/1773 500,000 1/15 D. D. & L. A.D.S.S./Forms/C. 2118.

WAR DIARY
or
INTELLIGENCE SUMMARY.
(Erase heading not required.)

Army Form C. 2118.

Hour, Date, Place	Summary of Events and Information	Remarks and references to Appendices
	Casualties during the month	
	Officers — Nil	
	Other ranks — Killed — three (3)	
	Wounded — 27.	Nil.

WAR DIARY
or
INTELLIGENCE SUMMARY.
(Erase heading not required.)

Army Form C. 2118.

96

Hour, Date, Place	Summary of Events and Information	Remarks and references to Appendices
SHELTER WOOD (SOUTH) 10/1/17	Appendix! Foot powder was substituted for whale oil — the use of latter being forbidden. Method of use. The men's feet to be thoroughly washed in warm water with specially prepared soap. Feet to be dried and then a clean dry pair of socks to be put on after sprinkling the inside with powder.	

12th Batt'n,
The Highland Light Inf'y.
February, 1917

15.M.
Schut

Army Form C. 2118.

WAR DIARY
or
INTELLIGENCE SUMMARY.
(Erase heading not required.)

97

Instructions regarding War Diaries and Intelligence Summaries are contained in F. S. Regs., Part II., and the Staff Manual respectively. Title pages will be prepared in manuscript.

Hour, Date, Place		Summary of Events and Information	Remarks and references to Appendices
ALBERT.	1/2/17 – 3/2/17	Squad, company drill during the forenoon. Recreational training carried on in the afternoon.	
	3/2/17	Sec. Lieut. L. Hammond rejoined the battalion and posted "A" Coy.	
WARLOY	4/2/17	Battalion marched from ALBERT to WARLOY via LA BOISSELLE.	
	5/2/17 – 11/2/17	Training carried on under company arrangements. Company drill, bayonet fighting, musketry, attack practice during forenoon. Recreational training in afternoon.	

329
SB

Army Form C. 2118.

WAR DIARY
or
INTELLIGENCE SUMMARY
(Erase heading not required.)

98

Instructions regarding War Diaries and Intelligence Summaries are contained in F. S. Regs., Part II., and the Staff Manual respectively. Title pages will be prepared in manuscript.

Hour, Date, Place	Summary of Events and Information	Remarks and references to Appendices
WARLOY (cta) 12/2/17	Exercise carried out by brigade in conjunction with contact aeroplanes	
BEAUVAL 13/2/17	Battalion marched from WARLOY to BEAUVAL via PUCHEVILLERS. Brig: General Matheson took over temporary command of the Division: Col: Sellar DSO. took command of the Brigade.	
GÉZAINCOURT 14/2/17	Battalion moved from BEAUVAL to GÉZAINCOURT	
BOURET 15/2/17	March resumed to BOURET.	

Army Form C. 2118.

WAR DIARY
or
INTELLIGENCE SUMMARY.
(Erase heading not required.)

99

Place	Date	Hour	Summary of Events and Information	Remarks and references to Appendices
IZEL-LEZ -HAMEAU	16/2/17		Battalion moved from BOURET to IZEL-LEZ-HAMEAU.	
	17/2/17 -21/2/17		Training under companies carried on at IZEL-LEZ-HAMEAU. Bayonet fighting, musketry, &c and especially practising a battalion in attack and specially company in attack. Recreational training during afternoon.	
	20/2/17		Brig. Gen. Matheson returned from the Division to the Brigade.	
ARRAS	22/2/17	3.30 am	Battalion marched to ARRAS and billeted in cellars.	

WAR DIARY
or
INTELLIGENCE SUMMARY.
(Erase heading not required.)

Army Form C. 2118.

Hour, Date, Place	Summary of Events and Information	Remarks and references to Appendices
ARRAS		
23/2/17 - 25/2/17	Owing to the majority of men being confined to McLellan little could be done beyond a daily inspection of the men's feet, gumboots and arms. Working parties were supplied to the New Zealand Tunnelling company.	M.
26/2/17	Battalion relieved the 7/8th K.O.S.B. in the Relief complete by 8 pm	

Army Form C. 2118.

WAR DIARY
or
INTELLIGENCE SUMMARY.
(Erase heading not required.)

101

Instructions regarding War Diaries and Intelligence Summaries are contained in F. S. Regs., Part II. and the Staff Manual respectively. Title pages will be prepared in manuscript.

Place	Date	Hour	Summary of Events and Information	Remarks and references to Appendices
ARRAS	28/2/17 (cktd)		Dispositions. "D" left front coy: "B" right front coy.	
			"C" coy in support	
			"A" coy in reserve in ARRAS.	
	27/2/17		Reserve company engaged in carrying up rations of "B", "C" + "D" coys to coy cookers	M.
			Support coy employed carrying rations to "D" and "B" from cookers.	
			Front coys engaged in improving front line and also Ingles St., Income Tax and Invalid Lane.	

A.5834 Wt.W4973/M687 750,000 8/16 D. D. & L. Ltd. Forms/C.2118/13.

WAR DIARY
or
INTELLIGENCE SUMMARY.
(Erase heading not required.)

Army Form C. 2118.

102

Place	Date	Hour	Summary of Events and Information	Remarks and references to Appendices
	28/2/17		Carrying parties by support reserve coys as usual. Front line coys improved front line and cleared communication trenches.	
			Officers	
	28/2/17		Capt A.R. Chislett and 2nd Lieut M. Paterson joined the Bn and were posted to "C" Coy.	
			Casualties during month Officers — nil O.R. Killed — 2 Wounded — 1	

[Signature]
Lt. Col.
O.C. 102nd Can. Inf. Bn.

16.M.
11 sheets

Confidential.

Vol 16

War Diary
of
12th High. L. I.
for
March 1917.

Army Form C. 2118.

WAR DIARY
or
INTELLIGENCE SUMMARY.

(Erase heading not required.)

12th L.L.I

Place	Date	Hour	Summary of Events and Information	Remarks and references to Appendices
Areas.	1/4/17		Received in trenches at 1.3 Sectn Klan 9/8. In relief in areas the Reserve.	Q.
	2/4/17	7.30	Q Buzancy Reserve in areas at Proceeded to Hyzette arriving there at 11.30 am.	
Hyzette	3/4/17		At Hyzette. Day spent in cleaning up.	
do.	4/4/17		At Hyzette. Parades & Coys arrangements.	Q.

Army Form C. 2118.

WAR DIARY
or
INTELLIGENCE SUMMARY.
(Erase heading not required.)

Instructions regarding War Diaries and Intelligence Summaries are contained in F. S. Regs., Part II. and the Staff Manual respectively. Title pages will be prepared in manuscript.

Place	Date	Hour	Summary of Events and Information	Remarks and references to Appendices
NORELETTE	5.3.17		Snow fell during night of 4/5" March - About 2" deep - About 11-0 AM Thaw came - and the snow rapidly disappeared under strong sunshine - Frost commenced about 10 p.m. 17 O.R arrived from Base.	
	6.3.17		Slight frost during night of 5/6" March followed by bright sunshine.	
	7.3.17		Hard frost all day. Windy.	
	8.3.17		Hard frost. Bright sunshine. No wind. 2nd Lt Hammond left to join R.F.C. at Hendin.	
	9.3.17		Slight snow in morning. Slight frost. Heavy thaw in evening. Commandg officer (Coy Commander) attended an exhibition attack by 44th Brigade. Capt R.P. Easton reported here for duty as 2nd in command. Adjutant & Coy Commanders attended a lecture on "The employment of Tanks in Warfare."	
	10/3/17		Bed & sick (slight) all day. 2Lt/Capt Johnston left for hospital. 2nd Lt Jagh took over Adjutancy. C.O. 2nd in Command & Coy Commanders attended a lecture at St Pol on "The employment of Tanks in warfare."	
	11/3/17		The Battalion left Norelette for Mezières at 10.30 arg marched via Norelette Siracourt, Crosette, Anceine, arriving at Mezières at 2 p.m. Clear day. Settled in billets. To day was fine & sunshine. Strong Z.W. 4-30 when rain fell at intervals till night time. The men fell out on the march.	

A5834 Wt.W4973/M687 750,000 8/16 D. D. & L. Ltd. Forms/C.2118/13.

Army Form C. 2118.

WAR DIARY
or
INTELLIGENCE SUMMARY.

(Erase heading not required.)

Instructions regarding War Diaries and Intelligence Summaries are contained in F. S. Regs., Part II. and the Staff Manual respectively. Title pages will be prepared in manuscript.

Place	Date	Hour	Summary of Events and Information	Remarks and references to Appendices
Negreier	12		Divisional Training at Regnieg. Weather dry.	
	13		do do do	
	14		do do weather wet.	
	15		Battn spent day in cleaning up & inspection.	
	16		Divisional training as above.	
	17		do do	

WAR DIARY
or
INTELLIGENCE SUMMARY.
(Erase heading not required.)

Army Form C. 2118.

Place	Date	Hour	Summary of Events and Information	Remarks and references to Appendices
H⁺ Maquise	18.		Battn. left Maquise to move by route march at Div: H⁺s. were mined at Wormories for dinner and at Scrivens for tea. 8 men fell out on the march and were transported. Battn arrived at Arras at 8 p.m. and were billeted near the Foundry. Plenn in cellars. 2 prisoners, Pte Ramay + Pte McLaughlin escaped at Divisans. Battn in Arras.	G.
Arras	19.	10 A.M.	Battn. moved off about 6 to take over line at I–3.	W.
		12 N.	Took over from 7th (3 Coys) Inniskilligs + 8/10 Gordons Scipionoris. A. Coy in front line with sight of railway in I–3 sector. B. Coy in reserve & Coy in support. E. Coy took over Country defences.	
Arras	20.		Disposition as above. Weather wet and cloudy. Enemy + own artillery fairly active. Battn H.Q. lit twice by shell fire	G

WAR DIARY
or
INTELLIGENCE SUMMARY.

Army Form C. 2118.

Place	Date	Hour	Summary of Events and Information	Remarks and references to Appendices
Arras	21		Very wet and foggy. Enemy N.W. wind. Artillery very active at intervals. A Coy took over front line.	G.
do.	22		Fine weather - very clear. Intense bombardment of enemy trenches in the morning and strong retaliation of the Germans later.	
do.	23	10 a.m.	Relieved by 10th R.S. & 17th H.L.I. in week in Arras at 1 P.m. Concentration for the tour. O.R. 4 killed O.R. 9 wounded (1 accidental) O.R. 1 gassed.	G.
	24	7/-	Working parties for Brigade.	
do	24		Weather fine - bright. One machine gun hors de combat at enemy's plane and drove 5 off from the landing place. Working parties supplying from Brigade. Major Osborn proceeded for duty 2 R.F.C. Jones left for R.F.C.	

WAR DIARY or INTELLIGENCE SUMMARY

Army Form C. 2118.

Place	Date	Hour	Summary of Events and Information	Remarks and references to Appendices
Arras	25/3/17	am	Working parties supplying for Brigade. Later - desultory shelling of known bivouacs in Fauvel Place our men slightly wounded. Our Lewis gun firing from Fosse Plane drove off 5 enemy of planes firing 950 rounds fired. Weather fine & dry. Heavy rain at night.	9.
	26.	am	Working parties supplying for Brigade. Very wet all day.	
	27	am	Working parties supplying for Brigade. 2/K wounded reporting from hospital. Weather very wet.	
	28.	am	Working parties supplying for Brigade. 2/K.S. Simpson, Campbell - recon relieved here for duty and posted as follows R. 2/Lts. Nelson & Simpson. C. Coy. 2/Lt. 13. Coy Campbell. 2/Lt A.S. Nieson C.G. left for duty to observer with R.F.C. Enemy sent shells into town at intervals during day. No casualties. Weather very wet. Occasional bright sunshine. Relieved 19/p Inf. Bde/3 Corps at 10 a.m. Disposition as follows. A. Coy in front line. B. Coy 3 platoons in support, 1 in reserve. C. in Reserve. Weather wet - slight mist. Situation normal. Tampoons of the P.A. and their on observation were dispersed.	9.

A5834 Wt. W4973/M687 750,000 8/16 D.D. & L. Ltd. Forms/C.2118/13.

Army Form C. 2118.

WAR DIARY
or
INTELLIGENCE SUMMARY.
(Erase heading not required.)

Place	Date	Hour	Summary of Events and Information	Remarks and references to Appendices
Trenches Area. S.E. Loos	30.3.17		In trenches. Weather day & clear. Much aeroplane observation. Our artillery and enemy artillery very active at intervals.	A.
	31.3.17		Rather weather wet, occasional sunshine. Cr. S. Coys. Adjutant attended a lecture in area of C.O.s who later relieved by 7th Camerons at 7.30 p.m. & then proceeded to billets in Mazingarbe. Casualties for the tour. 1 killed, 1 wounded.	

Eric Gore-Brown
Capt
12 H.L.I.

46/15 7/0
12/H.L.I. April 1917

WAR DIARY
or
INTELLIGENCE SUMMARY.
(Erase heading not required.)

Army Form C. 2118.

17. M.
51 sheets

Place	Date	Hour	Summary of Events and Information	Remarks and references to Appendices
Habarcq	1/4/17		In billets at Habarcq. 25 O.R. draft joined from Base.	
do	2/4/17		In billets at Habarcq. Baths were provided for batln.	
do	3/4/17		In billets at Habarcq.	
do	4/4/17		Batln moved to Arras at 3.30 pm arriving at 10 pm. to men per sec on the march.	
Arras	5/4/17		Batln billeted in cellars of Grande Place.	
Arras	6/4/17		Batln billeted as above.	
	7/4/17		Batln billeted as above. 7 men were wounded by our shell coming through roof.	
	8/4/17		Batln in billets as above.	

Army Form C. 2118.

WAR DIARY
or
INTELLIGENCE SUMMARY.
(Erase heading not required.)

Place	Date	Hour	Summary of Events and Information	Remarks and references to Appendices
ARRAS.	9/4/17	5.30 a.m.	Batt. assembled in clear GRANGE PLACE. and marched to outskirts of town via the Lion Sewer. Remainder of Bn. in Ref. J6 a.n. B.0061. Steins and Plates was evacuated to point of assembly. E of D.G.2. A fairly heavy artillery barrage was kept up by enemy on our main line & communication trench being particularly heavy carrying parties.	(1) Marching out State A. (2) Copy of operation Orders. B. (3) Sketch. Eg/ARRAS "C".
		9 a.m.	Batt. had arrived in area of assembly. Batt. Coys. in advance had got into pieces & were of Bois over to communication trenches.	
		11.10a.	Batts. advanced. Coys. gradually going into their proper positions.	
		12 noon.	The right flank of Batt. was held up by M.G. & Rifle fire from HENRY HOUGHIN Trench. The flank of Batt. being supported on 35th Bn. were checked in front. The wheeling was done with Q, A, & B Coy on flank. C & D Coy wheeling to the Bn. This swing movement on Left flank of 35th Bn. caused our rather heavy fire M.G. fire fairly heavy during.	
		12.30p.	Orders received from Bn. that advance upon Intermediate Objective would not commence at 12.10 p.m. in execution of orders the Bn.	H.T.

111

Army Form C. 2118.

WAR DIARY
or
INTELLIGENCE SUMMARY.
(Erase heading not required.)

Place	Date	Hour	Summary of Events and Information	Remarks and references to Appendices
BATTERY VALLEY	9/4/17		Lewis Corp. had commenced their attack soon after their recent was dispatched, but as it was too late for him to get behind our arty barrage, they lost cover. Our directly the barrage lifted pushed home their attack on BATTERY VALLEY.	
		1.50p	Report received from Lewis Corp. (A & H) had entered Valley. Their advance on enemy trenches has met with little opposition, but they were under heavy fire from 3 Field Batteries at H.26.b.35, H.26.d.69. & H.27.c.83. This fire came heavy casualties, the range and they were then 2000x & let's can of his Battalion. Mr. Harry McLean and 1 top blown off. The situation was admirably dealt with by his Co. & 2nd Lewis Corp. speeded by Lieut. CUDDEFORD. The gunners of an 3 Battalion were dispose of by rifle & L.C. fire. Mcd. [?] on their guns. a got into their dug out. Nine Field Guns were captured.	
		2.30p	The Batt. assembled & reorganised for attack on ORANGE HILL in BATTERY VALLEY. Touch was established with 5. Royal Berks. 35th Bd. on our right.	

WAR DIARY
or
INTELLIGENCE SUMMARY.

Army Form C. 2118.

113

Place	Date	Hour	Summary of Events and Information	Remarks and references to Appendices
ORANGE HILL.	9/4/17	3.30p.	The preliminary arrangements for the advance commenced. The Corps. gradually working up to the vicinity of BROKEN MILL. Then they commenced to come under heavy M.G. fire from N.E. Touch obtained with 10/K.R. About this time it became necessary for Leaving Coy. to commence to dig in. The Batt'n. pushed forward and when the Art'y. barrage lifted commenced the advance, at the same time as the 10.K.R. on the left. The enemy ran was practically absent, but a "TANK" nearer great assistance in knocking out nests of putting out of action seven M.G." which he caused great trouble. HIMALAYA Trench & the Support line, were only lightly held. hereafter by M.G. & Snipers.	
		5.30p.	The objective was practically taken. Then we knew were difficulty, as our right, on the 35th. Bde. had not gained their objective. Casualties were not heavy.	
		7.30p.	Consolidation was in hand. Our Snipers were active & cavalry reconnoitering. Strong point was constructed & 37th. Div. dug trenches in front of us.	P.1

WAR DIARY
or
INTELLIGENCE SUMMARY.
(Erase heading not required.)

Army Form C. 2118.

Place	Date	Hour	Summary of Events and Information	Remarks and references to Appendices
	9/4/17	11 p.m.	The night passed without any counter attack, but on the right flank was noisily shelled cold, showery, ground heavy. Snow at night.	
	10/4/17	12 a.m.	An attack was fixed by his advance of the 12th Div.	
			On front my quiet. Enemy evidently moving his guns back. The Batt. was holding the line 3 Coys in O.G.2. 1 Coy in O.G.1. Clean cold weather with a strong wind. Trying to clean & sleep at night. Carried during the day snow mostly from our own Artillery on our front trenches.	
	11/4/17	3.30 a.m.	Orders received from 46.I.B. that Batt would continue the advance at 5 a.m. and attack & capture the line 1.31.B.8.0. 13.1.B.7.0. The Batt. to be in Reserve.	
		5.30 a.m.	The Batt. less O.C. 2 & was in touch with 7/6 K.O.S.B. & advanced E. & N.E. edges of ORANGE HILL.	(4)
MONCHY		7 a.m.	The Batt. was halted. The late Lewis Coy. O/C had already gone forward with the 10th H.L.I. & 7/6 K.O.S.B. in the attack on MONCHY.	Sketch MONCHY

Army Form C. 2118.

WAR DIARY
or
INTELLIGENCE SUMMARY.
(Erase heading not required.)

Instructions regarding War Diaries and Intelligence Summaries are contained in F. S. Regs., Part II. and the Staff Manual respectively. Title pages will be prepared in manuscript.

Place	Date	Hour	Summary of Events and Information	Remarks and references to Appendices
MONCHY	11/4/17	8.30 a.m.	The his no Coy moved toward MONCHY under heavy Art. fire. On firing the T/o KOSB digging in & our horse movement stopped, commenced to dig in N.E. of them. This was satisfactory everywhere even heavy Art. M.G. & sniper fire, which he approaching Cav.? Bde. The position taken up was a good one with strong point in front of K.O.S.B.'s. The whole forming a strong front.	
	11 a.m.		'C' Coy had free itsely from the left & advanced in the village, & was occupying the issue ground as 'C' Coy. The shelling was very heavy, but we still advanced except. Amongst Cavalry faster them. Every Aeroplane was very active. An our offering my scheme.	
			It was in communication with T/o KOSB on right but not with the 8th or on left. Although there was a company of the Royal Scots. amongst them as stretches.	

WAR DIARY
or
INTELLIGENCE SUMMARY.

(Erase heading not required.)

Army Form C. 2118.

Place	Date	Hour	Summary of Events and Information	Remarks and references to Appendices
MONCHY	11/4/17	7h.	"D" Coy move thing from the village & relieved the position held by "B" & "C" Coys. The situation remained quiet in the night. Our M.G. shoots continued. The enemy shortened the day but he met with showers of snow, and during the night turned into a blizzard. The enemy proved quiet, and the Batt. was relieved at 11:30 a.m.	
	12/4/17	11:30 a.m.	by 10 W. YORKS. the relief being by 6 hours or so. The Batt. has experienced a hard time, and has performed some excellent service. Good music being done to our ranks.	(51) Casualty List E
ARRAS.		7p.m.	The Batt. arrived at ARRAS. being billeted for 3 hours at The Railway Triangle. Casualty lists attached.	

WAR DIARY
or
INTELLIGENCE SUMMARY.
(Erase heading not required.)

Army Form C. 2118.

114

Place	Date	Hour	Summary of Events and Information	Remarks and references to Appendices
Acres	13/4/17		In billets in Acres.	
do	14/4/17		Bn. marched to Steenau and were billeted in No 3 Camp here.	
Steenau	15/4/17		In billets as above. 2/Lt Jamison evacuated to hospital	
do	16/4/17		In billets as above.	
	17/4/17		In billets as above. Battle inspected by Brigadier General began at 11.30 a.m.	
	18/4/17		In billets as above. Drafts of 9 + 72 joined from base and were drafted to Coys. A 11, B 20, C 30, D 10	
	19/4/17		In billets as above.	

Army Form C. 2118.

WAR DIARY
or
INTELLIGENCE SUMMARY.
(Erase heading not required.)

(118)

Place	Date	Hour	Summary of Events and Information	Remarks and references to Appendices
Duisans	1917 April 20		Instructions to move to Arras received. Weather dry & fairly warm.	
		2 pm	Battalion marched to Arras, & billeted there.	

WAR DIARY or INTELLIGENCE SUMMARY

Army Form C. 2118.

149

Place	Date	Hour	Summary of Events and Information	Remarks and references to Appendices
ARRAS	22/4/17	8 p.m.	The Batt. left Arras Church on Offensive Order No. 1. Bivouacs in O.C. trenches H. of TILLOY at 10.20 p.m. A carrying party of 4 Officers & 130 O.R. was furnished for carrying 17.C. Arrels, and was on duty all night under heavy fire. Casualties 1 Killed & 5 Wounded. A good deal of enemy gun-fire was carried on by the enemy. The party. Some of whom did not rejoin the Batt. until morning the following day.	Offensive order (1) SS56 (2)
	23/4/17	9 a.m.	The Batt. were formed & bivouacs in O.C. Trenches S.E. of TILLOY.	
		10 a.m.	Green received to move into position of assembly H. of Brown Line. Brown Line Counter. Nil to report.	
		12 nn.	Arrive in vicinity of H. of Brown Line Counter. Nil to report. Everything was heavy & the Batt. dug in in shell hole & occupied O.C. trenches.	
		1 p.m.	Orders received regarding situation and availability of Batt. to be ready to repel Counter attack.	
		3 w.p.	Orders received to prepare to attack "Blue Line".	
		4 p.m.	Conference held at H.Q. 1.B. Bde. at O.C. Trenches. Brown Line & plan of operation discussed for attack on "Blue Line". Orders issued. Batt. in support to 7. & 8. R.Rifles	
		6 p.m.	Batt. left Brown Line in support to 10 R.Rifles at zero hour and moved forward. At zero hour, this advance was delayed. Batt. to halt his own & other Coys, and to further orders. This was carried out, men entered a	H.S.I.

Jam Carruthers

Army Form C. 2118.

WAR DIARY
or
INTELLIGENCE SUMMARY.
(Erase heading not required.)

120

Place	Date	Hour	Summary of Events and Information	Remarks and references to Appendices
SHOVEL Tr.	22/11/17	6.30p.	A heavy enemy Barrage on Bois him. Batt. suffers Casualties, infantry in neighbourhood of SPEAR LANE. SHOVEL Tr. in support to 10th Rifles in TANK Tr. & Batt. arrive in support.	Sketch (3)
		7p.	G.S. Rifles.	
		7.30p.	In support G.S. Rifles advanced to CAVALRY FARM. 1 Rifle interior to support & has since been in return to TANK Tr. The Batt. Coy. apparently coming under heavy fire in SHOVEL Tr. Batt. disposed as Sketch No 3.	
		9.30p.	From heavy BROWN LINE, & tales settling in SHOVEL Tr. Casualties from enemy sniping, of whom many reported, heavy frozen arrival up with us 1.B. The day was clear & bright and has arisen the night very cold.	
	24/11/17		A heavy Artillery fire was kept upon our position all night & particularly heavy on the enemy wiring 24" west Batt. H.2. were during the night in SPEAR Tr. like enemy further to the East of it.	
		4 am.	Position occupied by Batt. in SHOVEL Tr. improved, & trench adopted. Trust which was suspected was not continuous & about 3 ft. deep was taken up & about 5 ft. deep. Batt. now in touch with 1st R. PR. 1 hour. & with R.S.F. on left.	
		11a.	Enemy area visible to assist upon Bois him all up & over - ammunition to Cap. by 2 fm.	
		2.30p.	Orders (B2J) for attack on Bois him next. Batt. now moves to Cap. but own	Appendix (2) h.S.T

A.5834 Wt.W.4973/M687 750,000 8/16 D.D.&L. Ltd. Forms/C.2118/13.

Army Form C. 2118.

WAR DIARY
or
INTELLIGENCE SUMMARY.
(Erase heading not required.)

Place	Date	Hour	Summary of Events and Information	Remarks and references to Appendices
	26/4/16		were not relieved by Coy until Wed'day 3.45 & 3.45 pm. our Coy. g. Coy then offic: leaving the Blue line at 4.5 pm.	
		3.40pm	Heavy enemy barrage on SHOPEL T. & Reserve area. Our "Heavies" dropping short on Shrove T. Canadian keen Trench badly knocked about.	
		up	Attack on Blue Line commenced. Bosch already in kopje of K.O.S. Rifles. Our Coy "D" decided to dig itself with S. Pts. Dispositions about here "C" Coy r. "B" Coy a left: "A" Coy in Reserve. B Coy got over edges but under the heavy barrage had own platoon put out very soon. B & C Coy got into difficulties. Scarce arrived into a M.G. dest in the Trench which cut up 20 men from going over. After leaving the Trench, they got to went to the right of road. "B" Coy to the left. To spare from the French, to the Bosch area, for attack on our 5th Coy a difficult matter.	
		6.35pm	The attack they made considerably N. of our trenches. The Company had reached the Blue line. And every 2 heavy M.G. & sweeping from the whole front & particularly from Cavalry Farm & the C.T.N.E. our own riflemen & L.G. & shell like apparently on the line there in scattered M.G.	

MM(O.P.S.)
h S.J.

Army Form C. 2118.

WAR DIARY
or
INTELLIGENCE SUMMARY.
(Erase heading not required.)

Instructions regarding War Diaries and Intelligence Summaries are contained in F. S. Regs., Part II. and the Staff Manual respectively. Title pages will be prepared in manuscript.

Place	Date	Hour	Summary of Events and Information	Remarks and references to Appendices
BLUE LINE	24/4/17		The Coy's during the assault were heavy principally from Snipers & M.G. fire. The advance being made close up to our own Barrage without casualties, and only a few from enemy barrage. Our own barrage made tr's great a line from the front of enemy trench to Blue line, so missing them. It was possible to observe the Boche digging in & holding digging in & support. A few of the enemy in the sky line. The position appeared slightly to far East of our objective and in bad visibility can down by the CAMBRAI Rd. so must be all right. "D" Coy was never in position & digging in.	
		5pm	Report commences to come in from Companies showing that enemy M. Guns & Snipers were well established and that in large chances of enemy were out. Casualties from 17.5 pm to Snipers was heavy and included Lieut. CRICKETT, M. QUEEN & WATSON was killed. Conduct of these Coys was improving. The activity Coy was evidently at work in the right Bn. sector has been infilled by the Coys enemy that were also known posts in the sullen top of the Rd. between The Copse. This has been arranged for presently with Major S'Enneis the Co.	h.S.T.

Place	Date	Hour	Summary of Events and Information	Remarks and references to Appendices
			Shells oversents arrive. Our men carry the ammunition with which we are supplied and the bomb patrols are sent to examine the safety of the left flank. The enemy now is seen from (also in shell hole or shell hire) and prepare now to prevent us moving out of the gulch. M.G. fire + sniping kept us incessant pinned up of the gulch tion.	
			During the night, and previous, notwithstanding to consolidating but the line was not continuous. The day had been cold with a blast wind. The night clear but cold. The ground rapidly drying ever peril.	
	29/4/17 3.30am		A heavy barrage was put down by enemy's relation of own covering a few minute earlier. Our four bin's was not however damaged. By this time the flame line of support stands over liken up, and half of them taken into a Communication Tr N9 the CAMBRAI Rd Counterattack by the Batts by 40.	
			The 9th LONDON Hrs fate + return had not yet been received	

K.P.T

Army Form C. 2118.

WAR DIARY
or
INTELLIGENCE SUMMARY.
(Erase heading not required.)

122

Instructions regarding War Diaries and Intelligence Summaries are contained in F. S. Regs. Part II. and the Staff Manual respectively. Title pages will be prepared in manuscript.

Places	Date	Hour	Summary of Events and Information	Remarks and references to Appendices
	25/4/17		So it was impossible to screen them up to the line in the day time. Attempts to get made up were made, but sniping at these rays prevented it. The day passed without incident or attempt.	
	26/4/17	4:30a	Batt. relieved by 11th Argyll & Sutherland H'rs. and moved to MARLIERE in Div. Reserve.	
	27/4/17	10f	Marched to ARRAS in hired lorries.	
	28/4/17	3am	Arrived ARRAS.	
		12am	Marched to QUISSANT quarters in Kitchener Camp. Lists for parties of Officers & others. The behaviour of all ranks under trying conditions was most praiseworthy. The Officers in their own with great gallantry always forming keen to their objects. Especially conspicuous was situation, for which were previous instructions in invasion of Queens two ?.	Appended (S) ??

A 5834. Wt. W4973/M687. 750,000. 8/16 D.D. & L. Ltd. Forms/C.2118/13.

WAR DIARY
or
INTELLIGENCE SUMMARY
(Erase heading not required.)

Army Form C. 2118.

Place	Date	Hour	Summary of Events and Information	Remarks and references to Appendices
	29th		been carried over with communication with Batt. H.Q. previously cut off by enemy shell fire. The Batt. went into action short of Officers and efft. casualties this week showing up this morning as heavy. The N.C.O.'s and men fought & worked without cessation from the time of going into action on the nights of the 23rd until relieved and this game heroism upon the part by steen Officers is alone envied.	
	30th		Church Service. Inspection of Feet, arms & equipment. Men of A & B Company went to Baths at Montenescourt. Other two Companies had instructional training in offensive action. Arrived that the following given D.C.M. N.C.O's & Battalion have been awarded the Military Medal. See Routine Orders dated 2/4/17.	

Army Form C. 2118.

WAR DIARY
or
INTELLIGENCE SUMMARY.
(Erase heading not required.)

126

Place	Date	Hour	Summary of Events and Information	Remarks and references to Appendices
Dunano	April 30 1917		N.C.O.o No. 40223 Sergt. Dockery, T.J. 8264 " Gardner, J.A. 17879 " Robinson, A. 17833 " Kenny, G.M. 32451 Private MacDonald, H. 22353 " " Ross, W. 18823 " " Doyle, A. 12460 " " McLellan, J. 23068 " " Moore, J.S. 18426 " " Savello, A. 18553 " " Robertson, R. Of the above Private A. Doyle was killed. T Sergt. J. Dockery wounded 25/4/17. The following Officers proceed for duty with the Battalion were posted to Companies. Lieut. W.D.H. Green, 2/Lieut. J.E. Grover 2/Lieut H.E. Bethune, 2/Lieut G.M. Beauchamp 2/Lieut A.L. Alexander, 2/Lieut G.L. Leith A. Draft of 73 other ranks also arrived	

"B"

12th Battalion Highland Light Infantry.

OPERATION ORDERS No. 1

SECRET.

by

Lieut. Col. W. S. St. John, Commanding 12th Battalion H.L.I.

6th April 1917

Reference Maps. 1/10,000.
51 B. N.W. 3 & 4.

----

1. The object of the following operations by 15th Division is to capture the enemy Third Line from Road H.28.c.8.2. Northwards to the River Scarpe in H.22., also to capture the high ground in H.29. c and d., i.e., the Northern slope of ORANGE HILL. Divisional, Brigade and Battalion Areas are shown on maps issued previously.
In the attack, the 15th Division has on its right the 12th Division and on its left the 9th Division.

2. In the attack on FEUCHY CHAPEL by the 35th Inf. Brigade, 12th Division, three Battalions will be used. The fourth - the 5th Royal Berks - will move with its left on HOUDAIN LANE to bottom of Valley H.33.a.8.7. - H.27.a.5.5. Its role will be that of a Brigade Reserve echalloned on left rear of the main attack on FEUCHY CHAPEL, and protecting that flank.
It will be prepared to,-
(1) Reinforce main attack on FEUCHY CHAPEL.
(2) Attack Brown Line at H.34.central.
(3) Deal with counter attack from Brown Line.

3. ORDER OF MARCH AND ATTACK. H.L.I

   (1) From Sewers. D., A., B., C., H rs.

   (2) Assembly at Black Line.   Left.   Right.
                                  D.   A.
                                  B.   C.
                                     H rs.

   (3) At Blue Line. "D" Company in assault formation to take all objectives between Blue and Intermediate Line.
   "A" Company in Support.
   "B and C" in Reserve.
   20 N.C.O. and men- "Moppers Up" for the attack to the Intermediate Line - will be furnished by "C" Company under an Officer.

   (4) For the Brown Line "Moppers Up" for each objective will be detailed from the two assaulting Companies

   (5) From Intermediate Line for Assault on Brown Line.
   "D" Company on Left.   "A" Company on Right.
   "B" Company in Support.
   "C" Company in Reserve.

4. The Battalion will be disposed in cellars at Zero Hour, and commence to enter Sewer. at Zero+
At Zero Hour plus three 30 minutes the Battalion commences to debouch from the Sewer by the South exit "A". Each Company as it debouches will assemble at the Factory Wall, G.22.d.9.9½. and

4. contd.

immediately move to its position of assembly at the Black Line. (Routes given in Appendix 1.)

The forward movement, so long as it is by C.T's, viz., as far as the East of the Cemetery, will be by Platoons. When in the open it will be by half platoons, Artillery formation.

At Zero plus 4 hours the Battalion will be clear of O.G.2, halted with two Companies in front, in Artillery formation, covered by the two rear Companies.

If space permits or there is cover, the Companies will remain in Column of Companies in Artillery formation

5. ADVANCE ON BLUE LINE. At Zero plus 5 hours 40 minutes the Battalion will advance to the vicinity of the Blue Line.

As the Standing Barrage covering the front of 44th and 45th Inf. Brigades will be operating some hundred yards beyond their leading troops, the leading Companies of the Battalion will push through to them and get into position on correct alignment - lying down within 100 yards of Barrage.

Before carrying this out, the leading Company will be organised for the attack to the Intermediate Line, and receive the men for Mopping Up from the rear Company "C".

The rear Companies will remain in Artillery formation unless the situation renders it impossible to do so.

6. ATTACK ON BROWN LINE. The attack on Brown Line will commence at Zero plus 6 hours 40 minutes, and will be divided into two phases.
(1) The advance on an intermediate objective shewn by the red line in Battery Valley entered on Maps.
(This includes the capture of the FEUCHY REDOUBT by 7/8th K.O.S.B's.
(2) The clearing of FEUCHY VILLAGE and attack on Brown Line.

7. ADVANCE TO INTERMEDIATE OBJECTIVES. The leading Company will advance on a frontage of two platoons as laid down in "The Company in Attack."

The principle being, that should any trenches be held by the enemy, the first wave goes to the furthest objective.

It is important that during this attack communication is kept with the 10th Scottish Rifles on the left, and if possible, communication with 5th Royal Berks, 37th Division on the right.

The Commander of leading Company must be prepared, should circumstances admit doing so, to make his advance in a more open attack formation.

The ground to be advanced over will be covered by Patrols and Scouts from the leading Company.

The advance will be made under a Creeping Barrage which jumps back at the rate of 100 yards in 2 minutes.

During the advance the left of 10th Scottish Rifles will direct.

During the advance the 7/8th K.O.S.B's will capture the FEUCHY REDOUBT.

The 10th Scottish Rifles will take the Trenches South of the Railway in H.21.c.

The 12th H.L.I. will move on the right of 10th Scottish Rifles and deal with any opposition encountered in their Area.

Mopping up parties will be left in any trenches occupied by the enemy. These parties will be under the command of an officer of "C" Company. When their task is completed they will rejoin the Battalion under his orders.

- 3 -

8. **HALT AT INTERMEDIATE OBJECTIVE.** After the intermediate objective has been taken there will be a pause of one hour to allow of reorganization, reporting casualties, and to allow of touch being obtained with the 5th Royal Berks of 35th Inf. Bgde. on the right, and 10th Scottish Rifles on left.
A patrol will be sent along HIRSON LANE to get in touch with a similar patrol of the 5th Royal Berks (who wear a green triangle on backs). This patrol will be furnished from the leading Support Company, ("A" Company), who will also detail a patrol to get in touch with 10th Scottish Rifles on the left.
The line to be taken up by the Advance Coy. is roughly to the East of Battery Valley as shewn on Map.
Directly this line is reached the Commander of leading Company will push out patrols to front and flanks.
The exact position taken up by rear Companies; whether on the East or West of Battery Valley must depend upon the nature of the ground, and enemy Artillery and Machine Gun fire.
The main principles will be, to select a place affording cover to reassemble in, in security, and to arrange for protection by means of Scouts and Posts.

9. **ADVANCE ON BROWN LINE.** At Zero plus 7 hours 55 minutes, the Creeping Barrage will move back at the rate of 100 yards in 4 minutes, till it rests on HIMALAYA TRENCH.
The 7/8th K.O.S.B's will clear up FEUCHY VILLAGE. The 10th Scottish Rifles will assist with two Companies. The remaining two Companies, S.Rif. as soon as they see the attack on Village is progressing satisfactorily, proceed by most concealed route along the Railway in file or suitable formation, in support of this front.
At the same time as the rear Companies, 10th Scottish Rifles begin to move off, the leading Company 12th H.L.I. will move to a position West of Broken Mill at about H.27.b.1.0. to H.27.b.1.2.
Scouts and Patrols will be used during this advance and after. The formation this Company moves in must be one suitable for fire action, and yet suitable to make the assault on Brown Line Trenches.
The safety of flanks must be assured.
Two machine guns will accompany this Company at this phase, and One will enfilade the Trenches in continuation of Brown Line, North of River, the other to cover the advance of the Battalion at a later period on the Brown Line.
Touch with the troops attacking the village of FEUCHY, and 5th Royal Berks by the patrols from flanks of leading Companies must be maintained.

(1) In the attack on the Brown Line, the leading Company "D" which will be reinforced by "A" Company on its right, will work up to within assaulting distance, taking advantage of all cover, and will be ready to press home their assault simultaneously with the 10th Scottish Rifles and 7/8th K.O.S.B's.
Patrols will be sent forward by both Companies to reconnoitre gaps in wire in front of Brown Line.

(2) At Zero plus 9 hours the two leading Companies will assault the Brown Line, the Artillery Barrage having been lifted off Himalaya Trench, - the assault being covered by Machine and Lewis Gun fire,- the L.G. fire being arranged by 7/8th K.O.S.B's and 10th Scottish Rifles.

(3) The object of the 10th Scottish Rifles when assaulting Brown Line will be to force an entry into German trenches at the Railway. Send forward L.G. along Railway in rear of Germans. Pour down the trenches South of Railway, and assist them if necessary by an attack of the rear Companies out of Railway cutting through any gaps there may be in the wire.

(4) The Left Company (H.L.I.) will be the directing Company. The dividing line between these two Companies in the Brown Line will be where CABLE Trench cuts HIMALAYA Trench.
The Assault upon the Brown Line will be made in two waves, the first going to the 2nd Objective - The German Support Line. The attack to be pushed home with the greatest vigour.
Mopping up parties will follow the first wave, the first line of "Moppers Up" going to the 2nd Objective.
All positions captured at the Brown Line will be held at all costs. When FEUCHY CHAPEL and ORANGE HILL are captured, the 37th Division is to move into position for the attack on MONCHY.

(5) In the Assault upon the Brown Line, the Company in Support, "B", will move forward as they attack ready to support the Assaulting Companies, and when the first and second objectives have been occupied, will be prepared to assist in the consolidation

(6) The Company in Reserve ("C") must not move forward until the Commander receives instructions from Battalion Head quarters. When the Brown Line is occupied he must be prepared to move forward and dig in as Battalion Reserve. It may also be necessary to form Defensive flanks.

10. **ACTION AFTER BROWN LINE IS TAKEN** Artillery and Machine Gun Barrages are being arranged for to keep off counter attacks after the capture of the Brown Line.
Four Bangalore Torpedoes will be provided for each of the attacking Battalions for cutting wire. C.R.E. will arrange the necessary parties for using them.
Immediately the Brown Line is taken the work of consolidation is to commence. Every advantage will be taken of the possible period of quiesence to push on the work.
Strong Points will be constructed under the supervision of the 91st Field Co. R.E. approximately at following points:-
H.28.c.8.8. - H.28.d.0.3.

11. **CONSOLIDATION.** The work of consolidation will be covered by means of Strong Patrols with Lewis Guns, which will be pushed out by each attacking Company to the Northern Slopes of ORANGE HILL, approximately LINE, H.35.a.5.0. - H.23.c.2.5.
Communication with Battalion on either flank will be established.

12. In the event of the 44th and 45th Infantry Brigades not capturing the trenches at the Blue Line, the 46th Inf. Bgde. may be called on to assist.

13. TANKS/

13. **TANKS.** (a) Two Tanks of No. 4 Section, "C" Bn., H.B. H.G. Corps, under Captain Walker, will co-operate in the attack on the Brown Line. The Tanks will leave the Blue Line with the leading troops of the Brigade and will cover the distance to the Intermediate Line - they will be available to destroy any obstacles encountered. During this phase one Tank will operate to the North and one to the South of the Railway.

(b) Both Tanks will move just South of the Railway during the advance to the Brown Line, until they reach a position from which they can cover the assault - Special attention to be paid to the Trenches N. and S. of the Railway at H.22.a.4.9.

(c) After the assault on the Brown Line and when their services are no longer required, both tanks will move South along the Brown Line towards FEUCHY CHAPEL - other tanks will be moving N. along BROWN LINE from FEUCHY CHAPEL.

14. **STRAGGLERS POSTS.** The 12th H.L.I. will establish Stragglers Posts consisting of 1 C.S.M. and 3 O.R. within its own area in the vicinity of the Blue Line.
Warrant Officers in charge will be provided with written orders by their Battalions. These posts will stop all men proceeding to the rear, except on duty and will return them to their units taking their names for subsequent communication to units.

15. **REPORTS.**
Battalion Headquarters. -
(1) Until Battalion is clear of the Sewer will be at G.23.c.1/2.8.
(2) When Battalion arrives at Black Line - In dug-out under Railway Line at G.24.c.3.4½. and until Blue Line is taken with a forward Station at G.24.d.4.3.
(3) When Battalion reaches the Blue Line at H.25.b.7.9.
(4) When the advance on the Intermediate Line commences, Battn. H'rs will remain at H.25.b.7.9. with a forward report station at H.26.a.7.6.
(5) When the Battalion reaches the Intermediate Line - at H.26.b.2.5.
(6) Brigade H'rs will be at G.23.c.1/2.6. - Forward Station G.24.c.3.4½.

Reports, in addition to any others it is found necessary to send in, will be sent in by Companies reporting arrival and approximate Casualties at:-
        (a) Black Line.
        (b) Blue Line.
        (c) Intermediate Line.
        (d) Brown Line.

- 6 -

The following Appendices are attached:-
A. Route to be taken by Platoons from Sewer to Black Line.
B. Time Table Appendix.
C. Diagram of Barrage.
D. Lists of Dress, Equipment, Tools, S.A.A., Explosives etc.
E. Information and Instructions regarding Dumps and Supplies.

APPENDIX "A".

12th H.L.I.- Exit from Sewer, - "A".
Route. - Stretcher Trench - Interpreter or Image.
Destination in first instance. - Assembly positions in area between BLACK LINE and O.B.1 (exclusive).
Zero plus 1 hour 30 minutes. - 7/8th K.O.S.B's and 12th H.L.I. debouch from Sewer followed by remainder of Brigade, moving off independently to assembly position in Black Line Area as allotted.

Route to Sewer through cellar No.23, thence under Rue des Dmingains, thence through Cellars on N.E. side of square, thence by connecting passages to Sewer.

APPENDIX "B".

Zero plus 30 min.	Brigade will move into Sewers, K.O.S.B's leading followed by 12th H.L.I.
1 hour 30 min.	~~Rest of Brigade into Sewers, etc. Black Line-Sewer.~~ K.O.S.B's and 12th H.L.I. debouch from Sewer and proceed to positions at Black Line.
4 hours.	All Brigade will be clear of O.B.1.
5 hours 40 min.	Brigade will advance to vicinity of Blue Line, passing through 44th and 43rd Brigades, and will move as close up to Barrage as possible.
6 hours 40 min.	Advance to Intermediate Objective (shewn in red) 7/8th K.O.S.B. will capture FEUCHY Redoubt. 10th S. Rif. will take trenches S. of Railway in H.21.c. 12th H.L.I. will deal with any opposition they may meet. There will be a halt of an hour on or about Battery Valley.
7 hours 58 min.	K.O.S.B. and two Companies S. Rif. will proceed to clear up FEUCHY Village. Remaining two Coys S. Rif. will move up railway as soon as this attack is progressing favourably. 12th H.L.I. will then move one Company W. of Broken Mill and will afterwards move other Companies into position. They will then work up to assaulting distance of Brown Line.
9 hours.	Assault on Himalaya Trench.
9 hours 2 min.	Assault on Support Trench.
10 hours.	37th Division leave Brown Line.

APPENDIX "D".

Fighting Kit. - N.C.O's and men will wear and carry:-
        Steel Helmet.
        Equipment (without pack).
        Entrenching tool and carrier.
        Haversack worn on back containing two Iron
        Rations and unexpended portion one day's rations.
        Mess Tin.
        Water bottle filled.
        Oil bottle filled.
        Leather Jerkin.
        W.P. Sheet.

Wire Cutters, Rifle - Wire Breakers, Rifle - Wire Cutters, Hand - Rifle Bomb Cups, Bomb bucket, Bomb carrier,.

A½ full sized entrenching tools per man carried through left side of waistbelt.

S.A.A. 220 rounds carried by each rifleman.
     100 rounds per Bomber, Rifle Grenadier or Lewis Gunner.
     Battalion Reserve, 10,000.
     per Lewis Gun.- 20 drums, 1,000 loose. (Remainder of drums
                                  in Battn. Reserve.)

Grenades Mills.	-	2 per man.
do	-	12 per Bomber.
Grenades Rifle.	-	20 per Grenadier.
Flares.	-	80 per Company.
P. Bombs.	-	40 per Company.
Stokes Bombs. (for dug-outs)	-	4 per Mopping Up party.
Very Lights.	-	500 per Battalion.
Artillery Signals.		
Sandbags.	-	4 per man.

12th Battalion Highland Light Infantry.

SECRET OPERATION ORDERS No.2.

1. Reference Operation Orders No.1 dated 6/4/17.

(a) For para 9 sub para (5) substitute - "Support Company. "B" Coy. in support of the two leading Companies will assault the Brown Line in two waves,-
   The first to the 2nd Objective.
   The second to the 1st Objective.
After the reserve Company "C" has entered the first objective, the second wave of "B" Company will go on to second Objective. "B" Company will furnish Mopping Up Parties to assault with "D" and "A" Companies - 10 O.R. to each Company for first Objective, Brown Line."

(b) For para 9 sub para (6) substitute - "The Company in Reserve (C) will move in attack formation, if necessary giving covering fire to the leading Companies, and will follow the Support Company "B" and assault the Brown Line.
The assault will be made in two waves, both going to the first Objective."

2. Reference Instruction No.6.

For para 3, first sub para substitute -
"Flares will now be lit as follows:-

   On reaching
      ~~BLACK LINE....... at Zero plus one hour.~~
      ~~Blue Line........ at Zero plus 3 hours.~~
                         at Zero plus 8.30 hours.

      by leading troops wherever they may be at that
   hour
                         at Zero plus 9.30 hours.

                     (sd) Graeme Taylor, 2nd Lt. & A/Adjt.
                              12th High. L.I.
8/4/17.

12th Battalion Highland Light Infantry.

SECRET. INTELLIGENCE ARRANGEMENTS. Instruction No. 1.

1. **PRISONERS OF WAR.**
   (1) Prisoners taken in operations by 46th Inf. Brigade towards the "Brown" Line will be conducted by troops of that Brigade to the neighbourhood of either 44th or 45th Inf. Brigade H rs. where N.C.O. in charge of escort will ~~escort~~ hand over the Prisoners - the 44th or 45th I. B. supplying further escort.

   (2) <u>Procedure after capture</u>.

   (a) All prisoners will be disarmed.

   (b) Only Officers and N.C.O's will be searched, all their documents will be removed and handed over to the N.C.O. in charge of the escort who will deliver them to the Intelligence Officer at the PRISON and obtain a receipt.

   (c) Units capturing prisoners will report to Brigade H rs. as early as possible the numbers taken and Regiments to which they belong. Brigades will forward this information by "Priority" wire to the Division.

   (d) Prisoners will not be interrogated, except in cases of immediate tactical urgency, prior to their arrival at the Corps Collecting Station, where they will be examined by Officers of the Intelligence Corps.

2. **SITUATION MAPS.**
   A situation map on a scale of 1/20,000 will be issued each night showing the situation at 6 p.m. and any important information received during the previous 24 hours. An Intelligence Summary will accompany the map. As this information may influence the following day's operations, it is important that it should be passed down to units without delay.

3. **DOCUMENTS ON ENEMY DEAD.**
   <u>Searching of dug-outs etc</u>. All Head uarters and Dug-outs will be carefully searched, by special parties to be detailed by Commanding Officers, for documents and for any new type of telephone instrument.

7th April 1917.

(sd) Graeme Taylor, 2nd Lt. & A/Adjt.
12th High. L.I.

12th Battalion Highland Light Infantry.

S E C R E T.   SYNCHRONIZATION OF WATCHES.   Instruction No.2.

Following are arrangements for synchronization of watches:-
Time Signal sent from Army Headquarters daily at 9 a.m. and
6 p.m. commencing to-day.
All Signal Offices connected by telegraph will receive this
signal at same time.
Special additional arrangements will be made for Z day.

                    S I G N A L S.   Instruction No.3.

1. No.100 Squadron (Flying over Third Army Area under G.H.Q.
orders) which is to be used for night flying, is equipped
with F.E.2.b. machines painted as follows:-

Bottom Planes. (a) Bottom - all black with one white circle
                              underneath each wing instead of the
                              standard red, white and blue.
               (b) Top.   - all black with no circles.

Top Planes.   (a) Bottom.- all black with no circles.
               (b) Top.   - brown with standard red, white
                              and blue circles on each wing.

Nacelle.   Dark Grey.

Tail Plane and Rudder. Black.

2. With reference to communication between Infantry and aeroplane during operations; the attention of all Battalion
Commanders is to be called to the importance of the front line
of Infantry lighting flares when called upon to do so by signals
from the aeroplane.
The Signals are laid down on page 70 of S.S.135 " Instructions
for the Training of Divisions for Offensive Action", viz., a
succession of "A's" sounded on the Klaxon horn, or, if this
does not produce a reply, the firing of a white light.

3. Signals to Artillery.
   (a) The Signals with 1½" Very Pistols given below have been
       laid down by Third Army for use during operations between
   Artillery observers in the front line and batteries, in
       connection with covering fire (not the barrage covering an
       assault by our troops).

           Succession of Green Lights ....Open Fire.
           Succession of White Lights ....Lengthen Range.

   (b) These signals do not come into force until orders to
       that effect are issued from Divisional Headquarters.

   (c) As soon as these signals come into force they will also
       be applicable to Signals between Infantry and Artillery
       and will be carried out by the various means available,
       e.g. rockets, 1" Very Pistols, etc.

   (d) It/

SIGNALS.   Instruction No.3 contd.

(d) It will be understood from the above that the S.O.S. Signal which has hitherto been given by rocket only, will, when this system comes into force consist of a succession of green lights, whether from 1½" Very Pistols, 1" Very Pistols, rockets or other means is immaterial. This fact should be made clear to all personnel carrying any means of firing signal lights, so that they will fully realise the results to be expected if they discharge lights.
Care will also have to be taken that with so many individuals in possession of means of giving the S.O.S. Signal it is not used unnecessarily.

(e) The signal for lengthening range is primarily intended for use by Artillery personnel and should only be used by Infantry when urgently necessary.

Forced Landing of Aeroplanes.   Instruction No.4.

It is anticipated that some difficulty may occur in obtaining news of aeroplanes which have forced landings away from their aerodromes during open warfare.
When machines are forced to land, the occupants of which are either missing or incapacitated, a telegram should at once be despatched to No.1 Aircraft Depot stating:-
(a) The number of the machine and type, if possible.
(b) The names of occupants, if any.
(c) The co-ordinates on the 1/40,000 map of the place of landing.

   N.B. The number of sheet must be stated.

(d) Whether the machine is a total wreck, or appears to be only slightly damaged.

Bombing Parties Signals.   Instruction No.5.

The Signal in use in 15th Division when Bombing parties are working towards each other in a German Trench is the waving of a sandbag on the end of a fixed bayonet.

      (sd) Graeme Taylor, 2nd Lt. & A/Adjt.
             12th High. L.I.

7/4/17.

12th Battalion Highland Light Infantry.

SECRET.   S I G N A L S.   Instruction No.6.

1. **Between Infantry and Artillery.**
   (a) Very Light Signal.
       1" and 1½"
          Succession of White............ lengthen range.
                  "   " Green............ open fire.
   The above signals will come into force at 12 noon on 7th April.
   The present S.O.S. Rocket Signal (Green - Red - Green) will cease to be in force at above time and date.
   NOTE.
   In the case of white light, in order that it may be distinguished from the ordinary illuminating light, the succession should be rapid and from one spot.

   (b) **Flags.** (Yellow with Black St. Andrews Cross.)
   To be carried by each platoon. They must on no account be stuck in the ground, but should be waved to denote position of our Infantry.

2. **Aeroplanes.**
   (a) Contact patrol with Infantry.
   Markings.- One black band under both lower planes with streamers attached to each plane immediately behind the black bands.

   (b) Contact patrol with Cavalry.
   Markings.- The bottom of the lower planes will be painted black from the outer rib to the extremity of the planes.
   A blue streamer will be attached to the rear outer strut on each plane.

   For methods of communication between Aeroplanes and Infantry, vide S.S.135, paras 4 and 5 - Appendix B.
   Note. - The two letter code calls will be used.

3. **FLARES.** (red will be lit by the leading Infantry.
   (a) On Reaching:-   Black Line at Zero plus 1 hour.
                    Blue   Line   "   "   "   3 hours.
                   § Brown Line   "   "   "   9 hours 30 minutes.
   § To be lit by leading troops of the Brigade at that hour, irrespective of their position with regard to Brown Line.

   The 12th Squadron, R.F.C. will arrange for aeroplanes to be over these objectives at the anticipated times if flying is possible.

   (b) When called for by aeroplanes.

4. **KITE BALLOONS.** There will be two kite balloons up just behind ARRAS for receiving messages by Visual from the front line. All forward Visual Stations are to be notified that this is an additional method of getting through.
   The procedure will be as follows:-
   (a) Messages will be sent by lamp, either Lucas or French. The lamp is to be aligned on the basket by day, and on the light carried by the balloon by night.

   (b) Messages to be BxB DD - DD but acknowledgment will be given.

   (c) Messages/

- 2 -

(c) Messages where possible are to be confined to the code letters laid down for signalling to aeroplanes. Messages in clear will however be accepted, but should be short.

(d) The balloons will be up both day and night from Zero onwards and will receive messages at all times.

(e) The two-letter code-calls will be used for and by the Infantry.

(f) The Kite Balloon call will be "KB".

ESTABLISHMENT OF "H" DUMP.   Instruction No.7.

1. The R.S.M. will be in charge of Battalion Dump ("H" Dump.) This dump will be established at some suitable spot near Broken Hill. As soon as possible after the Brown Line is captured, two platoons of 10/11th H.L.I. will carry supplies to "H" Dump from Brigade Dump. ("B" Dump.)
The establishment will be:-
  S.A.A............15 boxes.
  Mills Bombs.......48 "
   "   R.G. ....14 "
  Very Lights.......
   White 1"   1 "
   "   1½"   1 "
  P. Bombs.......... 2 "
  Flares............ 1 "
  Rockets........... 8 doz.
As stores from "H" Dump are taken into the line, an equal amount of stores will be called from the rear.

2. Carrying parties will be supplied as follows:-
 (a) Sergt. Fleming and 15 O.R. from H'rs to carry to "D" Coy.
 (b) One Sergt. and 15 men from "C" Coy. to carry to "A" Coy.
One man will carry two boxes bombs. Two men will carry one box S.A.A. or one box Very Lights.
Company Commanders will send a runner with indents for what stores are required, and R.S.M. will see that stores are supplied evenly to all Companies until demands are satisfied. N.C.O's in charge of carrying parties will hand over stores properly to Companies.

SUPPLIES OF EXPLOSIVES.   Instruction No.8.

1. **Battalion Reserve.** The carrying parties under Sergt. Fleming, and N.C.O. from "C" Company will move up under R.S.M. in rear of "C" Company in Artillery formation and will carry the undermentioned stores:-
Sergt. Fleming, - 10 men - 250 bombs in sandbags of 25 each.
      5 Men - 2500 rounds S.A.A. in double sandbags of 500 rounds each.
N.C.O.(C. Coy.) 10 men - 250 bombs.
      5 men - 2500 rounds S.A.A.
These stores will be placed in "H" Dump and used as required. O.C. "C" Company will arrange to carry up 5000 rounds S.A.A. and place them in "H" Dump.
2. COMPANIES. In addition to explosives specified in Operation Orders No.1 Appendix "D", will carry 320 bombs, that is 20 in each Bomb Bucket.

SECRET   COPY NO. 6

                     46th Infantry Brigade Order No. 180
_____

Reference 51.b. N.W.   22-4-17
          51.b. S.W.
          1/20,000
----

1.   The enemy is holding the following general line on the Third Army front ;--

FONTAINE-LEZ-CROISELLES - GUEMAPPE - ROEUX - GAVRELLE.

        On the front of the 15th Division (according to information from prisoners) the 176th Regiment, 35th Division, holds GUEMAPPE and north of GUEMAPPE is the 18th Bavarian Infantry Regiment, 3rd Bavarian Division. The relief of the latter is suspected.

2.   The Third and First Armies are continuing their advance at zero hour on April, 23rd.
        On the right of the 15th Division is the 50th Division (VII Corps) on front N.30.b.2.8. to COJEUL River at N.24.a.4.8.
        On the left of the 15th Division the 29th Division (VI Corps) on front LA BERGERE (exclusive) round the eastern outskirts of MONCHY-LE-PREUX.
        The 3rd Division (H.Q. WARLUS) is in VI Corps Reserve.
        A map showing the objectives (Blue Line and Red Line) of the 50th, 15th and 29th Divisions has already been issued.

3.   Dividing line between ;--

    (a) 15th and 50th Divisions - The COJEUL River
    (b) 15th and 29th Divisions - N.12 central to small copse in O.8.central to south edge of BOIS DU VERT to road in O.9.b. central (Road to 15th Division).

4. (i)   The 15th Division will attack at zero hour on April, 23rd. The advance will be simultaneous along the whole front of the Division.

        44th Inf.Bde. (H.Q. N.16.b.1.8.) on the right
        45th Inf.Bde. (H.Q. N.10.d.3.7.) on the left
        46th Inf.Bde. (H.Q. H.31.central) in Reserve.

        Dividing line between 44th and 45th Inf.Bdes ;-- from bend in road N.18.a.6.7½ to north of buildings in C.14.a. central, to point of spur on second objective about C.15.b.3.4½.

    (ii) (a) The 44th and 45th Inf.Bdes. are to capture both the first and second objectives.
         (b) The advance from the first to the second objectives will commence at zero plus seven hours.
         (c) After the capture of the RED Line, patrols will be sent forward to cover the consolidation of the captured position and to obtain observation with a view to a further advance at a later date.

                                                        (iii) ....

2.

    (iii)   The 44th Infantry Brigade are detailing one battalion to deal with GUEMAPPE, the remainder of the Brigade pushing forward to the capture of the BLUE Line.

    (iv)   The 45th Infantry Brigade are to advance against the first objective - Right battalion in line with the 44th Infantry Brigade and Left battalion in echelon forward to connect with the flank of the 29th Division.

    (v)   The advance of both Brigades will at first be at the rate of 100 yards in three minutes, and subsequently at 100 yards in four minutes.

The 18 pr barrage maps will be issued later.

The leading Infantry will advance as close to the barrage as possible.

5. (i)   The 46th Inf.Bde. (less 46th M.G.Coy) will move to a position of assembly S. of the CAMBRAI Road and West of BOIS DES BOEUFS *to-day* in accordance with the attached March Table. Movements will be by Platoons at 75 yards distance. Sketches showing the areas allotted to units have already been issued to units.

    (ii)   The Brigade will be prepared to move to the BROWN LINE when vacated by rear Battalions of the leading Brigades, on receipt of orders to do so from Bde H.Q.

In the first instance units will move as follows :--

    10th Sco.Rif. to Southern portion of BROWN LINE, followed by 10/11th High.L.I. to Northern portion of BROWN Line.

    7/8th K.O.Sco.Bord. will then occupy area vacated by 10th Sco.Rif.
    12th High.L.I. will occupy area vacated by 10/11th High.L.I.

    (iii)   One Stokes Mortar 46th T.M.Bty. will be attached to each Battalion and will join before ZERO hour.

    (iv)   Brigade Headquarters will move to Headquarters, 44th Inf.Bde.(N.16.b.1.8.) and will be established in an adjoining dug-out.

    (v)   When Headquarters, 10th Sco.Rif. advance from BROWN LINE a cable will be laid forward from Advanced Brigade Headquarters by this Battalion.

3.

6. (i) The Divisional Artillery Group attacking under the orders of the Divisional Commander, consists of the 3rd and 15th Divisional Artilleries, the 232nd Army Field Artillery Brigade, and the 14th Heavy battery R.G.A.
The Division has a direct call on the 32nd H.A.G.

(ii) The preliminary bombardment is being carried out on the 21st and 22nd April.

(iii) After the capture of the BLUE Line, a battery of the 3rd Divisional Artillery and a battery of the 15th Divisional Artillery will move to Les FOSSE'S Farm VALLEY where the 232nd A.F.A. Brigade is in position.

7. Field companies R.E. and Pioneers will work under the orders of the C.R.E.
Sections of Field companies have been allotted to attacking Brigades for the construction of strong points.

8. Instructions have been issued regarding :-

(a) Machine gun barrage
(b) Consolidation of positions.
(c) Tanks.
(d) Communications.
(e) Medical arrangements.
(f) Prisoners.

9. Orders as to synchronization of watches and hour of ZERO will be issued later.

10. Arrival of units in positions of assembly in the TILLOY Area will be reported to Brigade H.Q.

11. Brigade Headquarters will close at RUE TROIS VISAGES, ARRAS at 5.30 p.m. and open at dug-out in HARFLEUR Trench (H.31.central) at the same hour.

Major,
Brigade Major,
46th INF.BDE.

Issued at 7.30 a.m.
through Signals.

Distribution overleaf ..

MARCH TABLE.

Issued with 46th Infantry Brigade Order No.186
dated 22-4-1917.

UNITS (in order of march)	STARTING POINT Place	Time	DESTINATION	ROUTE	REMARKS.
10th Sco.Rif.	ARRAS STATION G.28.b.2.2.	8 p.m.	Position of Assembly as ordered.	Through station - Road leading S.E. from G.28.b.3.9. to G.29.c.3.5.5 - thence by most convenient route.	Routes to be reconnoitred in daylight and guides arranged for by units as required.
10/11th High.L.I.	"	8.30 p.m.			
12th High.L.I.	"	9 p.m.			
7/8th K.O.S.B.	"	9.30 p.m.			
46th T.M.Bty.	"	10 pm			

SECRET   COPY NO. 6

46th Infantry Brigade Order No. 181

Reference VISEN - ARTOIS 1/10,000   24-4-17.
GUEMAPPE Trench Map.

1. The advance of the 15th Division will continue at 4 p.m. to-day. OBJECTIVE :— BLUE Line.

2. The 46th Infantry Brigade with 8/10th Gordons and 6th Camerons and 8 Machine Guns 44th Machine Gun Company, 8 Machine Guns 45th Machine Gun Company will carry out the attack and capture the " BLUE " Line. The attack will be pushed home with the utmost vigour.

3. On our right the 50th Division line at 11.30 p.m., 23rd April ran as follows ;—
N.30.b.5.8. - N.30.b.8.9. - O.19.d.6.2. - O.19.b.9.5. - O.13.d.8.4. .
The 29th Division on our left hold SHRAPNEL Trench .

4. (i) The attack will be carried out as follows ;—

UNIT	TASK	POSITION OF ASSEMBLY
10th Sco.Rif. Present H.Q. (N.18.b.5½.8½).	RIGHT Assaulting Battalion	Present Line.
12th High.L.I. Present H.Q. (N.12.c.9½.3½).	LEFT Assaulting Battalion.	Present Line.
8/10th Gordons 44th Inf.Bde. Present H.Q. (N.17.d.1.1.).	RIGHT Support	Present Line.
7/8th K.O.S.B. Present H.Q. (N.16.a.8.2.)	LEFT Support	Coy. in STRING Trench to join Battalion as it advances . Remainder to move to position N. of N.18.b.7.8. in rear of crest.
6th Camerons Hrs. (45th Inf.Bde.)	RESERVE.	Remain in present position.

.... (ii)

(ii) Machine Guns will be employed as follows :-

  46th M.G.Coy. 2 Guns with each of
    10th Sco.Rif. and 12th High.L.I.

  44th M.G.Coy. (N.16.a.8½.9.)
    2 Guns with 8/10th Gordons

  45th M.G.Coy. 2 Guns with 7/8th K.O. S.B.

  Remaining Guns available will cover the advance under the orders of Captain MORROGH, M.C. Present H.Q. (N.11.a.2.5.

  A Machine Gun Barrage will be placed on N. and S. GRID LINE between 0.14. and 15 on an S.O.S.Signal being sent up.

(iii) **FORMATIONS** Battalions will advance on a two Company frontage, each Company with two Platoons in front, well extended.

  10th Sco.Rif. will deploy 3 Coys in front line when they reach N. and S. GRID LINE between 0.13. and 14 squares. The company of 12th High.L.I. at present on right of 10th Sco.Rif. will attack under the orders of O.C., 10th Sco.Rif.

  12th High.L.I. (less 1 Coy.) will move into line on left of 10th Sco.Rif. from their present position unless they can move into position as they move forward in SHOVEL Trench before ZERO hour, unobserved by the enemy.

(iv) Dividing Line between Battalions – an E. and W. Line through 0.14.a.0.7.

(v) The Artillery Barrage. will advance at the rate of 100 yards in 4 minutes and will do so from the line 0.13.d.8.5. – 0.7.b.8.0. at 4.4 p.m., opening on that line at 4 p.m. Assaulting Battalions will advance so as to move close under the Barrage. The Barrage will halt 300 yds beyond the BLUE Line.

6. CONSOLIDATION.

(1) Consolidation is to commence immediately the objective is gained. New trenches will be dug, existing German trenches will not be occupied.

(2) Rifle and Lewis Gun fire are to be employed at once, without waiting for orders, whenever a Target presents itself.

(3) All positions gained are to be held – more casualties occur by retirements than if our positions are held on to.

(4) ....

(5) The main line to be consolidated will be on the Reverse or Western slope of the BLUE Line Ridge with Strong Posts pushed on to forward slopes.

(6) After the capture of the BLUE Line the front will be held by the 10th Sco.Rif. on right and 12th High.L.I. on Left . Supporting Battalions to dig in   in close Support about 100 yards in rear of Captured Line.

3.

(4) Communication is to be established with units on flanks by patrols as soon as the objective is gained.

7. (a) O.C., 7/8th K.O.Sco.Bord. will work his Battalion forward to positions allotted during the day by Platoons.

(b) When the assault commences every opportunity will be seized to work these Battalions forward in close support of the assaulting Battalions, ready to fill gaps as they occur. Each Battalion will tell off one Company to protect the RIGHT and LEFT Flanks of the Brigade respectively and to form defensive flanks on arrival at objective irrespective of whether Brigades on RIGHT and LEFT get up or not.

8. Dressing Stations exist at Northernmost House in MARLIERE and at LES FOSSES FM.

9. When Battalion Headquarters advance from their present positions Telephone lines will be laid by them and positions of Advaced Headquarters to be reported to Brigade Headquarters.

10. 10/11th High.L.I. will not take part in the attack and will withdraw after dark to the BROWN LINE, N. and S. of present Brigade Headquarters, Headquarters to that point.

11. Brigade Headquarters will be established at a dugout on Railway at H.11.d.7.4. before ZERO hour. Reports to this point.

Major,
Brigade Major,
46th INF.BDE.

Issued at 1 p.m.
through Signals.

Copy No.			
1.	War Diary	14.	151st Inf.Bde.
2.	File	15.	86th Inf.Bde.
3.	7/8th K.O.Sco.Bord.	16.	8/10th Gordons
4.	10th Sco.Rif.	17.	6th Camerons
5.	10/11th High.L.I.	18.	44th M.G.Coy.
6.	12th High.L.I.	19.	45th M.G.Coy.
7.	46th M.G.Coy.	20.	15th Divl.Arty.
8.	46th T.M.Bty.	21.	Liaison Officer, R.A.
9.	Staff Captain	22.	45th Fd.Amb.
10.	Bde Signals.	23.	8th Inf.Bde.
11.	15th Division	24.	73rd Fd.Coy.R.E.
12.	44th Inf.Bde.	25.	74th Fd.Coy.R.E.
13.	8th Inf.Bde.	26.	9th Gordons.

2. PERSONNEL WHO WENT FORWARD WITH UNIT ON "Z" DAY.

OFFICERS. 20.
OTHER RANKS. 623.
TOTAL 643

Secret

12.15.1

Herewith O.O.
Nos 1 & 2.
Please acknowledge
by Bearer.

Ralph McKay BM
46 IB.

8/4/17.

wishing you all
the best of luck
RM

List of Officers wounded.

		Date
2nd Lt.	L. McLean	9-4-17
"	J. R. Prentice	do.
"	S. I. Murdoch	do.
Lt.	H. I. Martin	do.
2nd Lt.	M. Wallace	11-4-17
"	D. Wood	10-4-17
"	D. W. Haldane	9-4-17
"	J. A. Penman	11-4-17
"	J. McKie	11-4-17
"	D. R. Sillars	10-4-17
Capt.	W. McHardie	10-4-17

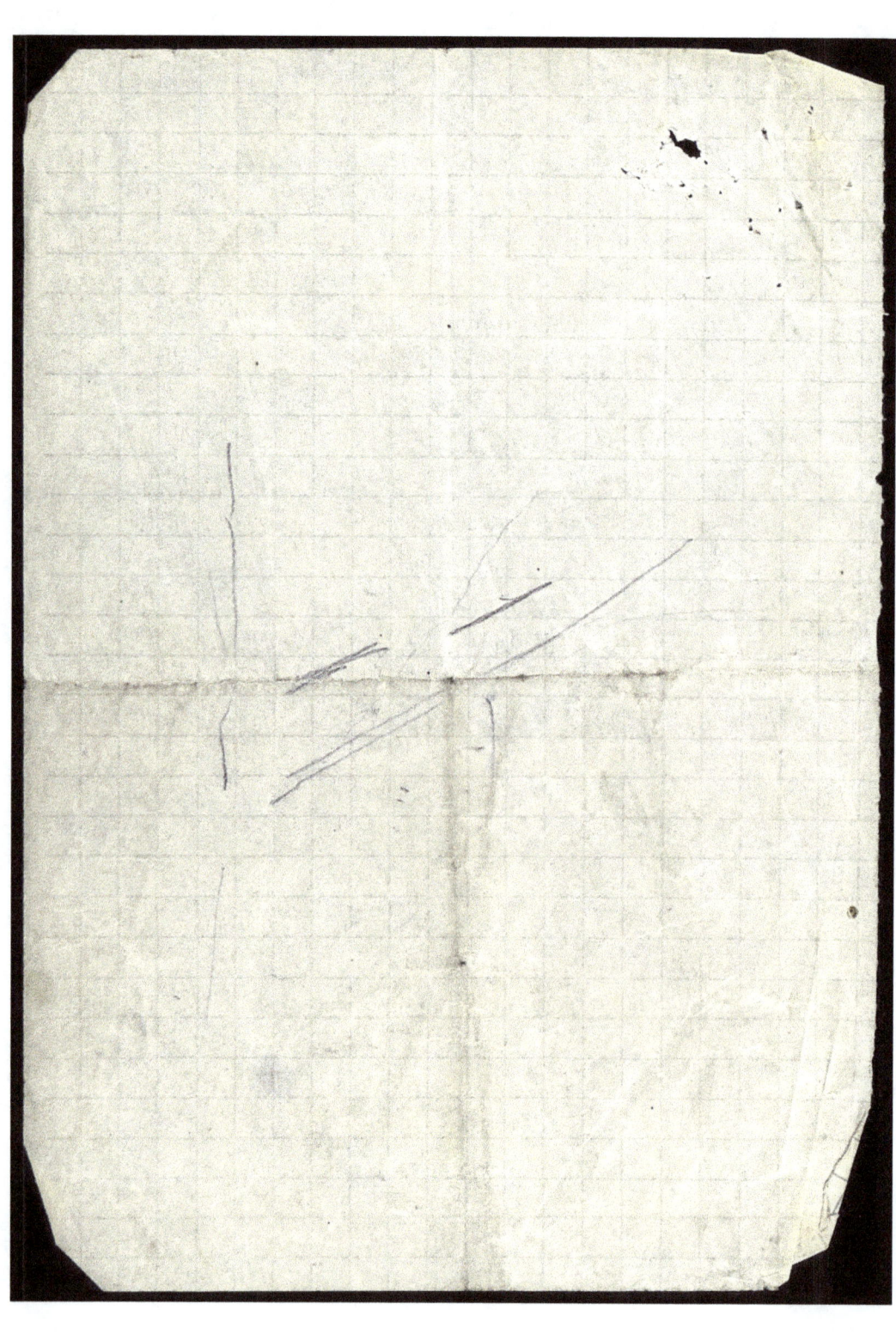

O R's CASUALTIES
22/24 7/7 (5)

KILLED
A Coy   3
B "   10
C "   9
D "   8   30

MISSING
A Coy   NIL
B "   4
C "   7
D "   1   12

WOUNDED
A Coy   20
B "   36
C "   23
D "   20   99

                TOTAL   141

Officer Casualties (5)
22/24. LVY

Lt.   A. R. J. Chislett.   KILLED 22 4/17
2nd Lt. J. Macqueen   KILLED 22 4/17
2nd Lt. M. C. Watson.   KILLED 22 4/17
2nd Lt. W. D. McCaul   WOUNDED 22 4/17
2nd Lt. D. Donley   WOUNDED 25 4/17
2nd Lt. W. Nelson.   SHELL SHOCK 23 4/17

TOTAL   6

Casualties Other Ranks
9/11 4 17

KILLED		TOTAL
A Coy	8	
B "	2	
C "	11	
D "	3	24

MISSING		
A Coy	1	
B "	1	
C "	4	
D "	1	7

MISSING (BELIEVED KILLED)		
A Coy	NIL	
B "	NIL	
C "	NIL	
D "	3	3

WOUNDED		
A Coy	52	
B "	36	
C "	59	
D "	52	199

GRAND TOTAL 233

OFFICERS
WOUNDED 11

PERSONNEL
WHO WENT FORWARD
WITH UNIT ON "Z" DAY.

(2).

OFFICERS   16.
OTHER RANKS   581.
                          597

AND SIGNALS. No. of Message

Code ... m. | Words | Charge | This message is on a/c of: | Recd. at ... m.
Office of Origin and Service Instructions. | | | | Date
Sent | | 943 | | From
At ... m. | | Service. |
To | | (Signature of "Franking Officer.") | By
By | |

TO **46. I. B**

Sender's Number: **Co 30** Day of Month: **2/21/17** In reply to Number: **A A A**

Attached Copy of Batt" Operation Orders
Now amended by No 2 of this date
in accordance with this Brig Gen'l
instructions.

Please return tonight as this is
the only Copy available for filing.

J. E. St John. Lt Col.
Cdg 12. H.L.I.

From
Place
Time

The above may be forwarded as now corrected. (Z)

Censor. Signature of Addresser or person authorised to telegraph in his name.
* This line should be erased if not required.

"A" Form.
MESSAGES AND SIGNALS.

Sender's Number.	Day of Month.	In reply to Number.	
*BM 480 (Ops)	23		AAA

Dividing line between 10 Lea R and 10/11 H1 - N14 a 69 - N7 d 61 ana 2 Vickers Guns will be attached to each of 10 Sea R 10/11 H1 12 H1 and Bde Hd will remain at 44 Bde (Hd) (N16 b 18) an advanced Report centre will be established about N12 c 81 an Dressing Stations an at Northern most House of MARLIERE and at LES FOSSES FM 10 Lea R 10/11 H1 + 12 H1 will lay out a line as they advance from Bde Hd

From	46 INF Bde
Place	
Time	5 PM

Rothern Payson

"A" Form.
MESSAGES AND SIGNALS.

*BM 490 (Cont)
Touch to be established with flanking Divisions aaa 50th Div S of River are attacking simultaneously aaa Bde will attack as follows aaa 10 Yorks R on R will clear GUEUDECOURT VILLAGE ~~with to their right — up to~~ ~~Stough Trench to junction with~~ ~~CAMP R~~ aaa 10/11/HLI will attack on left aaa 12/HLI will follow Yorks R in immediate support to their attack on Blue line and fill gaps as they occur aaa 7/8 KOSB will remain on Brown Line aaa

"A" Form.
MESSAGES AND SIGNALS.

	Prefix......Code......m.	Words / Charge	This message is on a/c of:	Recd. at............
	Office of Origin and Service Instructions.	Sent		Date............
		At......m.	............Service.	From............
		To		
		By	(Signature of "Franking Officer.")	By............

TO	FE	LS	LS	EU ✓
	DO	K2	RB	AR
	CA			

Sender's Number.	Day of Month.	In reply to Number.	
BM480	23		AAA

44 & 45 Bdes are to Capture S portion of SHOVEL Trench and GUEMAPPE Cemetery aaa Heavies to continue to fire on GUEMAPPE Village & isolate it aaa at 6 PM 18 pr barrage will open on line O13 c55 — O7 D46 and advance at 100 yards in 4 minutes aaa at 6 PM 46 Bde will pass through front line of 44 & 45 Bdes leaving GUEMAPPE on right aaa 46 Bde will Capture Blue line and Consolidate it

From
Place
Time

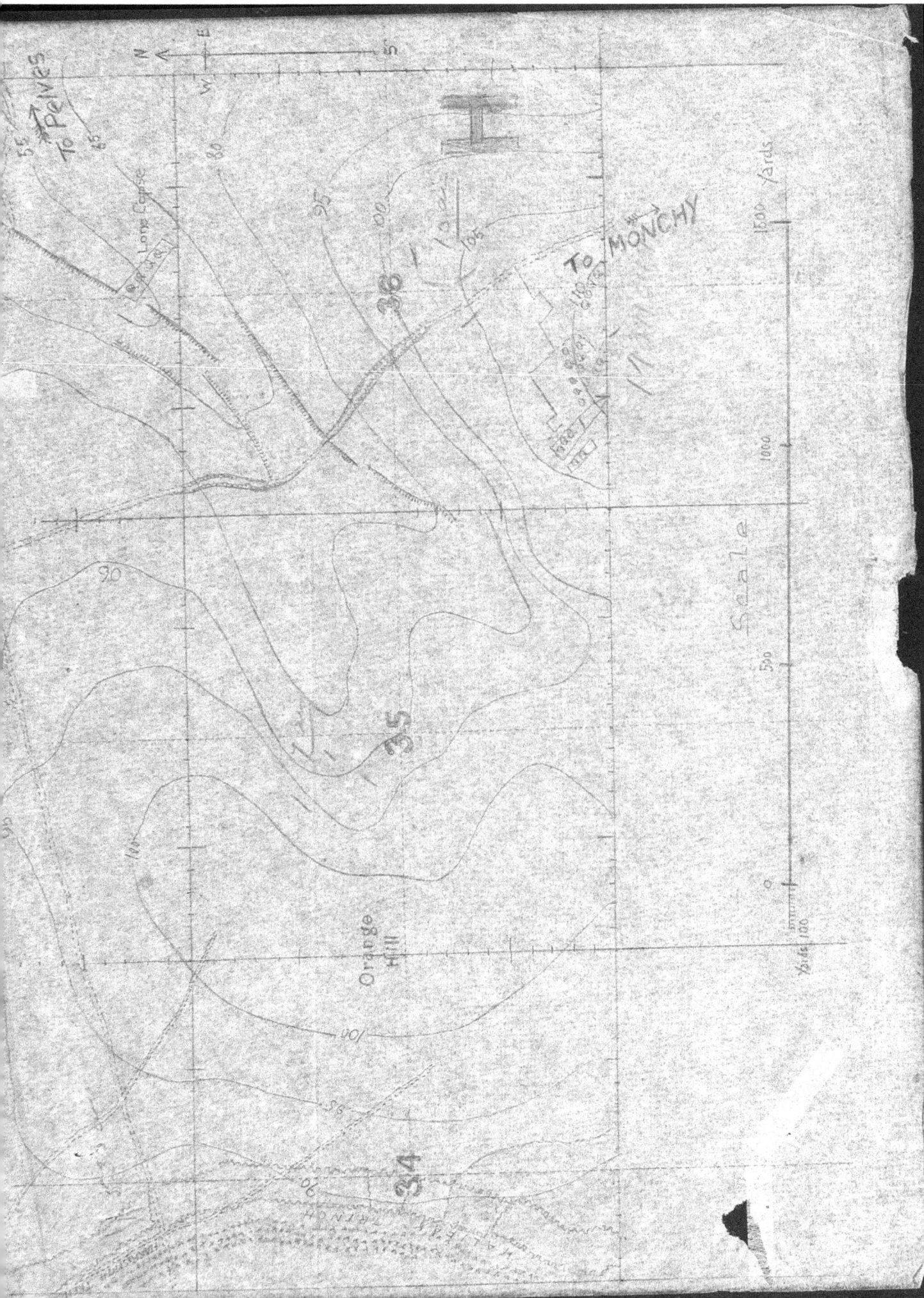

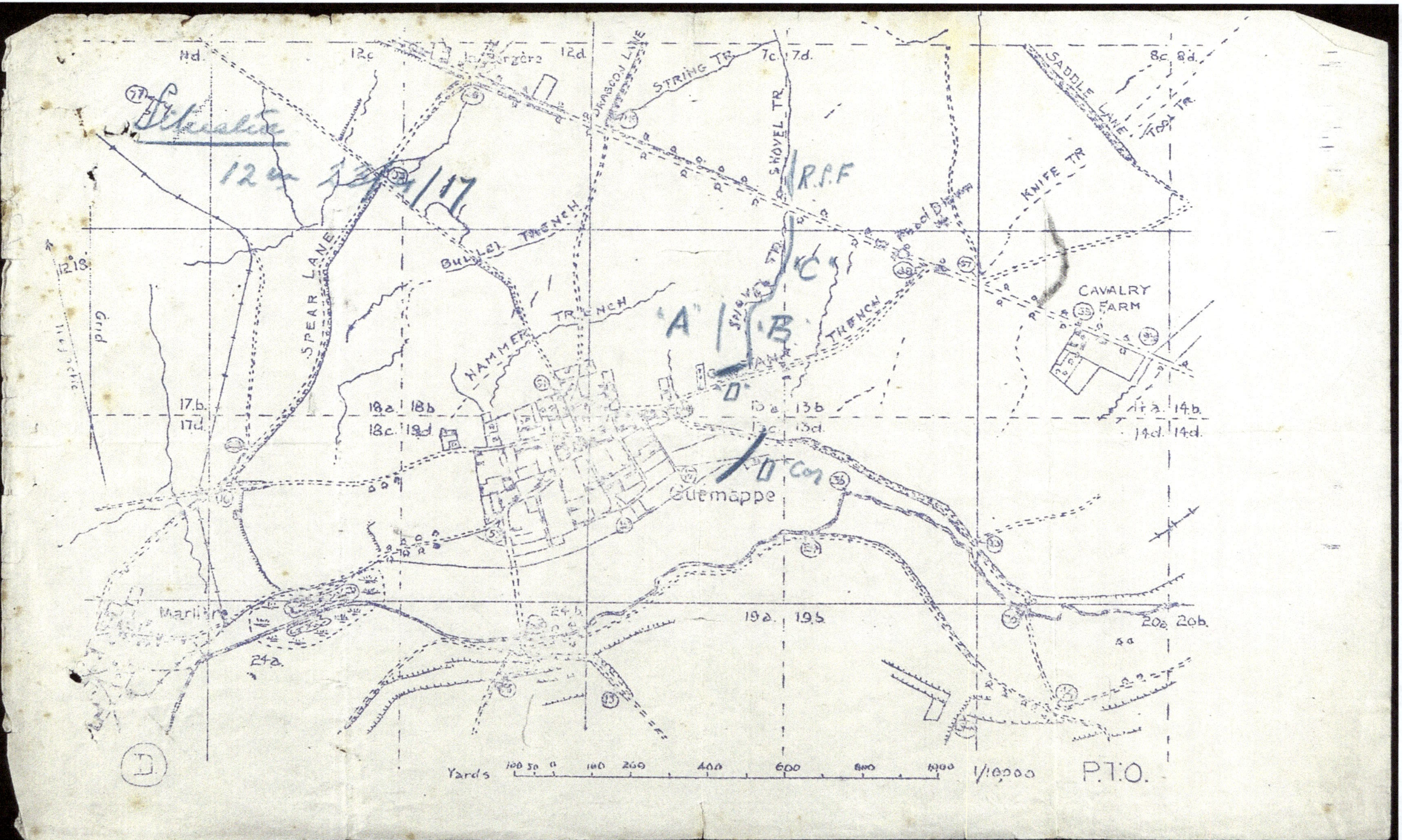

SADDLE LANE
KNIFE TR
CAVALRY FARM
STRING TR
SHOVEL TR
R.S.F
SPEAR LANE
BULLET TRENCH
HAMMER TRENCH
'A'
'B'
'C'
'D'
'D' Coy
Guemappe
Marlière
Grid
Yards
100 50 0 100 200 400 600 800 1000
1/10,000
P.T.O.

Report No

From   OC 'B' Coy
To   Adjt E A
Date   24/4/17
Time   8.0 p.m.
Am at
(mark on map)   — — — — —

In touch on
right with   } 'C' Coy at L. Jacons
                  road can be seen.

In touch on
left with   } Left flank falls back

Enemy withdrawing
to   — — — — —

Enemy massing at — — — —

Remarks Killed 2/Lt Watson
         2/Lt McQueen, 2/Lt Chisholm
         2/Lt Cuddeford believed wounded
         Casualties very heavy

                (Signature) F.F. Gardiner
Further details   OC 'B' Coy 2/Lt
late   E A

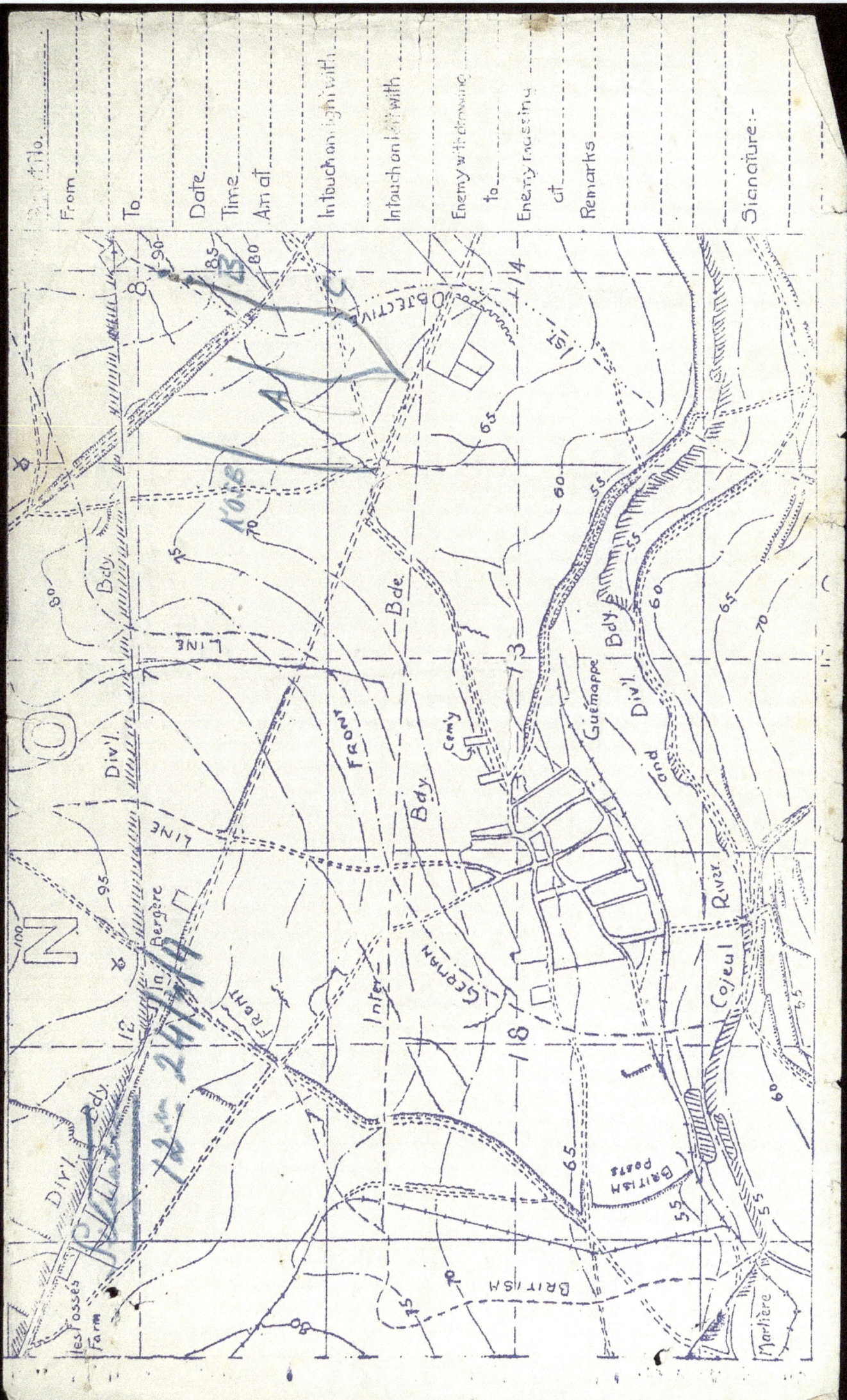

Confidential

Vol 18

18.M.
9 sheets

WAR DIARY
OF
12th High. L.I.

From 1st May to 31st May 1917.

Vol.

Army Form C. 2118.

WAR DIARY
or
INTELLIGENCE SUMMARY.
(Erase heading not required.)

1917

Place	Date	Hour	Summary of Events and Information	Remarks and references to Appendices
DUISANS	1917 May 1		Battalion in Hutments in No IV Camp (Division in Corps Reserve) Draft 71 O.R. arrived from Base. Draft good, a large proportion being men from Reg. War Battalions with long service, and men with previous service in the Battn. who had been evacuated wounded.	
	2		Three officers joined the Battn. from the Base 2/Lts. Stewart, Fennie & J. Young. Battn. at Duisans as above.	
	3		Warning order received. Battn. to be prepared to move at one hours notice. Battn. at Duisans as above.	
	4		Order received for Brigade to stand down. Battn. in Hutments at Duisans	
	5		do do	
	6		Draft of 22 O.R. arrived from Base. Battn. in Hutments at Duisans Brigade Church Parade at which Divl. General, General	G.O.C

WAR DIARY
or
INTELLIGENCE SUMMARY.

Army Form C. 2118.

128

Place	Date	Hour	Summary of Events and Information	Remarks and references to Appendices
Quivanes	6		A Major General McCrocken, attended. After service Brigade marked past the Divisional General.	
Quivanes	7	9.15 AM	Battalion marched to FOSSEUX - rest area 18th Corps, arriving 12.40 pm. Battalion disposed in hutments and billets.	
FOSSEUX	8		Batt. in hutments & billets.	
FOSSEUX	9		do do and training in France	
	10		Rullecourt Area. Draft of 54 O.R. arrived. Batt. in hutments & billets. The following officers reported for duty. - Capt. S.A. Rex. 2/Lts. A.W. HARDIE, W. DUNSMOR, R.E. SANDERS, J. TROTTER, T. RADIE, C. MILLAR, L.S. GRAHAM, F.B. FOSTER.	
	11		Batt. in hutments & billets.	
	12		Rullecourt Area. do Continue training in France	

2/Lt. W. Maclean reports for duty on the 12th.

J.O. Ith

Army Form C. 2118.

129

WAR DIARY
or
INTELLIGENCE SUMMARY.
(Erase heading not required.)

Place	Date 1917	Hour	Summary of Events and Information	Remarks and references to Appendices
FOSSEUX	May 13		Draft of 12 O.R. received from FREVENT. 2/Lt. N. MACLEAN rejoins Battn. Battn. in hutments & billets.	
	14		do. Battn. training in Grenade Ruttecourt Area.	
	15		do. Battn. in hutments & billets	
	16		do. Fuze firing at BARLY.	
	17		do. Training in Grenade Ruttecourt area.	
	18		Battn. in hutments & billets.	
	19		Battn. in hutments & billets. Draft of 18 O.R. received	
	20		do. 2/Lt. T. DADIE leaves Battn. to report at INDIA Office, LONDON. 2/Lt. STEVENSON returns for duty with the Battn. from #6th Trench Mortar Battery.	
	21		Battn. moves by march route to GRANDE RULLECOURT, arriving about 12 noon.	

> H.E. BETHUNE goes to hospital.

Army Form C. 2118.

WAR DIARY
or
INTELLIGENCE SUMMARY.
(Erase heading not required.)

130.

Instructions regarding War Diaries and Intelligence Summaries are contained in F. S. Regs., Part II. and the Staff Manual respectively. Title pages will be prepared in manuscript.

Place	Date 1917	Hour	Summary of Events and Information	Remarks and references to Appendices
GD. ROULLECOURT	MAY 22		Battn. in billets at GRAND ROULLECOURT. Battn. moves by march route to BOUQUEMAISON arriving about midday.	
BOUQUEMAISON	23		Battn. in billets at BOUQUEMAISON. Battn. moves by march route to BUIRE AU BOIS, arriving about 11 A.M.	
BUIRE AU BOIS	24		Battn. in billets at BUIRE AU BOIS. Draft of 15 O.R. arrives from FREVENT.	
do	25		Battn. in billets at BUIRE AU BOIS. do do Lieut. R.P. EASTON 10/11th H.L.I. arrives and assumes 2nd in Command of the 13th.	
do	26		Battn. in billets at BUIRE AU BOIS. B Coy. goes on Detachment to BACHIMONT to work under Canadian Forestry Coy.	
do	27		Draft of 14 O.R. received.	
do	28		Battn. in billets in BUIRE AU BOIS. The following Officers join the Battn. for duty:- 2/Lt. J.A. PENMAN, A.J. FERGUSON, W.A. MEIKLE, C. NEIL.	J.W.H.

A 5534 Wt. W4973 M687 750,000 8/16 D. D. & L. Ltd. Forms/C.2118/13.

WAR DIARY
or
INTELLIGENCE SUMMARY.

(Erase heading not required.)

Place	Date	Hour	Summary of Events and Information	Remarks and references to Appendices
BUIRE AU BOIS	1917 MAY 28		Draft of 8 O.R. received from FREVENT. The Battn. holds a Sports Day of which the following are the outstanding events on the Programme.	
			(1) Inter Company Football Match. — Winning Coy — "C" Coy	
			(2) 100 YDS Flat Race — Winner — Pte. Fieldie	
			(3) 1 Mile Flat Race — do — Bomb^r. Gray	
			(4) Boxing Competition — Heavy — Pte. McIlvennan	
			Middle — do — Duff	
			Light — do — Donnelly	
	29		Battⁿ. in Billets at BUIRE AU BOIS.	
	30		do	
	31		2/Lt. J. G. HAMILTON joins the Battalion for duty. Battalion in Billets at BUIRE AU BOIS. The following Officer & N.C.Os are awarded decorations as under. 2/Lt. D.A.M. MAIN Military Cross No.11312 Co. S.M. H. WARRINGTON, Y No.17661, Sergt. A. RAMAGE, Distin^g. Conduct Medal	[signature]

Confidential.

19.M.
7 sheets

N⁰ 19

WAR DAIRY

OF

12ᵀᴴ HIGHLAND LIGHT INFANTRY.

FROM :- 1ˢᵗ June 1917

TO :- 30ᵀᴴ June 1917.

VOL :-

Army Form C. 2118.

WAR DIARY
or
INTELLIGENCE SUMMARY.
(Erase heading not required.)

132

Place	Date 1917	Hour	Summary of Events and Information	Remarks and references to Appendices
BUIRE AU BOIS	June 1		Battalion in billets at BUIRE AU BOIS. Engaged in Field Firing. 2/Lt J.G. HAMILTON is transferred to 10/11 H.L.I.	
do	2		Draft of 12 O.R. received from FREVENT. Battalion in billets at BUIRE AU BOIS. 2nd Lt. W.S. GREGOR joins the Battn. is posted to "B" Coy. Capt R.P. EASTON relinquishes the duties of 2 i/c in command & rejoins the 10/11th H.L.I. Major H.C.N. DeBERRY is transferred to England, sick.	No. 45
do	3		Battalion in Billets at BUIRE AU BOIS.	
do	4		do	
do	5		do	
do	6		do 2/Lt. W.M. DIXON joins the Battn. is posted to "D" Coy.	No. 45
	7		Battn in Billets at BUIRE AU BOIS	

Army Form C. 2118.

WAR DIARY
or
INTELLIGENCE SUMMARY.

(Erase heading not required.)

133

Place	Date	Hour	Summary of Events and Information	Remarks and references to Appendices
BUIRE AU BOIS	1917 June 8		Battn. in billets.	
	9		do	
	10		do	
	11		2/Lt. G. TAYLOR rejoins the Battalion from hospital. 2/Lts. J.C. GRANGER "B" Coy. & 2/Lt. A.P. STEVENSON "C" Coy. are transferred to "A" Coy. Draft of 24 O.R. received.	
	12		Battn. in billets.	
	13		do	
	14		Draft of 2 O.R. received. C.S.M. H. LAWRIE joins the Battn. & takes over duties of R.S.M. Battn. in billets	16/2/15
	15		Draft of 14 O.R. received. Battn. in billets. One O.R. received.	
	16		Battn. in billets.	

Army Form C. 2118.

WAR DIARY
or
INTELLIGENCE SUMMARY.
(Erase heading not required.)

134

Place	Date	Hour	Summary of Events and Information	Remarks and references to Appendices
BUIRE AU BOIS	1917 June 17		Battn. in billets. Draft of 6 O.R. received.	
ERIE CAMP	18		Battn. marches to FREVENT & entrains for new area arriving at 9 p.m. at DOPOURE Station. Battn. arrives in ERIE CAMP after a march of 4 miles & are accommodated in huts. Battalion in Brigade Reserve.	
	19		Battn. in huts in ERIE CAMP. The following Officers, N.C.O's & men were mentioned in Sir Douglas Haig's Despatch 3rd April 1917. Temp/M. Captain W. McMARDIE. Temp/M. 2nd Lt. (Ach Lt) R.R. MARSHALL. Lieut. & Qur. Mr. Lt. J. CARPENTER. No 17933, Sergt. G.M. HENRY. 17796, " C. McGARRY. 23149, Pte. T. PORTER. 2/Lt. N. MACLEAN & 100 O.R. are attached to 254th Tunnelling Boy. R.E.	No. 2/1
TORONTO CAMP	20		Battn. moves to TORONTO CAMP. Battalion in Brigade Reserve.	
	21		Battn. in huts in TORONTO CAMP.	
	22		2/Lt. A.L. BRYSON is detached for duty on Divisional Water Supply. Battn. in huts in TORONTO CAMP. 2/Lt. FERME & O.R. detached for duty with 254th Tunnelling Boy. R.E.	

135

WAR DIARY
or
INTELLIGENCE SUMMARY.
(Erase heading not required.)

Army Form C. 2118.

Place	Date	Hour	Summary of Events and Information	Remarks and references to Appendices
TORONTO CAMP	1917 June 23		Battn. in huts in TORONTO CAMP.	
	24		do	
In the LINE	25		Battn. moves by train & march route to the YPRES SECTOR the LEFT SUB-SECTOR. Battalion Front line holding from POINT C.29.c.6.2, S. of WARWICK FARM to POINT I.5.b.2.b, and relieving the 10/11 th H.L.I. who move into support. The following dispositions are made:-	
			B. Coy. in left front line, from C.29.c.6.2, to junction to CURSON ST & front line, two platoons in front line, & two in immediate support.	
			C. Coy. in right front line from CURSON ST. to Point I.5.b.2.0., two platoons in front line & two platoons in immediate support.	
			"A" Coy. in ST. JAMES TRENCH. In support.	
			"D" Coy. in reserve, one platoon in MILLSCOTT, one platoon in POTIJZE REDOUBT & two in dugouts in POTIJZE ROAD.	16.7/15
			DETAILS under Capt. D.G. WATSON, M.C. left in huttments at TORONTO CAMP.	
	26		Battn. in the line as above Major W.H. ANDERSON reports for duty with the Battalion, to Details at TORONTO CAMP.	

Army Form C. 2118.

WAR DIARY
or
INTELLIGENCE SUMMARY.
(Erase heading not required.)

136.

Place	Date	Hour	Summary of Events and Information	Remarks and references to Appendices
IN THE LINE	1917 JUNE 27		Batt'n in the line as above.	
	28		Draft of 36 O.R. received at TORONTO CAMP by Details. Capt. J. R. COWAN-DOUGLAS reports for duty to Details. TORONTO CAMP. Batt'n in the line, dispositions of Coys. being changed as follows:— "D" Coy. in reserve relieves "B" Coy. in front line (left) A Coy. in support " " " C " (right) C Coy. is held in support B Coy. is held in reserve	
	29		Battalion in the line as above. 2/Lt. MacLEAN is attached with 220 O.R. to 73rd Field Co. R.E. 2/Lts. FERME & FERGUSON return from tunnelling Co. rejoin Details.	
	30		Battalion in the line as above.	[signature] Lt. Col. O/C 12th R.S.

46/13- Vol 20

20.M.
16 sheets

WAR – DIARY

12th. (S) Bn. Highland Lt. Infantry.

for the month

July 1917.

Army Form C. 2118.

WAR DIARY
or
INTELLIGENCE SUMMARY.
(Erase heading not required.)

137

Place	Date	Hour	Summary of Events and Information	Remarks and references to Appendices
IN THE LINE	1917 July 1		Tour of duty in the line terminates and the Battalion is relieved in the left Sub-sector of the Brigade front by the 9th Black Watch. Relief completed by 2 A.M. The Battalion moves by platoons to ERIE CAMP. Total Casualties for the Tour from 20th June to 1st July inclusive Killed 3. Wounded 27. Missing nil. One officer, Capt. R.R. BROWN, slightly wounded on the 1st. Draft of 6 O.R. received by O.C. Details at TORONTO CAMP.	
ERIE CAMP	2		Battn. in Hutments	
	3		Battn. moves by march route to WATOU AREA where the men are accommodated in billets	
WATOU	4		Battn. in billets as above	
	5		Draft of 5 O.R. received Battn. in billets as above. 2/Lt H.E. BETHUNE is struck off the strength having been transferred to	

Army Form C. 2118.

WAR DIARY
or
INTELLIGENCE SUMMARY.
(Erase heading not required.)

Instructions regarding War Diaries and Intelligence Summaries are contained in F.S. Regs., Part II. and the Staff Manual respectively. Title pages will be prepared in manuscript.

Place	Date	Hour	Summary of Events and Information	Remarks and references to Appendices
WATOU AREA	1917 July 5		England rich. 2/Lt F.S. SUTHERLAND joins the Battalion	
	6		Battalion in billets as above.	
	7		do MAJOR W.H. ANDERSON assumes duties of 2nd in command	
BROXELLE AREA.	8		do. Capt. D.G. WATSON resumes duties of Adjutant. Draft of 40 O.R. received. Battalion moves by march route to BROXELLE AREA, arriving at 11 A.M., and are accommodated in billets.	
	9		Battn. in billets as above. Training on RUBROUCK AREA.	
	10		do Training on BROXELLE AREA.	
	11		H O R (Signallers) received. RUBROUCK AREA	
	12		Battn. in billets as above. Training on RUBROUCK AREA	
	13		do	
	14		do	
	15		do	

Army Form C. 2118.

WAR DIARY
or
INTELLIGENCE SUMMARY.
(Erase heading not required.)

139

Place	Date	Hour	Summary of Events and Information	Remarks and references to Appendices
BRUXELLE AREA	1917 July 16		Battn. in billets as above. MAJOR R.S. DIXON rejoins the Battn. for duty.	
	17		Battn. moves to WINNIZEELE area, less "C" & "D" Companies which remain in training area to practice raid over tape trenches.	
ERIE CAMP	18		Battn. less "C"& "D" Coys. moves to ERIE CAMP arriving about 9.45 P.M.	
	19		Battn. "C" & "D" Coys. rejoin Battn. in ERIE CAMP.	
	20		Battn. in hutments in ERIE CAMP.	
H.16.Y.17			Battn. in hutments in ERIE CAMP. Moves into Brigade Reserve at H.16 (BELGIUM 28)	
RESERVE CAMP. H.16	21		Battn. in Brigade reserve in billets & hutments.	
	22		Battn. moves into the line, taking over from 10 Scottish Rifles & occupying left sub-sector of Divisional frontage. H.Q. at ECOLE.	
	23		Battn. in the line as above	
	24		do The two reserve Companies moves up to front line in preparation for raid.	

WAR DIARY
or
INTELLIGENCE SUMMARY
(Erase heading not required.)

Army Form C. 2118.

140

Place	Date	Hour	Summary of Events and Information	Remarks and references to Appendices
IN THE LINE	1917 24 July		INSTRUCTIONS FOR RAID — Reference map Sheet 28 BELGIUM N.W 1/10,000	Extract map showing Route when Raised 2 places page 150
			1. A daylight raid will be carried out on July 24th by two companies of the 12. H.L.I	
			2. The objects of the raid are (1) To secure identifications (2) ascertain effect of Bombardment on hostile trenches and wire with special reference to wire in front of the RESERVE LINE — Number positions and condition of dug outs (3) To harass the enemy	
			3. The 8th and 55th Divisions are either to carry out raids at the same time or will simulate them	See page 144 Reference K
			4. OBJECTIVES. The trenches to be raided are shown on attached map — The enemy front trench will be entered between I 5 b 7.3. and I 5 b 45.80. The raiders will penetrate as far as IBERIA RESERVE on front I 6 a 2.6 — I 6 a 05.95 — There will be no advance beyond the line of the TRENCH TRAMWAY 50 yards East of IBERIA RESERVE	See also page 22 page 143
			5. Strength of Raiding Force Capt MYLES in command — "C" Company under command 2nd Lt BANNATYNE 9. 3 Officers. "D" Company under command Capt HANNAH & 4 officers	
			6. Artillery Co-operation — Detailed programme of artillery co-operation will be issued later. The creeping barrage will lift back from Enemy front trench at ZERO + 4 minutes and will move at the rate of 100 yards in 2 minutes	See page 145 Ref. L

Army Form C. 2118.

WAR DIARY
or
INTELLIGENCE SUMMARY.   141

(Erase heading not required.)

Place	Date	Hour	Summary of Events and Information	Remarks and references to Appendices
IN THE LINE	21 July		Instructions for Raid *(Continued)* (b) Artillery Co-operation *(Continued)* in two minutes – a Box barrage is being placed round the area to be raided and a standing 18-pounder 4.5" How. barrage on the enemy front system on the Divisional front – a smoke barrage is being placed between the enemy front system and the FREZENBERG LINE on which fire is also directed – smoke is also being placed on the high ground S. of the ROULERS. RAILWAY. 7. **MACHINE GUN Co-operation.** The 44th and 46th M.G. Companies will co-operate under O.C. 44th M.G. Company as follows – (a.) 2 guns will enfilade CAMERON AVENUE and CAMERON DRIVE from ZERO – ZERO + 50 minutes (b.) 2 guns will enfilade ICE LANE from ZERO – ZERO + 50 minutes (c.) 4 guns will place a barrage on IBERIA RESERVE on the front to be attacked from ZERO – ZERO + 2 minutes subsequently searching back to the line WILDE WOOD – BILL COTTAGE where barrage will remain until 50th min. ZERO plus 50 minutes. 8. **STOKES MORTARS.** The 44th and 46th Trench Mortar Batteries will co-operate, under O.C. 46 Trench Mortar Battery as follows – (a). 1 Mortar to fire a burst of rapid fire on enemy Machine Guns under railway about I.6.a.1.0., and is to deal with this gun should it open fire at any moment during the raid. (b). 2 Mortars to fire obliquely from positions North and South of PICCADILLY on ground between STABLES and enemy front trench. One burst of 10 rounds rapid fire at Zero will be fired by each Mortar. A second burst being fired 30 seconds later. Subsequently these guns will search the ground between front and deal with any hostile M.G. within range which opens fire. (c). 2 Mortars each to fire 10 rounds rapid at Zero on the MOUND and vicinity. A second burst being fired 30 seconds later. (d). 2 Mortars to fire on Machine Gun in enemy front line about the POTIJZE ROAD at Zero and subsequently if a Machine Gun should fire from this trench. (e). The Brigade on our left will be asked to deal similarly with KAISER BILL. 9. **DURATION OF RAID.** The time allotted is 50 minutes. 10. The Brigade Signalling Officer will arrange for direct telephonic communication between Battalion Headquarters of MILLS CUTTS and Brigade Headquarters during the raid. 11. Watches will be synchronised at Brigade Headquarters, (I.8.d.1.6.) at 8 a.m. on 24 July. One Officer from each unit concerned will attend. 12. Zero hour will be notified later. 13. **ASSEMBLY.** The raiding force will be assembled before Zero in the front line trench. Every effort is to be made to conceal the presence of an abnormal number of troops from enemy observation.	O. P. see ins note see ins note OVER.

Army Form C. 2118.

WAR DIARY
or
INTELLIGENCE SUMMARY.   142.
(Erase heading not required.)

Place	Date	Hour	Summary of Events and Information	Remarks and references to Appendices
IN THE LINE	30th July		{13. ASSEMBLY (CONTINUED)} As many men as possible must be kept under cover until as late as possible. Men to be detailed to him places in attack ladders and gaps, and gradually drible to their places.	
			14. METHOD OF EXECUTION. Both Companies will be assembled in our front line trench, or front shown on attached map. The whole organised under Company Officers, so that at Zero the men standing at ladders will commence to move over our parapet, pass through the gaps in the wire shown on attached map, and form into and move forward in four waves. There will be no halt during forming waves. The first men to go over our parapet will do so upon the signal of the O.C. The Raiding Party. The first wave will be followed immediately by the second, third and fourth. The first wave will keep as close as possible to the barrage as possible. The first and second waves will push through to the trench (S4/2) dugline (enemy reserve trenches). The third to the second (Support Trenches & EITTEL FRITZ FARM). The fourth wave to the first (enemy front line). Officers will as far as possible move in line with their men. The O.C. Raid will make his Headquarters in GERMAN SUPPORT LINE. O.C. "C" Company will proceed to final objective. O.C. "D" Company will use his discretion as to whether he places himself in enemy front or support line. Waves will form blocks in trenches as shown on map. Six positions of Lewis Guns as shown on map. Compass bearings will be taken.	
			15. Parties for searching dug outs and obtaining identifications. Parties will be detailed by each Company for the purpose of searching dug outs and securing identifications. These parties will be provided with P. Bombs and Smoke Bombs. Dug outs are not to be destroyed. Search parties are not to stand in front of the entrances to dug outs on to enter them until cleared.	
			16. During the Raid the front line will be held by 3 Lewis guns of "B" Company. Signallers and stretcher bearers of Raiding Company. Officer i/c Further during Raid 2nd Lt JARDIE will be in command of the front line Parties during the Raid.	
			17. Each Officer will detail a N.C.O. to take his place should he become a casualty, who must know all details of the task of his party.	
			18. CASUALTIES each Officer and Sergeant will have a roll of their parties which will be checked in every opportunity and later with arrival. After the front line and support line have been taken O.C. D Company will send parties forward STRETCHER PARTIES TO CLEAR NO MANS LAND TOWARDS RESERVE TRENCHES, and will use to evacuate any casualties in his own Company as well. Walking wounded will, if unfit to continue fighting, return to our front line. During with withdrawal the Officer i/c each party will bring back all wounded, and collect any troops in rout.	
	19			

WAR DIARY
or
INTELLIGENCE SUMMARY.

Army Form C. 2118.

143

Place	Date	Hour	Summary of Events and Information	Remarks and references to Appendices
IN THE LINE	24 July		INSTRUCTIONS. FOR. RAID. (contd)	

19. To direct the Raiding Party returning made will be placed in front of our gaps in wire by Trench party under 2nd Lt HARDIE.

20. PRISONERS. All prisoners will be disarmed at once, searched for arms and sent back to our front line trench under escort — upon arrival they will be reached for papers etc, attention being paid to the pocket at the back of their tunic and trousers — a check will be kept of the number of prisoners brought in — They will be sent to ECOLE as early as possible — When A.P.M. 15 Division will accept and give receipt — An injunction in searching and forwarding prisoners will be under 2nd Lt HARDIE.

see p. 144 Ref M

21. MEDICAL. Separate instructions will be issued —

22. OBJECTIVES. (CONTD) The front line wave will not push further forward than the TRAM. LINE - EAST of Enemy Reserve trenches except to form the block in the C.T. running from it N.E. Company commanders will divide up the frontage of objectives so that platoons have objectives of equal frontage.

see p. 140 para 4

23. WITHDRAWAL. All parties will work in unison with arrival in accordance with time table — Officers or N.C.O.s i/c of Platoons are responsible for seeing that all groups employed as blocks or on other duties are recalled before their Platoons leave, and that their commands are clear of the positions occupied by the specified time — Withdrawal will be commenced on the signal of the O/C "C" Company — a blast from a SHUNTERS HORN upon which the most advanced men as the front system will commence to withdraw — All Lewis Guns which may have had their teams put out of action will be brought back —

see p. 145 Ref N

24. REPORTS. All Officers of the Raiding Companies will be required to furnish reports on conclusion of the raid. It is therefore important that they should make mental note regarding all key stones, regarding condition of enemy trenches etc; particularly Reserve Line Wire. After the return of the Companies to the front line the O.C. Raid and Battalion commanders will give Major Dixon verbal particulars of the raid. Detailed reports will be rendered as early as possible.

25. AFTER RAID. The Raiding Companies will resume holding the front line until Relief. The Lewis Guns of "B" Company will remain in front line.

26. DRESS AND EQUIPMENT. Skeleton Equipment. 50 rounds ammunition. Rifle and Bayonet.
Gas Appliances at alert. Wire Cutters.
All officers dressed and equipped as other ranks. No identification of any kind on Officers or men. Officers will wear but his is complied with, that no thing do not carry letters etc, and no one is in possession of any map or instruction.

27. ALL REGIMENTAL STRETCHER-BEARERS and Stretchers will be employed with the Raiding Party. Stretcher bearers of "C" Company "A" Company will be attached to "C" — 16. "B" Company will be attached to "D" — 16; "D" Company bearers will be seen as "B" Company will not commence to clear any wounded until within 30 yards of enemy wire. front & support trenches have been taken, and then Bearers forward towards Reserve trenches and evacuate any wounded from there. Prisoners will be used as Stretcher-Bearers.

Army Form C. 2118.

WAR DIARY
or
INTELLIGENCE SUMMARY.

(Erase heading not required.)

Instructions regarding War Diaries and Intelligence Summaries are contained in F.S. Regs., Part II. and the Staff Manual respectively. Title pages will be prepared in manuscript.

Place	Date	Hour	Summary of Events and Information	Remarks and references to Appendices
IN THE LINE	24 July		28. MISCELLANEOUS INSTRUCTIONS. In cleaning our front trench after raid to its normal garrison, it may be safer to proceed our often, not down C.T. It is possible that enemy may put his barrage down upon his own front line, as that it may be advisable to hold Reiva as lightly as possible. The enemy may too invade his wire at the Reiva Line. Where practicable that objective should be prepared to withstand such action, possibly using the communication trench. Owing to our heavy barrage there may be considerable smoke and that rendering it impossible that objects quite close and, during the early stage of the raid taken to landmarks is lead on. N.C.O's and men will be cautioned that in the event of captives no information must be given to the enemy, should they become casualties, beyond giving their Regimental No. Name and Regiment.	Esp. 3/E.
			ADDENDUM N°1. TO INSTRUCTIONS FOR RAID.	
			1 <u>1/6 Infantry Brigade</u> wire No. 199.	K. see p 140.
			(1) <u>Patrol</u> In conjunction with the raid to be carried out by the 12.H.L.I (Left Battalion) on 24 July 1917 - 7.th Camerons (Right Bn) will detail a patrol of strength not exceeding 15 other Ranks under an Officer, to move out from our front line Trench at ZERO plus 3 minutes 15 Cafr and an enemy machine gun believed to be posted in a tunnel under the Railway about I 12.a.10.95 and to ascertain how enemy front Trench is held.	
			(2) During the Raid the Right Battalion 7 Camerons will keep a sharp look out to their front for any hostile targets which may expose themselves to rifle or Lewis gun fire.	
			(3) The Raid to be carried out by the 168th Infantry Brigade on our left will be made by one Company 5th Kings Liverpool Regiment.	
			2 <u>Referring</u> by Major Bieron - Major Bieron will report to Battalion Headquarters by telephone as follows:- When all Companies have left our Trenches - The Code word "GOOD" in - The Code word "BETTER" Prisoners by numbers when prisoners are brought in - The Code word "BEST" when raiders have returned to our Trenches.	O. see p 141.
			3 Officers will know that men do not risk the success of the raid by searching for trophies. They must confine themselves to their allotted tasks.	
			4 One officer from "C" and "B" Companies will report at Bat.n Headquarters MILL COTTS. at 9 A.M.	
			5 Para. 23 WITHDRAWAL add "When the trash missed to C. Company has been completed, the tram line has been reached and all dugouts have been searched at the Final Objective the O.C. raiding party may order the withdrawal to commence. - 23/7/17. sgd. D.g. WATSON. Capt.: adj. 12 H.L.I.	
			ADDENDUM N°2. TO INSTRUCTIONS FOR RAID.	M see p 143
			MEDICAL. All Stretcher Cases - walking wounded - wounded Prisoners will proceed to R.A.M.C. Collecting post POTIJZE ROAD (which will be used as the Battalion First aid Post.) via HAYMARKET S.t JAMES 24/7/17. sgd. D.g. WATSON. Capt.: T.O. & adj. 12 H L I.	

Army Form C. 2118.

WAR DIARY
or
INTELLIGENCE SUMMARY.
(Erase heading not required.)

145

Place	Date	Hour	Summary of Events and Information	Remarks and references to Appendices
IN THE LINE	2nd July.		Reference para 14.— ZERO hour will be 1 p.m. July 24th.	P. Note p. 141
			ADDENDUM No 3 to 46 Infantry Brigade Min. No 199. – 23/7/1917	
			Reference para 14.— ZERO hour will be 1 p.m. July 24th. Appx R.V.S. Htn Majn. Bishmayn 46 I/B. Issued at 8 p.m. cypher.	Reference to 140
			RAID. TIME. TABLE	N. Ref. p. 143
			ZERO to plus 4 minutes Creeping barrage on enemy from line 1st Objective.	
			ZERO +4 minutes to plus 6 minutes Creeping barrage on enemy on a line 100 yards within Reserve line. 2nd Objective.	
			ZERO +6 to plus 8 minutes Creeping barrage on a line 100 yards within Reserve line. FINAL OBJECTIVE.	
			ZERO +8 to plus 10 minutes Creeping barrage on Reserve Line. FINAL OBJECTIVE.	
			ZERO +10 to plus 35 minutes — Barrage remains on a line 150 yards beyond RESERVE LINE	
			ZERO +35 Creeps back to RESERVE LINE	
			ZERO +33 WITHDRAWAL. All troops must be clear of final objective RESERVE LINE by—	
			ZERO +43 All clear of Support line	
			ZERO +47 All clear of Front Line	
			23/7/17.	
			Sgd D.G. WATSON Capt + Adj 12. H.L.I.	
			REPORT ON RAID by Lt. Col. W.E. St JOHN. Commd 12 H.L.I.	
2nd July	1. p.m.		1. Strength of Raiding party 10 Officers and 186 other Ranks. Under command of Capt. T. MYLES.	2n/a/apx 140-143.
			2. Party left our trenches at ZERO hour (1 p.m.) in accordance with arrangements issued by me.	
			3. 1·15 p.m. FIRST LINE Trenches taken – no opposition. Enemy was prevented no probable. The Trenches were badly damaged and unfit for use. — Two held each containing 6 men. These and four casualties only one one' and other exiled upon to kill the assaulted to get away, was short at unnoticed and recaptured. On the right when blocks were placed on bostant M.G. fire. Bombed a number of prisoners taken in this line. On the left opposition was stronger than bombers. This was one time.	
			4. proceed to taking the FRONT LINE the MOUND and STABLES were dealt with without opposition — no wire was found in front of the mound but the whole of the top was covered with wire — a Trench with walls surrounding it led to a concrete shelter in near in which 12 Bosches were taken — an O.P. (cement) was found outside shutting 4 on 5 men.	
			5 Support line no opposition was met with at the Support line and no Bosches were taken. EITEL. FRITZ. FM. The trenches continued no dug outs. The Support line was not inspected but locally approached. —	
			Two large craters dug into one heavily annealed.	

MyR

Army Form C. 2118.

WAR DIARY
or
INTELLIGENCE SUMMARY.
(Erase heading not required.)

Instructions regarding War Diaries and Intelligence Summaries are contained in F. S. Regs., Part II. and the Staff Manual respectively. Title pages will be prepared in manuscript.

146

Place	Date	Hour	Summary of Events and Information	Remarks and references to Appendices
	14 July		(Report Continued)	

6. RESERVE LINE (final objective) was reached at 1:10 p.m. Line was badly smashed and presenting no obstacle. The IBERIA AV. and IBERIA WALK. Leading to the Roeux Trenches was newly smashed out was about knee high in the Roeux Trenches than his own trenches capable of holding about 20 men each – approximately 50 prisoners were taken from these shelters. They came out freely when called upon & also – The TRAM LINE beyond the Roeux Trenches was hardly remarked – There were no works of any kind – within the Tram Line and Roeux Trenches – There was no M.G. emplacements uncovered – When the final objective was taken a few men were seen retiring about 300 yards ahead and were fired on.

7. WITHDRAWAL. The withdrawal commenced at 1:25 p.m. and the raiding party had reached our line about 1:38 p.m.

8. OUR ARTILLERY. All barrages were excellent – O/C Raid and O/C's Coys. spent in the highest terms of the artillery co-operation – There were two enemy shells from our creeping barrage during the advance to the first objective which have been thought as being enemy by some shots falling short, but as the wires were working exceedingly close after barrage (3 wounded from 35 to 50 yards) it does not appear there was from the front of the artillery – SMOKE BARRAGE The screen produced does not appear to have caused any embarrassment even from rifle.

9. ENEMY ARTILLERY. No immediate retaliation appears to have been put up – It is reported that on the troops left in trenches a few enemy shells fell, but this does not appear like any part of his artillery programme – During the time described by the raid my little interference seems to have been occasioned by artillery fire – A few stray shots were put into his own front line about 1:15 p.m. and after the withdrawal he shelled it – Lala & Shelled on front line near CAMBRIDGE ROAD.

10. OUR M.G.S. The barrage is reported as being effective.

11. Enemy M.G.S. Generally speaking the fire was very slight – One on our left at some short and fired inaccurately upon us – more M.G. fire experienced opposite the front from a great distance.

12. LEWIS gun + Rifle fire – Own Lewis gun fire, was in enemy – have seemed any Rifle fire, there appears to have been of valuable assistance. There appears to have been killed.

13. PRISONERS. The estimated total number of prisoners taken is – 2 Officers & 65 O.R. through A.P.M. and 12 O.R. wounded passed thro' own dressing station – Number estimated by medical officer. Total 2 Officers and 77 O.R. (estimate) all 90 FUS. REGT.

Army Form C. 2118.

WAR DIARY
or
INTELLIGENCE SUMMARY.
(Erase heading not required.)

147

Place	Date	Hour	Summary of Events and Information	Remarks and references to Appendices
	24 July		Report (continued)	

14. CASUALTIES. – The estimated casualties actually during the raiding force are:– 17 wounded O.R. mostly slight – 3 missing O.R. – 1 killed O.R. It is quite possible that the missing may yet be accounted for as having passed through a dressing station. – All three casualties occurred between enemy front line trench and front objective. – **ENEMY DEAD.** No enemy dead appear to have been seen by us, though doubtless many were buried by our bombardment.

15. GENERAL. All reports indicate that the artillery preparation is very severe. The whole country is described as being churned up. The success of the Raid reflects great credit on the O.C. Raiding Party – officers, NCOs & men engaged in it – undoubtedly very little actual opposition was encountered but the manner in which all ranks carried out their allotted tasks and firm resolve under all conditions was most satisfactory. I have as yet, owing to the difficulties of communication caused by heavy enemy artillery fire, been able to obtain few minor details of the raid – all of the parties reached by officers – NCOs in command were excellent (including No signal arrangements were available from 13th H.Q. to 46 I.B. but owing to the initiative of 2/Lt W.F. BORTON. Communication between our supports in was established and reports by Lieut T.H. CAMPBELL. R.A.M.C. were excellent in on support line by our artillery – 2nd By in the progress of the raid were all the movements on our supports in occasionally promo to reaching were continuously kept up by being shelled in our support line by our artillery – 2nd By having to withdraw from our front line to enable the heavy trench mortar Battery to open fire on the enemy trenches – resulting in our own trenches being blown in by our own fire.

24/7/17.

OCA. W.E. St John. Lt Col
Cmnd. 12 H.L.I.

W.J.C. Inyr.

FURTHER REPORT ON RAID.

Army Form C. 2118.

WAR DIARY
or
INTELLIGENCE SUMMARY.
(Erase heading not required.)

Place	Date	Hour	Summary of Events and Information	Remarks and references to Appendices
	24 July		FURTHER REPORT ON RAID. Carried out by 12th Bn. H.L.I. on 24th July 1917. By Lt-Col W.E. St John. Comdg 12th H.L.I. Following on my report of 24-7-17, additional information has been received as under:—	

1. SUPPORT LINE. Hard to recognise. No revetting. Battered in many places. and is not passable by day.

2. COMMUNICATION TRENCHES. Cpl the mar 3 feet deep. In a very bad state of repair.

3. THE STABLES. Simply a ruin. A small dug-out exists but this shows no sign of recent occupation.

4. THE MOUND. Ground slightly raised, running about 75ft out into No Mans Land. There is a small trench (covered) but badly damaged. Water has collected. It does not appear to have been in use for some time. Positions, probably M.G. have been neglected and are not fit for use.

5. M.G. POSITIONS. Position behind the MOUND — poor. Concrete position at junction of SUPPORT and IBERIA WALK — in bad condition and not fit for use. Positions beside dug-outs in front line behind STABLES. — In good condition.

6. O.P. In front line, behind MOUND, 6-7 feet high, and about 4 feet square.

7. DUG-OUTS. (a). Front line, left (Behind MOUND). Large surface concrete shelter, in good condition. — 15 prisoners taken.
  (b). Front line, right (20-25 yards S. of IBERIA WALK), similar dugout, badly damaged, not fit for use.
  (c). Centre of frontage, 4 low strong concrete shelters, 2 smashed, other 2 in good condition. — 10 prisoners taken.
  (d). Near EITEL FRITZ, concrete dugout, completely damaged.
  (e). A concrete dugout 15'×10'×6', 50 yards in rear of Reserve Line and about 30 yards to right of IBERIA AVENUE. was found to contain 3 wooden cases, each containing 10 small shells, "Wh 33 Nano" Kpz.
  (f). There were several dug-outs in Reserve Line. There was built in behind the Reserve Trench in dip of ground, and are about 30 feet long by 8 feet broad. They are about 6 feet high in front, obtaining down to 4 feet in rear.
  (g). There is a deep dug-out in IBERIA AVENUE about 50 yards E. of Support Trench. This dug-out was not entered but was bombed.

8. RAILWAY. The narrow gauge Railway runs along behind front line as well as Reserve line, but it has all been badly blown about.

9. RESISTANCE OF ENEMY. Very poor. — When the objective was gained the enemy attempts at stuns along his front line £Sy 2/£. from the south, but an attack party gained superiority and prevented him from advancing. — A few other stuns were bombed but with no effect.

10. Enemy aeroplanes rose to be seen during the Raid — one hour after the Guns ceased three enemy planes were flying very low over his lines —

11. S.O.S. Signals were observed on our front.

12. Map of ground raided is attached.

26/7/17.

sgd W.E. St John. Lt-Col
Commd 12. H.L.I.

Army Form C. 2118.

WAR DIARY
or
INTELLIGENCE SUMMARY.
(Erase heading not required.)

Place	Date	Hour	Summary of Events and Information	Remarks and references to Appendices
IN THE LINE	26 July		Recd:- The following telegrams were received:-	
			(1) B.M. 396. The Brigade Commander wishes to send you heartiest congratulations on your splendid success today – in which all ranks of the Brigade will join with him in doing –	
			(2) B.M. 398. Please convey to Col St John and officers and N.C.O. and men of my congratulations on their very successful raid and the patrol of 7 Cameron on their successful exploit from General THUILLIER.	@ 12. H.L.I. ↑ my
			(3) To 46th & 46th Bde. Following copy of a memo dated 26 July received from 5th Army General Staff is forwarded for communication to all concerned:- "The Army Commander wishes his emphatic admiration conveyed to the 12. H.L.I. – the 7th Cameron Highlanders and the artillery who assisted them on the success of the day's operations carried out by them on July 26th. The organisation of the raids and the manner in which they were carried out reflect great credit on all the officers and men concerned.	15 Div no 132 (3) 9.6. 28.7.17
			sgd. H F BAILLIE Lt Col. General Staff 15 Div.	
			26 July 1917.	

Army Form C. 2118.

WAR DIARY
or
INTELLIGENCE SUMMARY.
(Erase heading not required.)

Place	Date	Hour	Summary of Events and Information	Remarks and references to Appendices
IN THE LINE	1917 July 25		Battalion in the line occupying left Sub-section of Divisional Front.	
	26		do	
	27		do	
	28		Battalion relieved by 10 Scottish Rifles, & march to ERIE CAMP. 19 O.R. received from Divisional Depot.	
ERIE CAMP	29		Battalion in hutments in ERIE CAMP, move to RESERVE CAMP at H.16. leaving camp at 9 p.m.	
RESERVE CAMP H.16.17.	30		Battalion in huts in reserve camp, details left in ERIE CAMP.	
IN THE LINE	31		Battalion moved overnight to battle position in ST JAMES TRENCH & CAMBRIDGE & POTIZZE Defences. Operations commence on a large scale.	

Note: these operations cover a period of several days - Franchin etc. are attached to the August diary -

W.K.H. mjr.

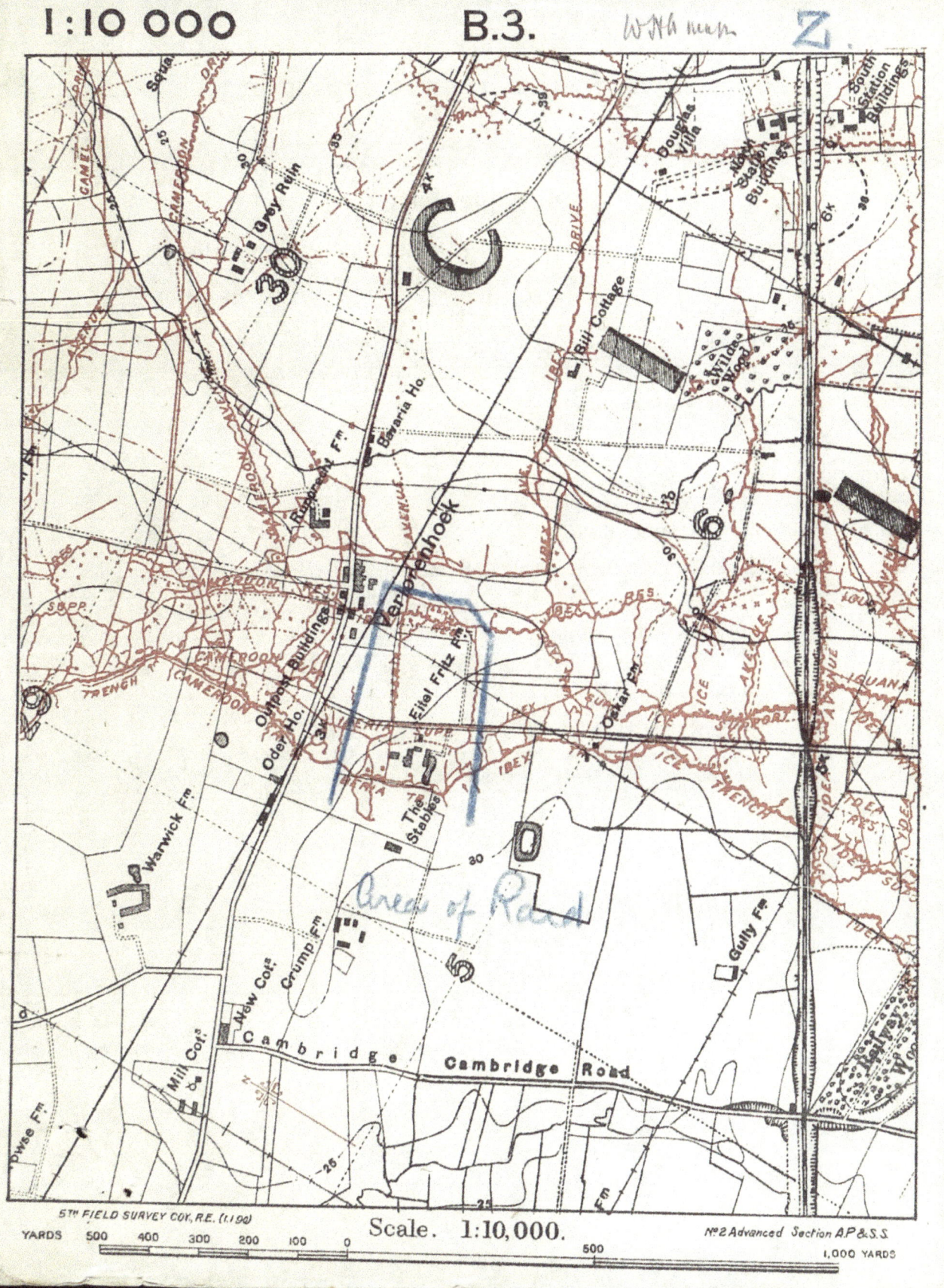

Message Form.

..............Division.

Map reference or mark own position on Map at back.

I am at..

I am at..and am consolidating.

I am at..and have consolidated.

I need :—Ammunition.
        Bombs.
        Rifle Grenades.
        Water.
        Very lights.
        Stokes shells.

Enemy forming up for counter-attack at..

I am in touch with..........................on $\genfrac{}{}{0pt}{}{\text{Right}}{\text{Left}}$ at..........................

I am not in touch on $\genfrac{}{}{0pt}{}{\text{Right.}}{\text{Left.}}$

Am being shelled from..

I estimate my present strength at..............rifles.

Hostile $\left\{\begin{array}{l}\text{Battery}\\\text{Machine Gun}\\\text{Trench Mortar}\end{array}\right\}$ active at..........................

Time   a.m. (p.m.)   Name..
Date..   Platoon.............. Company..............
Place..   Battalion..

WAR DIARY
of
12th (S) Bn Highland Lt. Infantry.

for month of AUGUST. 1917

Army Form C. 2118.

WAR DIARY
or
INTELLIGENCE SUMMARY.
(Erase heading not required.)

154

Instructions regarding War Diaries and Intelligence Summaries are contained in F. S. Regs., Part II. and the Staff Manual respectively. Title pages will be prepared in manuscript.

Place	Date	Hour	Summary of Events and Information	Remarks and references to Appendices
ECOLE YPRES	1917 AUGT. 2		Battalion returns from the line and are accomodated in the ECOLE YPRES	
WINNIZEELE AREA	3		Battalion embuses to WINNIZEELE AREA & arrive about 3 p.m. Draft of 50 O.R. arrive from Divisional Depot MERCHENHEM.	
	4		Battalion in tented camp. The following message of congratulation received:- "G.O.C. wishes to congratulate all Infantry Brigades on the magnificent manner in which they have fought to-day." 31/7/17. Battalion in tented camp as above. Draft of 8 O.R. received.	
	5		2/Lt J.A.PENMAN is appointed to temporary command of "C" Company vice Captain T.B.MYLES. killed in action. to take effect from 12 " ins. Brigadier-General D.R.SLADEN C.M.G. D.S.O. Kings Own Scottish Borderers assumes command of 46th I.B. from 2/8/17 vice Brig-General E.A.FAGAN D.S.O. invalided - gazed - to ENGLAND.	
	6		The under-noted N.C.O's & men have been awarded The MILITARY MEDAL by the Corps Commander for Acts of Gallantry in the field. 17910. SERGT P. McBREARTY 42633, P.G. S.BUNNETT 9297, SERGT H. COOK 42604, B.ORMSBY.	W.A.M. Major

Army Form C. 2118.

WAR DIARY
or
INTELLIGENCE SUMMARY.
(Erase heading not required.)

155

Place	Date	Hour	Summary of Events and Information	Remarks and references to Appendices
WINNIZEELE AREA	1917 Aug. 6		Battalion in tented camp as above. Draft of 7 O.R. received.	
	7		do Battalion sports held.	
	8		do 2/Lt E.H. WUENSCH rejoins the Battalion from England.	
	9		Battⁿ in tented camp as above. Inspection of the Battalion in mass by Divisional Commander, at which he expressed himself highly satisfied by with the works done by the Battalion, & by the continued high standard of efficiency.	
	10		Battⁿ in tented camp as above. The Field Marshall Commanding-in-Chief under authority granted by his majesty the King awards the MILITARY CROSS for Gallantry in the Field to the under-noted Officers —	M.W....

T/LIEUT (A/CAPT) T.B. MYLES.

Army Form C. 2118.

WAR DIARY
or
INTELLIGENCE SUMMARY.
(Erase heading not required.)

№ 156

Instructions regarding War Diaries and Intelligence Summaries are contained in F.S. Regs., Part II. and the Staff Manual respectively. Title pages will be prepared in manuscript.

Place	Date	Hour	Summary of Events and Information	Remarks and references to Appendices
WINNIZEELE AREA	1917 Aug 11		Battn in tented camp as above. 2/Lieut. D.R. DRURY-LOWE reporting for duty.	
	12		do. Draft of 55 O.R. received	
	13		do. Draft of 27 O.R. received	
	14		do.	
	15		do. 2/Lieut. D.R. DRURY-LOWE evacuated to hospital	
	16		do. Battn entraining at ABEELE & the Batt" entrained at ABEELE & proceed by march route to BIVOUAC CAMP at H.19 (Sheet 28 Belgium N.W)	
	17.		Orders received to move from H.18. and take up position in 0.9.1. 12 H.L.I. to relieve the 1st R. MUNSTER Regt in Right subsector in IBEX RESERVE TRENCH. Relief completed at 12.48 A.M.	
	18.	12.48"	18th D Coy in BILL COTTAGE. Remainder digging in in 0.9. lines and m.g. posn in 0.9. lines and m.g. position. - Casualties 3. O.R.	
		6.15 P.M.	Casualties 11 O.R.	
	19.	4.45 A.M.	Heavy Bombardment and punitive barrage for two hours. Some retaliation by Enemy. Casualties 3.	

A 5834 Wt. W4973 M687 750,000 8/16 D. D. & L. Ltd. Forms/C.2118/13.

Army Form C. 2118.

WAR DIARY
or
INTELLIGENCE SUMMARY.
(Erase heading not required.)

157

Place	Date	Hour	Summary of Events and Information	Remarks and references to Appendices
IN THE LINE	20 Aug.	12 Midnight	Headquarters and two Companies Relieved by 13 Royal Scots. and returned to Bivouac Camp at H.16	
	21 Aug.	A.M.	D Company relieved by M.M.G.'s/13th Royal Scots. Withdrew from line. a.m. Clean up and re-equip.	
	22 Aug.	4.45 AM	Bn. Moved to ECOLE. A.	
		7.15 AM	Move cancelled	
		10 AM	Orders to move at 2 ERO + 6 hours cancelled	
		1.40 PM	Orders to move forward to O.B.1. and received warning orders to attack at 8. P.M. C.O. to MILL COTTS.	
		3.45 PM	Bn. in position in O.B.1.	
		6.30 PM	Orders to attack cancelled	
	23 Aug.	6.15 PM	Orders Recd. to occupy line BILL COTTAGE & BAVARIA HOUSE	
		6.10 PM	Above orders cancelled by telephone	
		6.30 PM	Orders to take over 4.5 J.B. FRONT. Right the Railway D.25.d 9.2. Left Opst of Beck.House D.19.c 9.5	
		9.30 PM	Move commenced. (FREZENBERG 1/10000)	
	24th Aug	4.15 AM	Relief complete — Dispositions Right D Coy Center C Coy Left B Coy. Reserve A Coy in Trenches round Bill Cot. Head Quarters Bill Cot.	
		9.30 PM	Large working parties in front of Left & Center Coys. to dig advanced posts. Heavy barrage put down by enemy causing several casualties to parties.	
	25th Aug.	12 noon	Heavy French Mortar report direct hit on Beck House & garrison seen retiring. Ordered "B"Coy to occupy it if possible.	
		1 P.M.	Officers Patrol Reports Beck House still held.	
		5.30 PM	Casualties 39.	
		11 P.M.	Hurricane Bombardment from attack on Gallipoli Fm. Slight retaliation working parties same as last night.	

Army Form C. 2118.

WAR DIARY
or
INTELLIGENCE SUMMARY.
(Erase heading not required.)

158.

Place	Date	Hour	Summary of Events and Information	Remarks and references to Appendices
Battle line	26th Aug	9p.m.	Five advanced posts completed and occupied. Patrols in touch with enemy posts during night. Relief of Battn: by 3.B.M. 45th I.B. commences. Right 6th CAMERON'S Centre 13th ROYAL SCOTS Left 11th A.&S. High'rs Weather Bad, Heavy rain, night very dark. Trenches muddy & slippery.	
	27th Aug	1.A.M.	D, B, A & H.Q. Coys relieved, move to Camp H.17.	
		4.15.A.M.	Only 1 platoon 13th Royal Scots arrived to relieve C Coy, remainder lost. C Coy left in line till night.	
		9.p.m.	Relief of "C" Coy commenced.	
	28th Aug	7.A.M.	"C" Coy arrive in Camp H.17. Clean up & re-equip.	
	29th Aug	1p.m.	Marched from Camp H.17. to take over Right sector from 6th CAMERON'S & 13th ROYAL SCOTS. Right The RAILWAY D.25.d.9.2. Left NORTH of LOW F.m. D.25.a.8.8 (FREZENBERG 1/10,000)	
	30th Aug	1.30.A.M.	Relief complete. Dispositions Right B Coy Centre A Coy Left B Coy. Reserve C Coy in trenches near B.11. Col: H.Q. WILD WOOD.	
		8.45.p.m.	S.O.S on right - probably about GLENCORSE our front quiet.	
		9.15.p.m.	Situation apparently normal	
		8.p.m.	Guides meet relieving Battn: 5th LANCS. Fusiliers at MENIN GATE. YPRES.	
	31st Aug	12.40.A.M.	Night fine. Tracks dry. Relief Complete. Move to Camp H.16.	
		3.A.M.	Battn in Camp.	

Army Form C. 2118.

WAR DIARY
or
INTELLIGENCE SUMMARY.
(Erase heading not required.)

159

Place	Date	Hour	Summary of Events and Information	Remarks and references to Appendices
THISTLE CAMP	1917 Augt. 26		Summary of Drafts 15th to 31st Augt. 1917. Draft of 137 O.R. received Lt. Col. A.A. HEYMAN. D.S.O. Establishment Commanding Officer rejoins. Handing over by Lt. Col. W.E. ST JOHN delayed until conclusion of operations 2nd phase. Lt. Col. HEYMAN assumes command.	
	31		Summary of Casualties for 2nd Phase	
	Augt. 23		2/Lt L.S. GRAHAM wounded & evacuated to Hospital where he died on 29th Total casualties for this phase — O.R. 68	

W. Heyman
Lt. Col.
C.g. 1st Arg. Bn. L.

Vol 22

22.M
3 sheets

12 (Service) Bn. Highland Lt Infantry.
WAR DIARY for
SEPTEMBER. 1917.

Army Form C. 2118.

WAR DIARY
or
INTELLIGENCE SUMMARY.
(Erase heading not required.)

Place	Date	Hour	Summary of Events and Information	Remarks and references to Appendices
FIELD.	Sep. 1		Bn embusses at VLAMMERTINGHE at 5 A.M. and proceeds to VERMEZEELE area. Spends night in billets = Draft of 59 O.R. joins the Bn.	
	2		Entrain at CASSEL Stn. at 4 P.M. Division moves from the 5th to 3rd Army and is transferred to XVII Corps.	
	3		Arrived at DUISANES. Bn. billeted in hutted camps. The undermentioned officer Warrant Officer NCOs & men have been awarded decorations to acts of gallantry in the field. Military Cross T/Capt R.L. HANNAH. Distinguished Conduct Medal. No 6923. C.S.M. J.W. McDONALD — 9287 Sgt H. COOK. = Second bar to military medal No 12460 Pte J. McLELLAN = Bar to military medal No 17833 Sgt G.M. HENRY. Military medal No 40231 Sgt D.C. ARMOUR. No 21634 Sgt J. MAXWELL No 41851 Sgt T.P. BROWN. No 22264 Cpl D. O'HEA. No 41862 Cpl J.W. WHINHAM. No 43140 L/Cpl W. JACK No 18031 Pte H. EDDOWES. No 26137 Pte R. WILSON No 19525 Pte W. McCART. (extract from Bn orders No 7 dated 3 Sept 1917) Draft of 71 O.R. Reports	
	4		in huts	
	5		in huts	
	6		The Division 1st Relieves the 4th Division in centre sector of XVII Corps front. Bn moves to BAROSSA CAMP. 9.18 a.s.s. in divisional Reserve = Relieves 6. Cameron.	
	7		Bn moves to gents in SCOTS VALLEY, duty Bn in Bde Support (location H.25 c & 3) Coy C. Coy to Bn HQ in LANCER LANE. 2nd Lt R.E. SAUNDERS evacuated to base.	
	8		in Camp. Routine parades and training	
	9		—do—	
	10		—do— C. Coy Relieved and rejoins Bn	

Army Form C. 2118.

WAR DIARY
or
INTELLIGENCE SUMMARY.
(Erase heading not required.)

162

Place	Date	Hour	Summary of Events and Information	Remarks and references to Appendices
FIELD.	Sept. 10.	—	The undermentioned NCO's & men have been awarded decorations in acts of gallantry in the field: **BAR to Military Medal.** No 23065 Cpl. J. McMASTER. 8743. Pte. F. FOX. **Military Medal.** Pte. D. ROSE. 25305 Pte. W. SANDISON. 42548 Pte. J. DUFFY. 25318. Pte. A. ROBINSON. (extract from 13th Divs. Jnl. 10 Sep 1917) In camp. Working parties, training etc.	
	11		"	
	12		Cpl. JOHNSTONE. proceeds to ETAPLES. 2 Lt. SIMPSON takes on command of A Coy.	
	13		In Camp	
	14		"	
	15		On the night of 15th/16th Bn. Relieves 10/11 H.L.I. in left subsection of front line	
	16		Join in LINE Continued. B.I.D. Coys from line. A Support. & C. Reserve.	
	17		Draft of 46 O.R. arrives. The following officers reported to duty 2 Lieutenants. R. CRAWFORD. A.T. WILLIAMSON. W. McKENZIE	
	18		in line	
	19		in line	
	20		2 Lts. T. WILLIAMSON. R. CRAWFORD. W. McKENZIE Report to duty with Bn.	
	21		2 Lt. H. COWAN. J. BROWN. Report to duty with Bn.	
	22		in line	
	23/24		On night of 23/24. 46 J.B. Relieves by 45 J.B. = 12 H.L.I. being relieved by 6. CAMERONS. Casualties during tour. 5. O.R. wounded.	W/H.A.
	24/29		Bn. in Brit Reserve. Bn. doing training in vicinity of BALMORAL. CAMP. Draft of 5 O.R. reports into duty with Bn. — Ext. of Bn. orders 29 Sep 1917. "The undermentioned NCO's men have been awarded decorations in acts of gallantry in the field. — The MILITARY MEDAL	
	30		and in Dist Reserve. 1798 Sgt. H. MUIR 27474 Cpl. G. BRIAN 40234 Pte. V.W. AGNEW 24561 " J. TESS	

M. Wingrave
Lt. Col. Comm.
12 H L I

A.5834 Wt. W4473 M687 750,000 8/16 D.D. & L. Ltd. Forms/C.2118/13.

WAR DIARY

OF

12th (Service) Batt. Highland Light Infantry.

FOR

MONTH OF OCTOBER 1917.

Secret

To. 46. I.B.

Herewith War Diary of 12. H.L.I.
for month of October 1917.

W H Cunninghame Major
2i/c

31 Oct. 1917

Army Form C. 2118.

WAR DIARY
or
INTELLIGENCE SUMMARY.
(Erase heading not required.)

Instructions regarding War Diaries and Intelligence Summaries are contained in F. S. Regs., Part II. and the Staff Manual respectively. Title pages will be prepared in manuscript.

163

Place	Date	Hour	Summary of Events and Information	Remarks and references to Appendices
In the field	Oct. 1.		B.n in Support in STIRLING Camp. Two Coys toward at Bn H.q.	
	2		- do -	
	3		The undermentioned N.C.O. has been awarded the Military Medal for Gallantry in the field No 9678 Sgt T. MOORE	
	4		B.n in Support	
	5		do.	
	6		do.	
	7		do.	
	8		do. 2nd Lt J. LAMB. reports in duty. draft of 56. O.R.	
	9		do. 2nd Lt C. NEIL to hospital Sick	
	10.		B.n relieved 10th. H.L.I. in the line. Right subsection of left section of divisional front	
	11		" during the line 2nd Lt W. SIMPSON. to hospital sick	
	12		" do 2nd Lt W. DUNSMORE. wounded whilst out on patrol and evacuated	
	13		" do 2nd Lt D.G. WATSON. Reports in duty - draft of 25 O.R.	
	14		do	
	15		do	
	16		" do	
	17		B.n relieved by the 6/7 Royal Scots Fusiliers. Casualties 1 officer & 2 O.R. wounded.	
	18		B.n in Billets in ARRAS. Training carried on.	
	19		do	
	20		do	
	21		do Inspection by The Hon. The LORD PROVOST of GLASGOW. Sir T. DUNLOP. Bart.	
	22		do	
	23		do Lt P.B. MILLIGAN. reports in duty. draft of 4. O.R.	
	24		do No 9086 Sgt James TURNER. awarded the Military Medal. B.O. in O.R. para 7	
	25		B.n Returns 9,10 gallons in Brigade Reserve WILDERNESS. CAMP.	
	26		B.n in Bde Reserve. 2nd Lt A.B. IRVINE to Base unfit	

Army Form C. 2118.

WAR DIARY
or
INTELLIGENCE SUMMARY. (M 164

(Erase heading not required.)

Place	Date	Hour	Summary of Events and Information	Remarks and references to Appendices
Field.	27 Oct	—	Bn in Bdu Reserve. WILDERNESS CAMP – Training working parties	
	28.	—	do do	
	29.	—	do do	
	30.	—	do do	
	31.	—	do do	

W.H.A. Major

Anderson Lt.Col.
Comdg. 13. "Highland Light Inf."
31.10.17

Sent.

To 46. Inf. Bde.

Herewith war diary of 12. H.L.I. for month of
November 1917.
 It is regretted that the ~~consecutive~~
consecutive numbering has been mislaid
The pages are numbered N1 to N7.
 It will be a favour if the filing
authority will add the consecutive numbers
and advise what they are.

4 Dec. 1917.

 A.M. Bergman
 Comd. 12" Highland Light Infy.

WAR DIARY
of
12th Bn Highland Lt. Infantry
for month of
NOVEMBER 1917.

Army Form C. 2118.

WAR DIARY
or
INTELLIGENCE SUMMARY.
(Erase heading not required.)

Instructions regarding War Diaries and Intelligence Summaries are contained in F.S. Regs., Part II. and the Staff Manual respectively. Title pages will be prepared in manuscript.

Place	Date	Hour	Summary of Events and Information	Remarks and references to Appendices
ARRAS	1917 Nov. 1		Battⁿ in Billets in ARRAS.	
	2		Battalion moves into the line by March Route from WILDERNESS CAMP, taking over from the 10/11th H.L.I. in the LEFT SUB-SECTION of the RIGHT SUB-SECTOR of the Divisional Front. Relief carried out by daylight & completed by 2 p.m. Details accommodated in billets in ARRAS.	
IN THE LINE	3		Battalion in the line, distribution being as follows:- LEFT FRONT "D" Coy. RIGHT FRONT "B" Coy. SUPPORT "C" Coy. RESERVE "A" Coy. H.Q. in WELLFORD RESERVE. LIEUT. P.B. MILLIGAN wounded by gun-shot.	
	4		Battalion in the line as above. LIEUT. A. GILCHRIST joins the Battalion for duty & is posted to "C" Company. At 11.45 p.m. Intelligence Officer returning from patrol reports the presence of a body of the enemy who were advancing in the direction of a Sap in our Wire. He estimated the number to be about 40. & reports that they are divided up into three parties. O.C. "D" Coy in front of whose front of the line the Sap in the wire is ordered to run Lewis Gun fire to be opened, & the party was dispersed after throwing bombs into our wire & front line. 2/LIEUT. R. CRAWFORD wounded by splinter of a bomb.	
	5		Battalion in the line as above	
	6		Battalion in the line as above. Inter-Company Relief carried out during the morning, the Dispositions of Companies then being as follows. LEFT FRONT "C" Company RIGHT FRONT "A" Coy. SUPPORT "D" Company RESERVE "B" Coy.	

Army Form C. 2118.

WAR DIARY
or
INTELLIGENCE SUMMARY.

(Erase heading not required.)

Instructions regarding War Diaries and Intelligence Summaries are contained in F. S. Regs., Part II. and the Staff Manual respectively. Title pages will be prepared in manuscript.

Place	Date	Hour	Summary of Events and Information	Remarks and references to Appendices
IN THE LINE	1917 Nov. 7		Battalion in the line as above	
	8		Battalion in the line as above. Previous to 1.40 A.M. the hour at which the K.O.S.B. were to raid the enemy's line at DEVIL'S TRENCH, the men in the front line trenches were withdrawn, to shelters & dug-outs, leaving only men on duty & Lewis Gunners. At Zero Hour Lewis Gunners swept the enemy's parapet with Lewis Gun fire. The enemy's retaliation was extremely light, consisting of TRENCH MORTARS & a few shells on our FRONT & SUPPORT LINES. The Battalion had no casualties from the retaliation. Raiding Party left & safe on the RIGHT Coy's front & returned by the FRONT of the RIGHT SUB-SECTION.	
	9		The Battalion occupying the RIGHT SUB-SECTION.	
	10		Battalion in the line as above.	
	11		Battalion is relieved by the 6th Cameroons. Relief complete by 1.30 p.m. Battalion moves by March Route to ARRAS & are accomodated in billets. Battalion in Billets in ARRAS	
ARRAS	11		Battalion in Billets in ARRAS	
	12		ditto	The day being Sunday was devoted to Cleaning up and Divine Service
	13		ditto	

Army Form C. 2118.

WAR DIARY
or
INTELLIGENCE SUMMARY.
(Erase heading not required.)

N3

Place	Date	Hour	Summary of Events and Information	Remarks and references to Appendices
ARRAS	Nov. 12	~	Bn in Billets in bit Factory, Place St Croix. Training carried out at the Butte de TiR. Daily Routine Reveille 6.30 A.M. Breakfast 7 A.M. unlit Room 12 noon. Sick parade 7.30 am. Training hours 8 am till 12 noon. 2-4 p.m. Recreational Training. Specimen training programme. 8-8:30 March discipline. 8:30-9. Physical Training. 9-9:30 Tm Discipline. 9:30-10 Bayonet Fighting - Brick 10:15-10:30 Anti Gas drill. 10:30-11 Bombing. 11-11:30 musketry and Report fire. 11:30-12 Anti aircraft guards — Recreational Training in the afternoon. Specialists Scouts, Snipers, Signallers, visual Specialist Mining - Wiring Training under a Tactical Tr. from Bn.	
	13		Training as above. Bn paid. As above. A+B Coys attended the Sml Range. 8-1 p.m. Football match C Coy v D Coy. Draw 1 all. - Bad Frost. 3 months firm time. Weather continues fine and most use cloudy.	
	14		As above. with exception of Range.	
	15		As above working parties commenced 1 officer 170 o.R. under DTMO. Carrying Bombs and duty munch. 20 o.R. " Bn Train. Coal fatigue. Army party only Draft of 17th Draft 6. o.R. But fm officer from latrine 16 all N.Co & 2 p.m. Lieut football match v Chinese team in 17th Draft 6. O.R. arrived. Covered 6 pm till 8 p.m.	
	16		As above training in similar lines. Weather fine. Additional working parties. a. N.Z. Tunnelling Coy. 1 officer 8 n.c.o. 115 our when 16. 17. 18. 19. making avy ors b. do do 1 sgt 130 OR. — do — Baths allotted 10 B".	
	17		As above training on similar lines = 2 M.A. LEARMONTH. Reports for duty from Divisional Training Bn. Bn Football team plays 1st B" East Lancs. Revert. Win. h 12 H.z. 1. 4- Goals to 1. Heavies of hitops. Cont mus feet, from ar sick parade.	

A.5834 Wt. W4973/M687 750,000 8/16 D. D. & L. Ltd. Forms/C.2118/13.

WAR DIARY or INTELLIGENCE SUMMARY.

(Erase heading not required.)

Army Form C. 2118.

Place	Date 1917	Hour	Summary of Events and Information	Remarks and references to Appendices
FAMPOUX.	Nov. 18.		Bn. Relieve 7. Camerons as Bn. in Bde. Support. Distribution as follows. C. Coy. LANCER. AVE. A. Coy at STIRLING. CAMP. B.H.Q. v HQ. in Reserve entrenchment. Relief completed by 11 a.m. Working Parties taken over.	
			"C" Party – 33 O.R. marching dug outs under N.Z.T. Coy. 6.15 a.m.	
			D " 33 do 2.15 p.m.	
			E " 2 A Co 20 – do 10.15 p.m.	
			F " 35 O.R. Carrying do – do – 7. p.m.	
			J. " 60 O.R. T.M. positions under D.T.M.O. 9 a.m.	
			R " 1 Offr. 44 O.R. under 73. Field Coy. R.E. work on CHINSTRAP LANE. 12.45 a.m.	
			S " 1 " 40 O.R. do do 4.30 p.m.	
			T " 1 " 40 O.R. do	
			R.E.8. " 1 " 30 O.R. do Constructing cook houses & shelters.	
	19.		Party F subsequently cancelled.	
			Parties C. & E. Cancelled.	
	20.		Parties R.S.T. Cancelled. (owing to running of German withdrawal and the necessity for all being in readiness for immediate pursuit)	
			Party R.E. 8. Cancelled. Some gas shells fell about 200 yards west of Bn. HQ.	
	21.		Parties R.S.T. Resumed. – Retired did not break until, normal condition Resumed.	
	22.		Situation normal. Weather clamp and misty. – A few shells dropped west and south of Bn. Billets causing no casualties	
	23.		– do – do	
	24.		at 12 noon a Report was received "With effect that An R.F.C. Reported enemy trenches full of men trying out" in Shell Holes in No Mans Land. Bn. took immediate action Shots duly in readiness. No action required. Working party dug new trench at COR04130 2 Sappers 150 x long.	
	25.		Situation normal. Working Parties as usual.	

Army Form C. 2118.

WAR DIARY
or
INTELLIGENCE SUMMARY.
(Erase heading not required.)

Place	Date	Hour	Summary of Events and Information	Remarks and references to Appendices
IN THE LINE	1917 Nov. 26		Battⁿ relieved 10/11th H.L.I. in Right Sub-Sector of Left Brigade Front — just South of River SCARPE. Relief complete by 9 A.M. Company Dispositions as follows Right Front "C" Company Left Front "A" Company Support Coy. "B" " in WELLFORD RESERVE Reserve Coy. "D" " in LANCER AVENUE. Trench Mortars active on Right Coy. Front in the morning. At 4 p.m. orders received from Brigade to send out one Fighting Patrol to secure identification. Weather fine, clear but cold. Wind N.W.	
	27		Battalion in the line as above. As ordered strong patrol went out at 2 A.M. under 2/Lieut. WUENSCH, entered enemy trenches at ANGEL TRENCH, but were not successful in effecting any captures. Weather conditions were unfavourable as there was a bright moon shining through the clouds & snow had fallen at 1 A.M. Remainder of day uneventful. At 8.15 p.m. hostile party were seen assembling in PELVES LANE. There dispersed by L.G. fire. At 8.30 p.m. green lights were sent up by enemy — followed by T.M. bombardment. Party in PELVES LANE again dispersed by L.G. Fire.	

Army Form C. 2118.

168

WAR DIARY
or
INTELLIGENCE SUMMARY.

(Erase heading not required.)

Place	Date	Hour	Summary of Events and Information	Remarks and references to Appendices
In the line	Nov 27.		Owing to this activity on the part of the enemy and the possibility of a raid - firing attempted Front line Companies stood to. No further activity however was shown and at 10 P.M. Stand down was ordered. Front line Companies resumed fighting patrols who again went out during the night but were unable to obtain identification of troops opposite C. 390 C. 15th Div. Following letter received from Bde. passed to men from Division from Corps:- attached 390C. 15th Div. "I wish to express to you and your Division my appreciation of the fine spirit which has characterised their work during the last ten days - "Our own to divert the Enemies attention from the preparations for the offensive on the Right (CAMBRAI) "the Third army this Corps was ordered to show as much activity as possible, and by harassing the "enemy to simulate the preparation of an attack on this front. "All ranks have co-operated most loyally in carrying out this task, and the various "patrol work of the Infantry with the support of the Artillery have done exactly what was needed - "The enemy has been worried night & day, has had prisoners and machine guns and has been "made generally uncomfortable. "This activity has entitled us to claim at any rate a small share in the success "of the Third Army and I shall be glad if you will convey to all ranks under your command "my appreciation of their energy and courage. 390 Charles Fergusson. Lt. Gen. Comd. XVII Corps. 24. Nov. 1917. (No 9.48/44.	Nil
	28.		Weather continued fine, warm and clean. Considerable artillery & trench mortar activity was shown on both sides - Casualties N73'' M.E. - At night patrols were again active but were hampered by the full moon clear atmosphere. Patrols again active at night but were not successful in obtaining low action have noied - Patrols again active at night but were not successful in obtaining identification	
	29.			
	30		The Company relief carried out commencing at 7 P.M. Relief was completed 9 P.M. and position of Corps as follows. 4th Front by B. Left Front by A. In Reserve C.	

Army Form C. 2118.

WAR DIARY
or
INTELLIGENCE SUMMARY.
(Erase heading not required.)

Place	Date	Hour	Summary of Events and Information	Remarks and references to Appendices
LINE	Nov 30	7 P.M.	Period of silence commences. No artillery fire or T.M. or M.G. permitted except in S.O.S. in retaliation. 10 A.M. Barrage placed on our front support lines, and during evening 700 shells were dropped into HAPPY VALLEY, near Bn. HQ. Patrols again active. Corps Commr. sent out greetings on parade on the occasion of St ANDREWS' NIGHT. G.H. Heygate Lt. Col. Commd. 12. H. L. I	

25. M.
16 volumes.

CONFIDENTIAL 12 H.L.I.
VA 25

War Diary of 12th H.L.I.
From 1st Dec to 31st Dec 1917

Volume XXX

Army Form C. 2118.
172

WAR DIARY
or
INTELLIGENCE SUMMARY.
(Erase heading not required.)

Instructions regarding War Diaries and Intelligence Summaries are contained in F. S. Regs., Part II. and the Staff Manual respectively. Title pages will be prepared in manuscript.

Place	Date	Hour	Summary of Events and Information	Remarks and references to Appendices
IN THE LINE	1917 Dec 1		Weather continues fine and clear. Period of silence continues, and the Saxon Division opposite have suitied down in consequence – at 7 p.m. normal conditions resumed. Artillery and trench Mortar activity recommenced on both sides. Constant patrolling has made enemy very alert at night. Ration parties shelled.	
	2		Weather fine and clear. Wind W. Gas Mortars erected in our support lines for discharge tonight. In the evening wind increased, discharge of gas therefore postponed. Ration parties come up RIVER SCARPE by Fraye. Again heavily shelled at point of debarging.	
	3		Weather fine & clear. Conditions normal. Gas installed in Support Line, but not released owing to unfavourable wind.	
	4		Weather continues fine. Orders received from Division to rehearse their wine along Support Line. Line taped out. Wind again unfavourable and Gas not released. Much enemy activity – heavy gas shelling of WELLFORD RES Y HAPPY VALLEY from 8 p.m. to 10 p.m. from 3 A.M. to 4 A.M. on 5th Draft of 20 O.R. received	J.R.

Army Form C. 2118.

WAR DIARY
or
INTELLIGENCE SUMMARY.
(Erase heading not required.)

Place	Date	Hour	Summary of Events and Information	Remarks and references to Appendices
IN THE LINE	1917 Dec. 5		Activity in front line noted at 3 A.M. Battalion stood to. Considerable T.M. activity continued throughout the day, becoming heavy about 8 p.m. on the Right front Coy. Wiring Support-line continued, and patrols as usual. Warning Order received from Brigade anticipating enemy withdrawal to QUEANT-DROCOURT LINE. Orders issued to Companies giving detailed instructions in the event of such an operation taking place. Copy attached marked "A".	A
		6	"A" Coy. & "C" Coy. relieving "B" Coy. on RIGHT FRONT. "A" Coy. relieving "B" on left front. "B" Coy. to Support & "D" to Reserve. At 8.30 A.M. while relief was in progress enemy opened heavy T.M. fire on Saps on RIGHT Coy. front. Two posts went flattened out. Casualties 1 O.R. & 6 wounded. Day afterwards quiet until 5 p.m. Events subsequent to this are narrated in a Special Report to rent to Brigade on the day following of which the following is a copy. "At 5.45 p.m. the enemy put down a very heavy Artillery and French Mortar Barrage on our front & support line	

Army Form C. 2118.

WAR DIARY
or
INTELLIGENCE SUMMARY.
(Erase heading not required.)

174

Place	Date	Hour	Summary of Events and Information	Remarks and references to Appendices
THE LINE	1917 DEC. 6		line paying special attention to C, D & E Saps. At 6 p.m. retaliation was asked for. Two S.O.S. signals were put up on our immediate right & the Officer on duty in our right Company — 2/LIEUT. LEARMONT — fearing an attack or raid and no retaliation having been received — put up an S.O.S. signal at 6.5 p.m. The S.O.S. was not sent over the wire. Messages received stating "Barrage on our lines & Retaliation required," would point out that the S.O.S. signal could not be seen from any post near Battalion HQrs in JOHNSON AV. and the first intimation I received was from the Reserve Company and then it was thought to have been put up on our right. Artillery barrage opened on our side at 6.12 p.m. At 6 p.m. the Reserve Company went forward to occupy WELFORD RESERVE over the open & was in position at 6.20 p.m. At 6.25 p.m. Major J.A. COX went forward to report	

Army Form C. 2118.

WAR DIARY
or
INTELLIGENCE SUMMARY.
(Erase heading not required.)

175

Place	Date	Hour	Summary of Events and Information	Remarks and references to Appendices
IN THE LINE	1917 Dec 6		report on the situation. At 6.30 p.m. the situation became quieter & gradually returned to normal. At 7.3 p.m. gas shells were reported by the Front Companies, but although as far as can be ascertained the enemy fired a few gas shells, some of our own gas trench mortar bombs were hit. Our casualties are slight but the Lewis guns in "D" Saf was again blown up. At present neither "D" Saf nor E. 1 Saf can be held but I am taking special precautions for the safety of this part of the line." Report ends. The Corps Commander authorised an issue of rum.	
		7	Situation quieter; total casualties 7 killed, 2 died of wounds, 18 wounded	
		8	Battalion relieved by 6/7th. R.S.F. relief complete by 6 p.m. Battalion billeted in ECOLE DES JEUNE FILLES, ARRAS.	
		9	Battalion in billets in ARRAS. Working Parties commence. "C" & "D" Coys. on BUTTE DE TIR range under Musketry Officer.	

Army Form C. 2118.

WAR DIARY
or
INTELLIGENCE SUMMARY.
(Erase heading not required.)

176

Place	Date	Hour	Summary of Events and Information	Remarks and references to Appendices
ARRAS	1917 Dec/9 11		Battn in billets in ARRAS. Training continued on ground South of BUTTE DE TIR & in grounds adjoining ECOLE DES JEUNES FILLES.	
	11		Battn in billets in ARRAS. The following officers report for duty, 2/LIEUT. J.E. LAING, 2/LIEUT. DUNLOP, 2/LIEUT. J.W. HARDY rejoined from hospital. Battalion receives warning order to be ready to move at half-an-hour's notice from 6.30 A.M. till notice is sent from Brigade H.Qrs. to stand down, breakfasts to be eaten before 6.30 A.M.	
	12		Battalion in billets in ARRAS. Training carried out as per usual programme after Stand down, - received at 8.45 A.M.	
	13		Battn. in billets in ARRAS. Range at MOAT RANGE allotted to the Battn: Inter-Battalion football match played at BUTTE DE TIR between the Battalion & the 1/6th H.L.I. resulting in a win for the Battalion by 7 goals to nothing. The Battalion team was made up as follows: - Pte. J. McNEIL, A Coy. Pte. H. McDONALD, C Coy. Pte. A.J. JENKINS C Coy., Cpl. J. THOMSON, A Coy. Capt. R.L. HANNAH, O.C. D Coy. A/Cpl. J. KELLY, A Coy., 2/LIEUT. W.S. GREGOR, B Coy., 2/LIEUT. C. MILLER, C Coy. 2/Lt. W. PRENTICE, D Coy, L/C P. FERGUSON, A Coy, Sgt. H. MUIR, D Coy.	

Army Form C. 2118.

WAR DIARY
or
INTELLIGENCE SUMMARY.
(Erase heading not required.)

177

Place	Date	Hour	Summary of Events and Information	Remarks and references to Appendices
ARRAS	1917 Dec 14		Battalion in Billets in ARRAS. Training carried out on ground adjoining billet. Special attention being given to Gas Drill, training of Rifle Grenadiers & Wiring. Lewis Gunners carry out Range Practice on Divisional Lewis Gun Range.	
	15		Battalion in Billets in ARRAS. Training carried out as above. Inter-Batt. football match between the Batt. & 146 M.G. Coy Result 6-0 in our favour.	
	16		Battalion in billets in ARRAS. The Battalion is detailed for duty & all ranks are confined to billets. Training carried out in vicinity of billet. Concert for the men held in the billet to which all ranks contribute. The following programme of which all ranks contribute. The following programme of items received from boys during the course of the concert, were announced by the Commanding Officer. MILITARY MEDAL No. 17. Pte. GEORGE BEAGRIE, Matchen Reaves 36118 ,, JOHN GRAHAM do	
	17		The Battalion Stand to at 6.0 A.M. and 8.45 A.M. When Brigade orders were received ordering "Stand Down". Commenced at 3.0 P.M. The Battalion marched by companies to "Q" Dump when it entrained for AMPOUX to less our front system from 9th Norm HIGHLANDERS in the Centre Section of LEFT BRIGADE.	

Army Form C. 2118.

WAR DIARY
or
INTELLIGENCE SUMMARY.
(Erase heading not required.)

174

Place	Date	Hour	Summary of Events and Information	Remarks and references to Appendices
ARRAS	Dec 1917 17th contd		Front, T.8.c.0.8. to T.1.d.7.3. — Relief completed at 8.10 p.m. — Disposition of Companies as follows:- 'A' Coy Right Front, 'B' Coy Left Front, 'C' Coy Support, 'D' Coy Reserve. HQrs are in CHILI AVENUE. — The 7/8 Kings Own S. Borderers are on our Right Flank. The 10/11 H.L.I. on our left. The 10th SCOTTISH RIFLES are in Brigade Reserve. — The night passed Quietly.	Copy of Trench map attached "Appendix X"
	18		Weather Dry and Bright with hard frost. — The Battalion "Stood to ARMS" at 5.0 A.M. Orders to STAND DOWN were received from Brigade HQrs at 8.45 A.M. The enemy was Quiet and took no part in the Trenches commenced. During the morning an ENEMY AEROPLANE came over our lines flying at a low altitude, and was hit by ANTI AIRCRAFT defence and came down at 11.15 A.M. The pilot fell out of the machine, the latter landed in the enemy's lines. — The remainder of the day passes without incident [Front Company and our Right]	
	19th	3.45 A.M	Heavy Trench Mortar bombardment opened on our RIGHT, HE was used at the commencement followed by Lachrymatory and LETHAL Gas Trench Mortar Bombardment lasted until 5.15 A.M.	
		6.0 A.M	Bombardment reopened — Consisted of Gas T.Ms & Artillery. Our Artillery retaliated with good results — CASUALTIES. — 3 O.R. Dies from effects of Gas. 1 Officer 2/Lt H. COWAN and 24 O.R. Gassed but owing	Sgd/-

A.5834 Wt. W.4973/M687 750,000 8/16 D. D. & L. Ltd. Forms/C.2118/13.

WAR DIARY or INTELLIGENCE SUMMARY

Army Form C. 2118.

179

Place	Date	Hour	Summary of Events and Information	Remarks and references to Appendices
ARRAS	19th		Weather during the day was cold and dry. Relief by 10th Bn The Scottish Rifles commenced at 4.0 pm and was completed by 6.15 pm. The Battalion moved into Brigade Support and is accommodated in HUDSON, MUZZLE and LEMON TRENCHES - Head Qrs in NORTHUMBERLAND LANE. Working parties commenced.	
	20th		Battalion in Brigade Support. Working parties were supplied whilst church Vars conducted - "STAND TO" commenced at 5.0 am. Stand down at 8.45 am. A half issue of RUM was issued this morning - weather raw dry; and foggy.	
	21st		Battalion still in Brigade Support - Weather is Dry cold and very foggy. Great difficulty was experienced in supplying personnel for the numerous nights of working parties. Order for relief received. The Battalion moves at 4.0 pm to take the Right Section of the Brigade front extending from ARRAS - DOUAI Railway not to CATH ALLEY. Dispositions B & C Coy RIGHT FRONT D. Coy LEFT FRONT A Coy SUPPORT B Coy RESERVE. The night passed quietly.	N.B. The Battalion relieved the 10th SCOTTISH RIFLES
	22nd		Battalion in RIGHT SUB SECTOR - Weather inclined to be milder in the morning but keener to frost at midday - There was much aerial activity. A message was received from Brigade Head Quarters giving warning of possible attempted raid on our hers received from them from an intercepted message - The enemy was quiet up to midnight	Hugh

Army Form C. 2118.

180

WAR DIARY
or
INTELLIGENCE SUMMARY.

(Erase heading not required.)

Instructions regarding War Diaries and Intelligence Summaries are contained in F. S. Regs., Part II. and the Staff Manual respectively. Title pages will be prepared in manuscript.

Place	Date	Hour	Summary of Events and Information	Remarks and references to Appendices
ARRAS	1917. Dec 23rd	1.0 AM	Heavy Trench Mortar and H.E. was opened by the enemy on our front line at 1.0 AM lasted till 1.20 AM. Barrage was reopened at 3.15 AM and lasted till 3.35 AM. At 5.40 AM a barrage of 4.2's was opened on Reserve Trenches & continued till 6.0 AM. The Day was dull to start with but brightened. Clearer towards noon - Visibility at noon was very good - Activity on both sides was considerable. At 1.30 pm an intense barrage was put down on our front and support lines but died down in 20 minutes. One Lewis Gun returned a burst his with a 4.2 Gun, the Gun was silenced. The enemy aeroplane flew over battalions area at 400 feet (approximately) and was engaged by Lewis Gun & Rifle fire without result.	hip

WAR DIARY
or
INTELLIGENCE SUMMARY.
(Erase heading not required.)

Army Form C. 2118.

Place	Date	Hour	Summary of Events and Information	Remarks and references to Appendices
ARRAS	Dec 23		The weather turned rather milder in the evening, but visibility was spoiled by a mist which hung low on the ground.	
		6.30pm	A heavy barrage was put down by the enemy at 6.30 p.m. consisting of artillery fire chiefly – on our lines South of the river. At 6.35 p.m. an S.O.S. signal was observed by the sentry on duty at Batt. HQrs; it appeared to have been put up from the MONCHY Sector. At 6.37 p.m. the S.O.S signal was again put up in the same sector, and was taken up in rear by two Very Lights. Our field guns and howitzers opened at once in answer. The enemy appears to be concentrating all his fire on the front South of the River SCARPE. The enemy put up towards breaking into two Red Lights at intervals opposite own front. It is supposed that these lights were intended to represent our S.O.S. signals and were intended to mislead our artillery. S.O.S signals were again put up at 6.50pm. The Right Company reports that our 18 pounders were shelling our own line at the RAILWAY CUTTING. The S.O.S. signals put up at 6.50 p.m. were discharged from the MONCHY SECTOR, and in answer to them our Corps Heavy Artillery opened fire. The Barrage continued to be heavy on both Sector until 7.0 p.m. when fire began to slacken	

Army Form C. 2118.

WAR DIARY
or
INTELLIGENCE SUMMARY.
(Erase heading not required.)

192

Place	Date	Hour	Summary of Events and Information	Remarks and references to Appendices
ARRAS	Dec 23	7.15 pm	Guns by 7.15 pm the enemy's fire had quietened down. Our own artillery continued until 7.30 pm. At 7.30 pm the situation had returned to normal. The night passed but has been quietly.	
	24th		Weather fresh and sky overcast, with signs of rain. - Situation very quiet. G.O.C. 1st Division visited Batt. HQn in the morning and went off to visit the CENTRE Section on our LEFT.	
	25th		Weather continued to be clear and frosty in the morning but became cloudy in the afternoon, and a fall of snow appeared to be imminent. Situation normal but the usual slight Trench Mortar activity. - The day on the whole was peaceful. Our 18 pounders fire salvoes at intervals during the day but there was no retaliation at all shown by the enemy.	
	26th		Weather. Dull all day, a slight fall of snow. Was on the ground at day break. The morning passes quietly except for small artillery activity on both sides. The day passes without incident.	
	27th		Dull weather continued - A slight frost hung all day and it was very cold. Situation was quiet - An Inter Company relief was carried out - The RIGHT FRONT Company was relieved by the SUPPORT Company, and the Company in Reserve relieves the SUPPORT Coy - The original RIGHT FRONT Company moved back into Reserve.	W.S.

Army Form C. 2118.

WAR DIARY
or
INTELLIGENCE SUMMARY.
(Erase heading not required.)

Place	Date	Hour	Summary of Events and Information	Remarks and references to Appendices
ARRAS 1917	27ᵗʰ		Relief was continued by 7.45 pm Companies are disposed as follows – LEFT FRONT "D" Coy. RIGHT FRONT "B" Coy – SUPPORT "C" Coy – RESERVE "A" Coy.	
	28ᵗʰ		Snow showers fell during the night which made the Trench lines very slippery. The frost was keen and a mist hung over the front line Trenches. During the morning there was some artillery activity on both sides. The Battalion was relieved in the afternoon & evening by the 10ᵗʰ Scottish Rifles – and moved into Brigade Support. On the readjustment of the Brigade front – an alteration took place changing a disposition from a 3 Battalion front to a 2 Battalion front. Our Company of the Battalion – "A" Coy – and two platoons of "D" Coy have been placed in COLT Reserve as immediate support to the front line. During the night a heavy barrage was placed on the Communication Trenches (CAMBRAI TRENCH) which was kept up by Relieving Bn – a working party of 11ᵗʰ Argyle & Sutherland H⁺s Coy during of about 100 O.R. were brought to them at the time and it is supposed that they were seen coming up by the enemy, hence the fire opened on the party – The Party suffered casualties of 2 killed several wounded.	

A5834 Wt. W4973 M687 750,000 8/16 D. D. & L. Ltd. Forms/C.2118/13.

Army Form C. 2118.

WAR DIARY
or
INTELLIGENCE SUMMARY.
(Erase heading not required.)

Instructions regarding War Diaries and Intelligence Summaries are contained in F. S. Regs., Part II. and the Staff Manual respectively. Title pages will be prepared in manuscript.

Place	Date	Hour	Summary of Events and Information	Remarks and references to Appendices
IN THE LINE	Oct 1917 29		The Batt. succeeded in completing the Relief without Casualties. Weather was foggy & not cold - working parties continued. The enemy shelled fine with heavy artillery on the Junction of CAGEY HUDSON TRENCHES on CLYDE Trench - the bombardment lasted all afternoon.	
	30		Weather continues foggy & cold. The Battalion relieves the 10th R.S.R. in the RIGHT sector of the Brigade front taking over three Company frontage with one Company in Support in Platoon 8th 10 S.R. in Reserve in COLT RESERVE. Companies are disposed as follows RIGHT FRONT "B" Coy. CENTRE "C" Coy. LEFT FRONT "A" Coy with "D" Coy in Support with one platoon in each about front & S.O. Relief completed by 7 pm. without incident.	
	31		Battalion in RIGHT SECTOR of Brigade front. Weather dull with snow lying, making patrols difficult. Situation quiet on both sides. Weather dull & cold with slight thaw. Arrangements completed for handing over to 3rd Guards Brigade. In the evening news full twenty navy guns. LIEUT O.R. SILLARS rejoins the Battalion from Ireland.	19/h

A5834 Wt. W4973/M687 750,000 8/16 D. D. & L. Ltd. Forms/C.2118/13.

Army Form C. 2118.

WAR DIARY
or
INTELLIGENCE SUMMARY.
(Erase heading not required.)

Place	Date	Hour	Summary of Events and Information	Remarks and references to Appendices
IN THE LINE	1917 Dec.		The undermentioned are included in the list of Sir Douglas Haig's mentions:—	
			Temp. 2/Lieut. J.M. BANNATYNE (killed in action at YPRES)	
			Temp. Bre. Thom. Capt. J. CARPENTER	
			2/Lieut. W. DUNMORS (wounded in action S. of SCARPE)	
			Temp. Capt. R.L. HANNAH	
			2/Lieut. J. TROTTER (wounded in action at YPRES)	
			No. 19389 Coff. K. DUFFY	
			19070 Reg.t Q.M. Serjt. J. STEVENSON	

Cowdy Lt. H.L.I.

Vol 26

26.M.
12 sheets

(6339) Wt. W160/M3016 1,500,000 10/17 McA & W Ltd (E1898) Forms W3091.   Army Form W.3091.

Cover for Documents.

CONFIDENTIAL

Nature of Enclosures.

WAR DIARY

OF

12ᵗʰ BN. HIGH. L. I.

FOR

JANUARY 1918

To 106 Bde 3.2.18

Notes, or Letters written.

Army Form C. 2118.

WAR DIARY
or
INTELLIGENCE SUMMARY.
(Erase heading not required.)

196

Place	Date 1918	Hour	Summary of Events and Information	Remarks and references to Appendices
IN THE LINE	JAN. 1		Weather clear & cold. Enemy activity slight. Battalion relieved by 1st Grenadier Guards. Relief completed by 10.30 p.m. One Officer per Company & one N.C.O. per Platoon left behind for 24 hours.	
ARRAS	2	1 A.M.	Battalion arrives in ARRAS & is accommodated in ECOLE DES JEUNE FILLES. At 1 p.m. the Battalion moves out by Companies at 100 yards interval & march to billets in BERNEVILLE, a small village lying about 5 miles west of ARRAS. Men are accommodated in barns & are not at all comfortable, the billets being in a very bad state of repair.	
BERNEVILLE	3		Weather very cold, with snow threatening. Day spent in trying to make the mens quarters habitable.	
	4		Slight fall of snow, with continuation of cold weather.	
	5		do	
	6		Inspection of the billets by Brigadier & Town Mayor, and authority obtained for a supply of Timber & R.E. material to be drawn. Men have NEW YEAR DINNER in huts. "C" & "D" Coys. at 12 noon & "A" & "B" Coys. at 2 p.m. One barrel of beer issued per Company.	

Army Form C. 2118.

WAR DIARY
or
INTELLIGENCE SUMMARY.
(Erase heading not required.)

Place	Date	Hour	Summary of Events and Information	Remarks and references to Appendices
BERNEVILLE	Jan. 7 1918		Battalion in Billets. Training of Platoons commenced. Weather dry & cold.	187
	8		do. Companies organized in 3 Platoons.	
	9		do. Training continued. Allotment of short range to Companies enables a certain amount of Range Practice to be carried out.	
	10		Battalion in Billets as above. Musketry Roll Call carried out. No. 17796 Sergt. C. McGARRY is awarded MERITORIOUS SERVICE MEDAL in recognition of valuable services rendered with the Armies in the Field.	
	11		Battalion in Billets as above. Training being carried out under adverse circumstances. Heavy showers of rain &c. Considerable amount of damage to billets, reported being done to Billets & Property of inhabitants. Additional picquets are detailed for duty overnight.	
	12		Battalion in Billets as above. Training of Platoons continued.	

Place	Date	Hour	Summary of Events and Information	Remarks and references to Appendices
BERNVILLE	1918 Jan. 13		Battalion in Billets. Numerous complaints are received on account of the poor accommodation, and every endeavour is made to improve it. Many of the billets are scarcely water-tight, and any wind blows raw snow into the men's sleeping quarters. Weather very cold with fall of snow. Training carried on as far as possible inside. In the afternoons men are free to carry on recreational training & a football competition among platoons is organised & every opportunity taken to play off ties.	
	14		Battalion in billets as above. Training carried on in the morning. Weather fresh & snow disappears. In the afternoon final of Brigade Football Championship is played off on ground in the neighbourhood between the 10th Scottish Rifles & ourselves, ending in a draw, no scoring.	
	15		Weather very wet & no training can be carried out. Men kept indoors all day. 2/LIEUT. C. NEIL rejoins for duty & is posted to 'A' Company	

Army Form C. 2118.

WAR DIARY
or
INTELLIGENCE SUMMARY.
(Erase heading not required.)

Place	Date	Hour	Summary of Events and Information	Remarks and references to Appendices
BERNEVILLE	1918 Jan. 16		Weather continues very wet & unsuitable for training. Range at SIMENCOURT although allotted to the Battalion cannot be used owing to the weather conditions.	189
	17		Weather very wet. WAILLY Training Area to which the Battalion was to have marched is cancelled & the Battalion remains in billets.	
	18		Battalion in billets as above. Company training proceeded with. Coys Commander visited "A" & "B" Coys. training areas & expressed himself as highly pleased with their work. In the afternoon the final of the Brigade Football Championship was played between 10 Scottish Rifles & ourselves, ending in a win for the Battalion by 2 goals to 0.	
	19		Company training carried on. Ground very wet & muddy, handicapping movement. Each Company carries out a Tactical Scheme, occupying usually about two hours. Schemes are prepared & handed in the previous evening. One Company a per day is allotted the range for firing practice.	

WAR DIARY
or
INTELLIGENCE SUMMARY.

Army Form C. 2118.

Place	Date	Hour	Summary of Events and Information	Remarks and references to Appendices
BERNAVILLE	Jan 18/16	10	Battalion in Billets. Companies prepare for G.O.C's Inspection to be held on the following day. G.O.C's inspection is carried out during the afternoon. Weather dull & threatening rain. About 10 A.M. rain began to fall, and it was decided to parade by Companies for G.O.C's inspection in accordance with orders received.	
		2.	"A" Company are inspected at 11.30 A.M. after a short address to the Officers given by the G.O.C. Division. "B", "C" & "D" Companies in succession at intervals of 20 minutes. The Transport and drawn up on the main St, are inspected before the G.O.C. leaves Stp. Satisfaction is expressed at the smart turn out of both the men & Transport. The Brigadier-General in a letter received the following day desired to express his congratulations to all ranks of their smart turn-out under very adverse conditions. A Summary of the G.O.C. Divisions remarks as conveyed in a letter received the following day is appended.	

WAR DIARY
or
INTELLIGENCE SUMMARY.
(Erase heading not required.)

Army Form C. 2118.

191

Place	Date	Hour	Summary of Events and Information	Remarks and references to Appendices
BERNAVILLE	1919 JAN. 21		Facilities for Preparation by Unit. Fair.	
			Weather Indifferent.	
			Physique Good.	
			Turn Out: Very Good, especially in two Companies.	
			Clothing & Kits: Generally serviceable & complete.	
			Equipment: In good order.	
			Transport: Waggons & mules in excellent condition & well groomed. Harness well fitting & well turned out. All carriages in good order & clean. The Transport of this Battalion is in every way an example. The Transport Officer, Sergeant Cook and all ranks deserve the highest credit for the appearance on parade to-day.	
			Rifles, Signals, etc. Generally well turned out.	
			General Remarks: Unemployed men require more parades & attention. Officers require to be more familiar with the contents of S.S. 143.	

Army Form C. 2118.

WAR DIARY
or
INTELLIGENCE SUMMARY.
(Erase heading not required.)

192

Place	Date	Hour	Summary of Events and Information	Remarks and references to Appendices
BERNVILLE	1917 Jan 21		A Boxing Competition in connection with the Championship of the Division was held in the evening in the CINEMA HUT. Two men of the Battalion won their fights. Pte. J. McLELLAN HEAVY WEIGHT, & L/C. RADCLIFFE, Feather Weight.	
	22		Battalion in billets. Training carried on. Companies carrying out usual Tactical Schemes, & practising throwing live Bombs, & firing live Rifle Grenades. 2/LIEUT. E.T.R.HANNAH joins for duty & is posted to "A" Company. "B" Company on the range. Other Companies carrying out further practice in Bomb throwing & firing Rifle Grenades.	
	23		Weather dry & sudden.	
	24		Weather very fine. A, B & D Companies on various ranges. "C" Company carries out usual Tactical Exercise.	

Army Form C. 2118.

193

WAR DIARY
or
INTELLIGENCE SUMMARY.
(Erase heading not required.)

Place	Date	Hour	Summary of Events and Information	Remarks and references to Appendices
BERNEVILLE	1918 Jan. 25		Battalion in Billets. Weather favourable for training. Companies carry out Tactical Schemes. Company in Attack. "E" Company is placed at the disposal of O.C. 10th Scottish Rifles to act as opposing force in Battalion Scheme.	
	26		Battalion proceeds to WAILLY Training Area for training. Companies carry out Tactical Schemes, practising Company in Attack, Consolidation, etc. 2/Lieut. W.A. MEIKLE is appointed Transport Officer temporarily in place of Capt. H.S. ROBERTSON, appointed to Divisional Labour Corps. 2/Lieut. E. NOBLE having joined the Battalion for duty is posted to "B" Coy.	
	27		Battalion in Billets as above. Weather dry & mild. Officers, N.C.O.s & men attend Church Parade.	

Army Form C. 2118.

WAR DIARY
or
INTELLIGENCE SUMMARY.
(Erase heading not required.)

Place	Date	Hour	Summary of Events and Information	Remarks and references to Appendices
BERNEVILLE	1918 JAN 28		Battalion in Billets. Weather dry & clear. Training carried out on WAILLY TRAINING AREA.	
	29		Weather dry & clear. Battalion takes part in Brigade Scheme of attack on system of trenches. General Idea is that enemy have broken through & that the Brigade is ordered to attack & drive enemy back to original line. Warning Order & General Instructions issued on night of 28th. Final Instructions received at 9.30 A.M. Attack takes place at 10 A.M. Battalion work is pronounced by G.O.C. 7 Brigade. Attack completed at 1 p.m. & men return to Billets at 2.15 p.m.	
	30		Battalion in Billets as above. The Battalion carries out a "Battalion Scheme". Orders for which are attached & marked "K". One Company of 10" S.A. form enemy. Attack carried out on Wailly Training Area in Ideal Weather.	

Army Form C. 2118.

195

WAR DIARY
or
INTELLIGENCE SUMMARY.
(Erase heading not required.)

Place	Date	Hour	Summary of Events and Information	Remarks and references to Appendices
BERNEVILLE	1918 JAN 30		The B.G.C. 46 I.N.B., on conclusion of the Scheme, commented on the success with which the attack had been carried out, & was flattering in his remarks on the work of the Battalion. Warning Order received to proceed to ARRAS on the 3rd Feb.	
	31		Warning Order received that Battalion in Billets as above. WARNING ORDER received to proceed to the Fourth Army on 3rd Feb.y. The Battalion will be transferred to PESELHOEK, & thence the move will be by rail from BEAUMETZ to the Fourth Army. Battalion carrying out under Orders of the Fourth Army, Battalion carrying out Range Practice at SIMENCOURT Range & Short Ranges.	

R.S. Dixon Major
Comdg. 12th (S) Bn. High. L.I.

www.ingramcontent.com/pod-product-compliance
Lightning Source LLC
Chambersburg PA
CBHW080924230426
43668CB00014B/2193